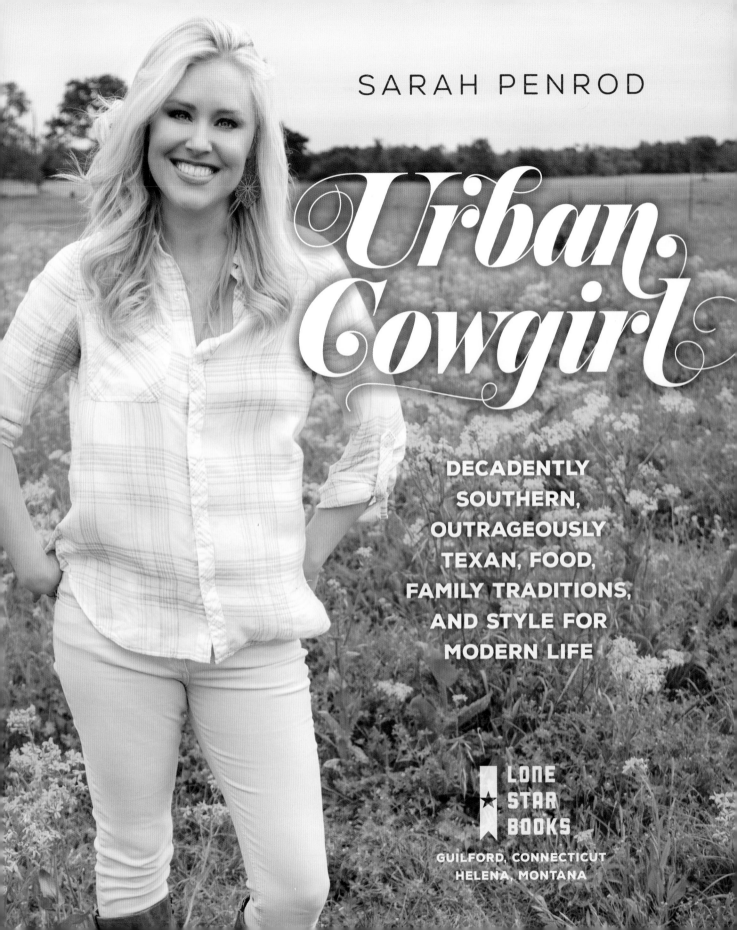

SARAH PENROD

Urban Cowgirl

DECADENTLY
SOUTHERN,
OUTRAGEOUSLY
TEXAN, FOOD,
FAMILY TRADITIONS,
AND STYLE FOR
MODERN LIFE

LONE
STAR
BOOKS

GUILFORD, CONNECTICUT
HELENA, MONTANA

LONE STAR BOOKS

An imprint of Globe Pequot
An imprint and registered trademark of Rowman & Littlefield

Distributed by NATIONAL BOOK NETWORK

Design by Katie Jennings Design
All photos by Liggett + Squier Photography except p. 108 (by Debbie Porter)
Food photography art director: Leann Squier
Food styling and additional photography: Sarah Penrod
Map on page 10 © Rowman & Littlefield

British Library Cataloguing in Publication Information Available

Library of Congress Cataloging-in-Publication Data

Names: Penrod, Sarah, 1983- author.
Title: Urban cowgirl : decadently Southern, outrageously Texan, food,
    traditions, and style for modern life / Sarah Penrod.
Description: Guilford, Connecticut : Lone Star Books, [2017] | Includes index.
Identifiers: LCCN 2016052583 (print) | LCCN 2017002865 (ebook) | ISBN
    9781493025619 (hardback) | ISBN 9781493025626 (e-book)
Subjects: LCSH: Cooking, American—Southern style. | Cooking—Texas. | LCGFT:
    Cookbooks.
Classification: LCC TX715.2.S69 P467 2017 (print) | LCC TX715.2.S69 (ebook) |
    DDC 641.59764—dc23
LC record available at https://lccn.loc.gov/2016052583

♾™ The paper used in this publication meets the minimum requirements of American National Standard for Information Sciences—Permanence of Paper for Printed Library Materials, ANSI/NISO Z3948-1992.

Printed in the United States of America

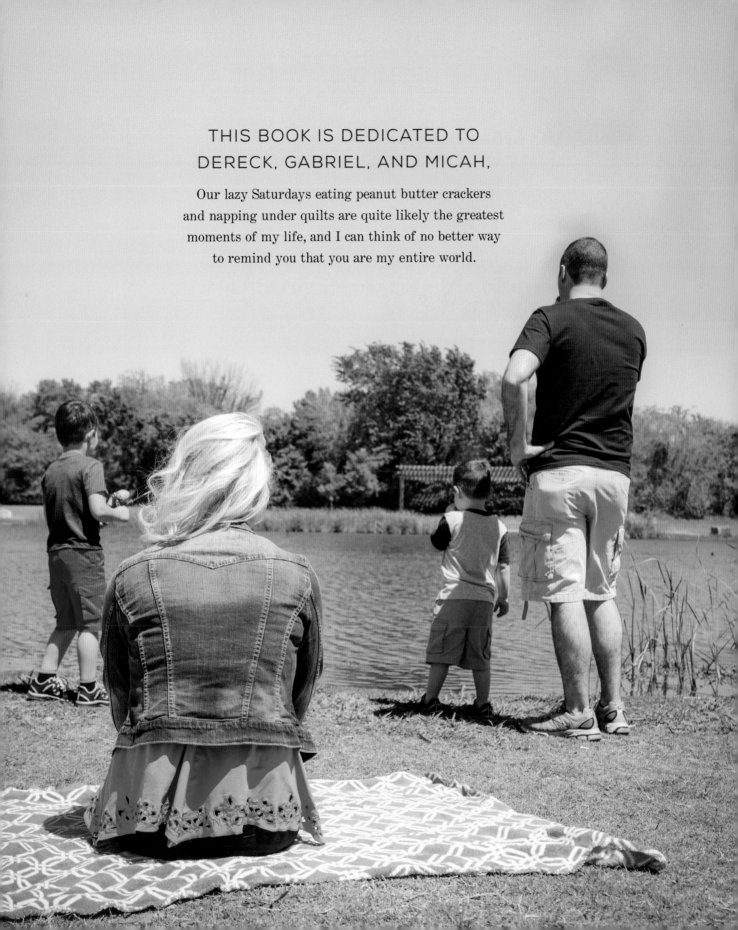

THIS BOOK IS DEDICATED TO
DERECK, GABRIEL, AND MICAH,

Our lazy Saturdays eating peanut butter crackers
and napping under quilts are quite likely the greatest
moments of my life, and I can think of no better way
to remind you that you are my entire world.

★ CONTENTS ★

Urban Cowgirl Traditions 230

The Urban Cowgirl

YOU ARE AN URBAN COWGIRL. YOU JUST DON'T KNOW IT YET.

Urban Cowgirls aren't born—they're created. This title isn't limited to your home state or your age, your hair color or your waist size. It's an in-the-heart-thing—a from the heart thing. I know you are one, because I know what it takes to really be one.

I know you.

You . . . have a designer coffee table littered with *Saveur* and *Bon Appetit* magazines, but the recipes you hold dearest are third-generation handwritten love letters from a grandmother you may have never met.

You . . . love fashion, trendy dresses, and sexy high heels. But you also value tradition, antiques, and the way vintage lace never goes out of style. Your wedding ring has the swankiest diamond he could afford placed into your grandmother's wedding band.

You . . . spend the evening in the city ordering martinis, but you still remember your first sip of homebrew.

You . . . love the little bottles of gourmet baby food, but you really want to learn how to make it yourself.

You . . . love the world and everything it has to offer, yet you're Southern and you have roots.

You . . . are a walking contradiction: a tomboy in a designer dress, a cowgirl that rides a Vespa.

Fiercely loyal to your heritage, you will do whatever it takes to preserve it. But it's not enough to just do it like grandma did. You are unique. You have to make it your own.

I know you because I am just like you. I love to create something from nothing but a set of ingredients and sheer willpower. If I find out something can be done at home, in the kitchen or in the garden out back, I jump in with both feet—be they bare, booted, heeled, or Ugg'd—and try it myself.

This book is a guide to doing and experiencing everything you hold dear. A how-to of everything you ever wanted to try and secretly always knew you could master. It's a celebration of Texas and of the South. It's a record of traditions that you cherish. It's a catalog of your favorite recipes made up with lipstick and wearing heels.

This world is full of gimmicks and littered with pesticides. Modern food is stuffed with fillers and additives. By going back to the roots of how things are made, we can bring our country hearts into the middle of our city life. And by committing to doing it from scratch, you will nourish your body and your mind, and rediscover the magic of temporarily bygone, but never forgotten, traditions

I'm Sarah Penrod, the Urban Cowgirl. I'm a seventh-generation Texan, a Daughter of the American Revolution, and for the last ten years a professional chef. I live the Urban Cowgirl life. It's big-city life that's designed around more than the hustle and bustle of "Likes" and "Favorites," nailing down Friday night's plans and listing Saturday's errands. It's more than e-mails constantly chiming, alerting me to deals I "just can't miss" and mascara that will give me "Marilyn eyes," or horns honking, traffic crawling, and children staring at screens in the car, in the house, at the dinner table.

Everything we will explore in this book has been fully vetted through my personal quest for a better quality of life in a fast-paced, commercial world that has forgotten that only one generation ago we made our own soap. I incorporate knowledge gleaned from my education, which has been honed with love and laughter. As a mother of two boys, my passion for wholesome food and healthy living runs deep. With this book, I want to impart some of my own sense of kitchen adventure, as well as share what I've learned about making an Urban Cowgirl home from my training as a chef.

It's time to write your own chapter. To turn off the noise. To listen to the little voice inside you promising more . . .

It's time to become the Urban Cowgirl I already know you are.

URBAN COWGIRL COUNTRY

THIS LAND IS OUR LAND.

For the purposes of the Urban Cowgirl life, when I refer to *the South* in this book, I am referring to the southern part of the United States. I am not referring to the Confederate South, a boundary line confined to a time in history, not a present reality. I am not referring only to parts of the country traditionally thought of as Southern, where the accents drawl and the air is humid and hot.

I'm talking about Southern California to Florida, New Mexico to Georgia. I'm drawing a line across this beautiful and complicated country, and I'm creating recipes that describe a newly defined world. My Urban Cowgirl identity is deeply connected to my native Texan-ness, but Urban Cowgirls aren't bound to a spot on the map. Urban Cowgirls can come from anywhere on the map because it's about more than location, it's about state of mind. Urban Cowgirls exist in New York City and the Colorado Rockies, but the food and philosophy is a union of the Southwest, Southeast, and, yes, even South of the Border.

Urban Cowgirl Country is a modern world where flavors roam free, and new traditions are made every day.

THE SOUTHWEST

THE MOTHERLAND

THE CLASSIC SOUTH

INSPIRATION COMES FROM HERE, BUT URBAN COWGIRLS ARE FROM EVERYWHERE.

How to Use This Book

NOW YOU'RE ONE OF US! GET IN HERE AND GRAB AN APRON.

This book is laid out in four parts:

THE URBAN COWGIRL including HOW TO USE THIS BOOK

An introduction to the adventures we're about to embark upon, where we'll cover a few basics that will help you along your way.

RECIPES FOR THE URBAN COWGIRL KITCHEN

Here is my treasure trove of recipes, from Coffee Shop Caramel Sauce to Catfish Diablo. They are organized by traditional chapters and are studded with tips, tricks, and stories along the way.

URBAN COWGIRL ARTISAN BEAUTY AT HOME

Soap recipes, lip balm, rose petal scrubs—all here for your home day spa enjoyment taken directly from my artisan spa line, Mommy Salts. This is the spoiler alert section, chock-full of the same recipes I use at home.

URBAN COWGIRL TRADITIONS

Here you will find my favorite celebrations, along with many great Texas and Southern traditions we all need a refresher course in. You'll find recipes, tips, and explanations on incorporating these into your own events. You could rename this section "How to be an Urban Cowgirl," because it contains all the things we hold most dear and enjoy with the most abandon!

IN THIS SECTION YOU'LL FIND:

URBAN COWGIRL TOOLS are a few gadgets and gizmos that have won my heart and become staples in my kitchen. You're probably familiar with a lot of them, but some are most definitely new to the cooking scene! Urban Cowgirls are always on the "new gadget front lines"! I'm a mommy chef as well, and many of these items make it possible for my sons to participate in the kitchen, because sharing our love in the kitchen is the most important thing we can do as food lovers.

URBAN COWGIRL COOKING SCHOOL will become your most dog-eared pages. In this section I go over some basic cooking techniques that I will refer back to in the rest of the book. Tricks like blackening corn without a grill, toasting nuts, and how to shingle an avocado are explained and easily referenced when you feel the need for a refresher course.

URBAN COWGIRL INGREDIENTS will explain and clarify some of the ingredients you see in the rest of the book. Items like Mexican chocolate, pepitas, or asadero cheese may be new to you, but not to worry, I provide a road map to what they are, where they can be found, and how best to use and care for them.

AND THROUGHOUT THE BOOK ARE
A FEW MORE BELLS AND WHISTLES:

MOM TIPS You'll see this icon when I have a tip that all moms will appreciate. It might be an easier way to clean, a smarter way to work through a recipe, or a reminder to save that extra coconut milk for a luxurious milk bath that night!

PRO TIPS You'll see this icon when I have a tip that will really elevate your cooking skills to the next level. This icon means take notice, there is a super cool tip coming up that will make you look like a total pro.

TINY TEXAN APPROVED You'll see this icon when a dish is particularly approved for kids or is a good time to bring the kids into the kitchen for a cooking lesson.

COZY FIREPLACE CHAT When you see this icon, you might as well picture us with cappuccinos in funny mugs in front of the fireplace with the rest of the tribe, because I'm about to really explain something in no-nonsense terms. This is the inner sanctum of the Urban Cowgirl world, a heart-to-heart in topics we care about.

URBAN COWGIRL TOOLS

TINY FOOD PROCESSOR: I accidentally came into possession of one of these tiny little things, and I have never been so delighted. It's just the right size for making roasted garlic puree, vinaigrettes, marinades, and fresh bread crumbs; for chopping nuts and larger amounts of garlic; and for other small tasks that you would never lug out a whole food processor. Easy to clean and lightweight, it's just been a dream of a find for under $20.

DISPOSABLE GLOVES: In restaurants, we use disposable gloves for tossing and plating salads, handling raw meat (think of mixing up a meatloaf), breading chicken-fried steak, and other messy, sticky things. They really make unpleasant tasks completely enjoyable. The same gloves are sold in the cleaning section of any grocery store near the dishwashing gloves, and come about ten to a package. You'll wonder how you ever got along without them.

JULIENNE PEELER: Sturdy, high-quality julienne peelers are sold online for under $15, and you'll love the fine, delicate ribbons of jicama, carrot, and zucchini. Slicing julienne for any dish is quite the labor of love, but these little tools (which look just like a vegetable peeler) do it in record time.

SMALL DICE CHOPPER: I actually love to chop vegetables, but when I discovered they were making home versions of expensive restaurant choppers, I was pleasantly surprised.

My mini chopper pushes out perfect cubes of apple, mango, onion, or anything else I can slide under there. I may be a chef but I'm also a busy mom, and these little choppers are quite handy for busy days—and for giving little helpers some work to do.

GARLIC PRESS: I love a good garlic press. I think you will too when you find a high-quality press with a firm grip handle and a small cleaning tool. You can certainly chop garlic, but I prefer the press when making guacamole.

INSTANT-READ THERMOMETER: To cook meats perfectly, you need a digital instant-read thermometer. The thermometer consists of a large metal spear that you insert into the thickest part of the meat. The device at the top instantly gives you a reading on the digital face. A regular meat thermometer with a dial will also work.

LASER THERMOMETER: Probably my favorite tool in the kitchen for one reason: A wonderful sear on a steak or a piece of perfectly golden fried chicken comes from getting the oil in the pan the perfect temperature and maintaining that level of heat. A laser thermometer looks like a little gun and shoots a laser that reads the temperature of any surface you shoot it at. It will not read the temperature inside of a roast or a steak, but it will tell you the temperature of the oil in a skillet, something that an ordinary thermometer cannot do. It's also less messy because the thermometer never touches the grease.

KNIVES FOR URBAN COWGIRLS

COZY FIREPLACE CHAT

BEFORE CULINARY SCHOOL, I DON'T THINK I HAD EVEN SEEN A TRULY EXCELLENT KNIFE, only well-marketed imposters. It's hard for a blossoming home cook to avoid the landmines of total junk knives being thrown in your face. *And look, it comes in a faux leather case!* Spare me. My kids' soiled diapers travel in a nicer bag than that.

These are all *products* marketed to home cooks. You do not need any of that. You need a real knife, like a real chef. With a little care you will use it your entire life and pass it down to the next fabulous family cook.

Do not buy anything on television or in a warehouse store. And do not buy the whole set!

Buy classic brands: Wusthof, Kikuichi, Global, Shun.

Specialized knife stores are a great resource. Indie stores have great deals and can mentor you on your purchases with wisdom.

If you don't have any indie knife stores around, you can purchase online for a nice price, or find a decent selection at kitchen department stores that cater to foodies.

Do not sharpen your knife with little garbage trinkets. Find a knife store that offers sharpening or a business that specializes in sharpening professional tools, or buy a knife sharpening stone and learn how to use it properly by watching tutorials online.

Despite that dream of unrolling all your knives and winning top chef you do not need all of those choices and they *will* cost a fortune. I cook hours and hours every day and I only use three knives . . . period, end of story, exclamation mark!

YOU NEED:

- 1 chef knife (pre-owned professional gear is better than new garbage)

- 1 paring knife or 3- or 4-inch "mini" chef knife (short, razor sharp, basically just a smaller version of the big guy)

- 1 serrated knife—This does not have to be a "super" brand. Replace it when it gets dull rather than having it sharpened.

- A magnetic knife strip on the wall to hang your knives. Don't keep them in drawers like a barbarian. They are your babies!

URBAN COWGIRL COOKING SCHOOL

ONCE YOU HAVE THE TOOLS, YOU NEED TO LEARN HOW TO USE THEM. Some tips and techniques for basic recipe instructions, as well as specific notes about handling ingredients special to the Urban Cowgirl way, will help you on your mission! Refer back to these pages as needed.

CHOPPIN' SCHOOL: HOW TO DICE, CHOP, AND MINCE

Here are a few basic chopping terms that will come in handy on your adventure.

LARGE DICE: About the size of a Cheez-it

MEDIUM DICE: About the size of an M&M's candy

SMALL DICE: About the size of a mini chocolate chip

MINCE: Tiny pieces, smaller then $1/8$ inch; but we're not in French culinary school here people, I just mean *small*.

ROUGH CHOP: A rough chop means just that, roughly chop it and don't worry about how pretty it is. It's probably going in stock or a sauce that is destined for the blender.

CRUSHED GARLIC: The flavor in chopped garlic is directly proportional to how much you chop or crush it. That's why I love my garlic press and use it quite a bit. Yes, you can mince it, crush it, and beat it into a paste, but for guacamole and many of my sauces, I'd much rather have a garlic press to make quick work of our favorite aromatic.

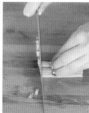

LARGE DICE: About the size of a Cheez-it

MEDIUM DICE: About the size of an M&M's candy

SMALL DICE: About the size of a mini chocolate chip

MINCE: Tiny pieces, smaller then ⅛ inch; but we're not in French culinary school here people, I just mean *small*.

ROUGH CHOP: A rough chop means just that, roughly chop it and don't worry about how pretty it is. It's probably going in stock or a sauce that is destined for the blender.

CRUSHED GARLIC: The flavor in chopped garlic is directly proportional to how much you chop or crush it. That's why I love my garlic press and use it quite a bit. Yes, you can mince it, crush it, and beat it into a paste, but for guacamole and many of my sauces, I'd much rather have a garlic press to make quick work of our favorite aromatic.

ESSENTIAL URBAN COWGIRL TECHNIQUES

HOW TO ROAST A PEPPER: Preheat the oven to 450°F. Wash the pepper, dry it well, and toss it in the oven to roast for 30 minutes. You can put it on a sheet pan if you want, but it's okay just to let it sit directly on the rack as we do in professional kitchens. Remove with tongs and toss it in a heat-safe bowl. Cover the bowl with plastic wrap (or a plate) and allow it to steam for 10 minutes. It's still cooking but it is also steaming the skin off. In a clean kitchen sink, under cold running water, remove the skin. (It should fall right off.) Pull open the pepper and take out the seeds. On a cutting board cut manageable slices off the roasted pepper and discard the stem. Now it's ready to use in any recipe—and ten times better than anything from a jar!

HOW TO BLACKEN CORN ON THE COB WITHOUT A GRILL: Move a rack in the oven to just under the broiler (with enough space that your corn will fit underneath). Preheat the broiler to high.

Line a cookie sheet with foil. On a cutting board cut the tip and stock off the corn. This should allow the husk to peel right off into the garbage can. Remove as much corn silk as possible and place the corn on the cookie sheet. Repeat with the remaining corn. Using a little bit of oil, rub the corn and the foil underneath to prevent sticking. Salt lightly.

Place the sheet of corn directly under the broiler and roast 10 minutes, rotating the corn twice to get bits of brown on the cobs. Stay nearby just in case things get smoky (broilers get so hot they need supervision!).

Remove the corn carefully and place on a cutting board to cool. Cut the corn off the stalks by standing the cob up on one end. Using a very sharp knife, slice from the top down, against the base of the corn kernels. Rotate and repeat.

Scoop up the corn and place it in a bowl. Discard the cob. (Or Pinterest will probably have ideas for how you can turn it into a bird feeder or Christmas decoration.)

HOW TO CUT AN AVOCADO: To cut an avocado you need a cutting board and a good sharp chef's knife. Place the avocado on the cutting board and cut into it vertically (up and down) until you hit the pit in the middle.

Carefully roll the avocado around the blade of the knife while pushing down on the cutting board, cutting it in half vertically. Remove the knife from the avocado. Pull it apart in your hands by turning it like a key. You should have one side with the pit still embedded in the avocado.

Using your knife, hit the blade to the pit and twist. The pit should stick to the blade and come out of the avocado. To remove the pit from your knife, knock the side of the pit into the sink and place it in the garbage. Do not remove the pit from the knife with your hands! Now you have two avocado halves . . .

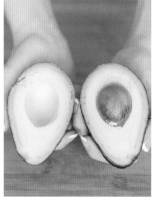

TO CUT AVOCADO CHUNKS: Hold the avocado in one hand and your knife in the other hand. Press the knife into the avocado just until it hits the skin on the other side. Cut it top to bottom in slices and then left to right creating squares. Put the knife down and, using a large spoon, scoop the avocado out of the skin. The chunks of avocado will fall right out.

TO CUT AVOCADO SHINGLES: Place one half of a pitted avocado flesh side down on a cutting board (peel facing up). Arrange the avocado so that it is lying horizontally in front of you. Cut a thin slice off the right end and a thin slice off the left end. Peel the skin off one of the edges and, gripping the avocado firmly, remove the rest of the skin briskly in one movement by pulling from left to right. Discard the skin.

Using a sharp knife, cut thin slices left to right into the meat of the avocado, but do not separate the slices (it kind of resembles an accordion). Using gentle pressure with your palm, press on the meat from left to right, causing the slices to shingle onto one another. Now the avocado slices will stick together, and you can slide your knife underneath the entire avocado to pick it up and place on a salad, sandwich, etc.

HOW TO WORK WITH JICAMA: Jicama is like a big apple with skin like a potato, so before we can do anything we have to remove the skin with a potato peeler. When all the skin is peeled off, you can cut it into slices and dice it, or using a julienne peeler you can peel thin, tender strips of jicama right off the root. This is my favorite method, because I think jicama is best used thin and crunchy.

To use jicama in a slaw, I use the cheese grater attachment on my food processor to shred several roots of jicama in minutes. You'll just have to cut the roots slender enough to fit through the chute of the food processor.

HOW TO FAJITA-CUT AN ONION: In these recipes we dice and mince our veggies just like in any other cookbook, but you will hear me refer to a fajita cut over and over again. Here's how to do it.

Using any color onion, slice the root and tip ends off. Place the onion on one of the flat bottoms you've just created. Slice the onion in half from tip to root end. Peel the skin off. Place both halves of the onion flat side down against the cutting board and make thin slices from top to bottom, cutting through the onion completely. When you pick the pieces up, they will naturally separate into thin slices of onion ready for caramelizing—or sautéing, exactly like the onions served with fajitas—and will not cling to one another.

HOW TO CUT A MANGO WITHOUT LOSING YOUR MIND: First, choose a soft, fragrant mango that gives just a little when you squeeze it in your hand. Peel the mango using a vegetable peeler. Take a glass (like you would use for drinking a cold drink) and, holding the mango in your hand, press the flesh of the mango (starting at the bottom of the mango) against the rim of the glass. The glass should slide into the flesh until it hits the hard core in the center of the mango. Then roll the mango down the glass rim, slicing off a piece of the fruit. The edge of the glass works just like a knife!

Rotate the mango and repeat.

HOW TO TOAST NUTS AND PUMPKIN SEEDS: Pour the nuts into a small sauté pan. Turn the heat to low to medium. Allow the nuts to begin to warm up, tossing them every minute or so. The nuts will begin to release their oils, toast, and become fragrant within a few minutes. Do not allow the nuts to burn. If they begin to get too hot, pull them off the heat and toss frequently.

Pumpkin seeds will turn from green to a toasted tan color and when shaken in a pan will begin to sound hollow as they toast.

Remove and cool before using.

HOW TO CANDY TOMATOES: Preheat the oven to 250°F. Slice the tomatoes in quarters and place in a large bowl. Coat the tomatoes in just a toss of extra-virgin olive oil, salt, pepper, and fresh herbs like thyme, basil, or rosemary. A recipe isn't really needed, just make sure every tomato is coated well in oil and seasonings. On a cookie sheet lined with foil, spread the tomatoes out in a single layer. Bake for 3–4 hours, reducing the heat to 225°F during the last hour. Remove them from the oven and allow to cool. The tomatoes can be refrigerated in Tupperware for extended use.

WHAT DOES IT MEAN TO SEASON TO TASTE?

I was twenty-three. I was standing in my second practical class (that means you're in the kitchens as opposed to the classroom), and we were making a clear vegetable soup. I salted the soup and tasted it. Good, but my tongue and brain were beginning to come together in a particular inner conversation that allowed me to know when a dish still needed more before perfection. It was amazing to me how the salt amplified the other flavors in the broth. If a soup included fresh thyme, I was quickly learning that I didn't always need another pinch of thyme in the soup, but sometimes an extra pinch of salt would "turn up the volume" on the thyme as well as all the other flavors. It's actually kind of magical if you think about it. What other ingredient has the ability to increase the flavor of other ingredients?

Most home cooks will stumble upon this revelation at some time in their cooking game, and it's exhilarating. You want to immediately shove something else in a pan to see if you can do it again. What I don't think you often stumble upon unintentionally, but are taught in classical technique, is that acidity does the exact same thing. Acidity, in most cases, is lemon juice or vinegar.

Allow me to take you back to algebra class and remind you of the x/y axis. It helps articulate this concept.

In algebra, we always work equations on the x/y axis. It's two dimensional. That is what salt and pepper are like. No matter how much more salt and pepper, or any other seasoning you add, you're still creating flavors in a two-dimensional world. Acidity is like getting to high school and learning about the z axis. It turns a square into a cube, a circle into a sphere. Our brain is wired to find bliss in this perfect zone of salt and acidity.

So how is it done? In this book you will find recipes that include "a couple drops of lemon juice."

When you see this, as you are seasoning the dish—adding salt, pepper, herbs, and other goodies—you will also want to squeeze in little dribbles of lemon juice as you go. Eventually you'll learn to harness this skill to hit the bull's-eye on any recipe (even recipes from other sources that didn't quite nail it). Those recipes will be no match for you because you will know how to fix them.

And when you reach that vivid "Eureka!" moment where you just know in an instant you've manipulated flavors to hit the peak for that dish, and you know you can replicate that over and over again, I hope you shout out to me, so we can celebrate together.

URBAN COWGIRL INGREDIENTS

URBAN COWGIRLS ARE EASYGOING, HAPPY-GO-LUCKY GALS, but we can be persnickety about a few things, and those things will dramatically enhance the way these recipes taste. Here are some guidelines for your trip to the market before we ever start cooking:

BLOCK CHEESE, PLEASE: The recipes in this book contain cheese from a block. Recipes are designed for you to grate the cheese and measure into a measuring cup. I also provide you with the weight, because you know that 4 ounces of sharp cheddar cheese is half of that 8-ounce package, which means you don't even have to measure at all.

Why grate cheese from a block instead of using pre-shredded packages?

I don't particularly have anything against packaged cheese, but it does behave significantly different than real cheese. A lot of the cheeses in this book don't come in pre-shredded form, and, honestly, I get excited to see freshly grated cheese. Somehow packaged cheese just doesn't make my heart go pitter-pat.

Plus, what job would I give my four-year-old if the cheese was already shredded?

BOXES OF HIGH PROTEIN STOCKS AND BROTHS: I use stock a lot in my recipes, and I look for a specific type: high protein content stocks, which are closer to homemade and taste fantastic when reduced. You'll know the difference by seeing four to six grams of protein listed in the nutritional facts as opposed to one gram.

But then again, if you're Ina Garten and happen to be home making fresh stock and hand feeding your honeybees all day, then you should definitely use that.

MEXICAN CHOCOLATE: Mexican chocolate can be found on the international aisle of the supermarket. Look for Ibarra or Abuelita brands. Mexican chocolate includes additional sugar, cinnamon, and nutmeg. It comes in a box containing several discs of chocolate. Triangles of chocolate can be snapped off the disc to portion, and many recipes will list the number of triangles to use rather than "1 cup chocolate." We use it to make hot chocolate, mole, and chili sauces.

COCONUT OIL: Oh, the legendary coconut oil. It's every mother's oil of choice, isn't it? Health claims range from curing diaper rash to weight loss. It's reached near maniacal status as a cure-all. Oh, your house is haunted? Let's just paint the whole thing in coconut oil. The devil hates coconut oil, you know.

Well, I don't know about all that, but a big jar is a permanent fixture on our stove. It is always soft—the consistency of soft butter. It melts clear in warm temperatures, it has a high smoke point, and it tastes good. You'll

find more on coconut oil throughout the book and with the recipes on creating your own baby food.

Avoid "liquid coconut oil," which is a product marketed on the heels of the coconut craze and is simply a byproduct of removing all the excellent fats like lauric acid, bottling what is left over, and marketing it to an uninformed public. If it isn't a solid white cream in cold temperatures, it is basically massage oil. (Even the extra-virgin coconut oil will melt in warm temperatures but will solidify at approximately 76°F.)

MEXICAN OREGANO: Mexican oregano is readily available now in the spice section of the supermarket. It has the same herbaceous qualities of the oregano found in the Mediterranean but with a brighter, more citrusy flavor. I would not say that they are suitable substitutes because most people associate the pronounced flavor of oregano with pizza sauce. Mexican oregano blends well with other flavors in soups, stews, chilis, and sauces to round out the overall flavor.

HOT SAUCE: Not to be confused with salsa (in Texas salsa is often called hot sauce), this ingredient means any type of vinegar-based cayenne pepper hot sauce such as Frank's Red Hot, Louisiana Hot Sauce, Tabasco, and all of the mom-and-pop hot sauce companies out there. Choose your favorites. We keep them in a basket on our kitchen table.

TIGER SAUCE: A moderately hot, hot sauce with a hint of tangy sweetness on the end. It's currently being used in competition barbecue quite a bit, and I use it every time we batter chicken in this book. If you can't find it, you can use any sweet hot pepper sauce.

PEPITAS: Pepitas are the Spanish name for pumpkin seeds. They are available raw or roasted with salt. Pepitas are high in iron and protein, which makes them a great choice for a snack that fits in your purse! Instructions for roasting your own are found in the "Urban Cowgirl Cooking School" chapter. Unsalted sunflower seeds would work in most cases if pepitas could not be obtained.

FRESH HERBS AND FLOWERING HERBS: It wasn't until I redesigned my flower beds full of fresh herbs that I realized how many herbs make beautiful flowers that never find their way into the grocery store. Cilantro grows like a weed and is covered with beautiful and edible white flowers. Sage buds baby blue in spring. While mint and oregano will crawl out and creep around stony areas, basil has beautiful white and purple flowers, and chamomile, lemon basil, and lemon verbena make excellent herbal teas. All these flowers and herbs are safe to use in cooking or as a beautiful garnish.

WHY DO I EVEN CARE ABOUT SMOKE POINTS? When an oil is heated beyond its smoke point, it creates free radicals, toxic substances, and toxic fumes that are extremely hazardous to your health, contribute to premature aging, and effectively destroy everything in that oil that is beneficial to your health. It may look just the same, but please, for your health, pour that poison out and start over.

WHICH OILS TO COOK WITH? A lot of oils are out there touting health benefits, high antioxidant levels, and exotic flavors, but what is practical enough for your kitchen and what is correct for our style of cooking?

I stock several for my recipes. For high-heat cooking like searing a steak, I always use coconut oil. I use coconut oil in everything from baby food to my homemade soap. It boasts a unique composition of fatty acids, and I love that the little jar of coconut oil is always the consistency of soft butter. Extra-virgin unrefined coconut oil has a lovely mild coconut flavor, while medium-refined coconut oil has no coconut flavor and a higher smoke point. I use both, or either.

For salad dressings, I use a flavorless oil like high oleic sunflower or grapeseed oil, which creates a blank canvas for some truly unique vinaigrettes inspired by our life in Texas. Oil for a salad dressing must be fresh or it will have stinky *off* flavors. Oil goes rancid very quickly once opened, at room temperature, and I keep many oils in the refrigerator to extend their shelf life. Sunflower and grapeseed oil are naturally high in vitamin E, which delays rancidity.

For frying, I use peanut, canola, or anything I can buy in a liter size (because Momma doesn't drive a Ferrari and frying correctly requires at least a liter of oil). I can also use the high oleic sunflower and grapeseed oil because they have high smoke points.

You will also see everyone's favorite oil, extra-virgin olive oil, popping up in these recipes. I love my small-batch Texas olive oils, but they do have a strong distinct flavor, so I usually do not use them in salad dressing.

For everything else there is butter! Because God loves us and wants us to be happy.

AVOCADOS: In this book I use Haas avocados. They cost slightly more but are larger and have better flavor for the applications in this book. Several options for opening and slicing them are found in the techniques portion of this book if you are unfamiliar with them.

TOMATILLOS: Though you'll find them near the tomatoes, they are actually a close cousin of the gooseberry. Bright green, firm tomatillos are bursting with tart citrus-like flavor. They are used fresh, roasted, and pureed into classic sauces like salsa verde. Roasting tomatillos provides a milder flavor and pairs well in sauces with chiles or avocados. Before using, remove the husk and wash them because they can be slightly sticky. I usually don't even remove the stem because it is fleshy like the rest of the body. After a good rinse you can chop them or roast them before incorporating into sauces and soups. Because tomatillos are picked ripe, you do not have to worry about choosing a ripe tomatillo.

JICAMA: Jicama is an edible root with a thin, papery skin similar to a potato. You remove the skin first and then chop or slice per the instructions for the recipe. Although it looks like a turnip, its mouthfeel and crunch are similar to an apple, though not as sweet. I prefer it sliced with a julienne peeler in salads and relishes.

QUELLING THE CONFUSION ON CHILI POWDER

IF YOU'RE NOT FROM THE SOUTHWEST, chili powder can be confusing. Climb up here with me and I will explain it from the top . . . down.

CHILE: A chile pepper, fresh or dried, is the fruit from a plant in the Capsicum genus. For the purpose of talking about powders, we'll assume the peppers have been dehydrated.

CHILE POWDER: This is simply powdered dry chiles. When you see a location (New Mexico, Arizona, California), it is simply referring to the varieties of chile in that area used in the powder. This could be any chile—from guajillo to chimayo to ancho—or a combination. Rather than racking your mind over finding the correct chile powder for a recipe, in most cases using any mild chile powder will do. What is a mild chile powder? It's not hot. Any of the combinations above will work. Stay away from cayenne pepper, which is technically a chile powder, but way too spicy to flavor a broth or chile gravy.

TEXAS CHILI POWDERS: Chile Powder + Other Seasonings (especially cumin) = Texas Chili Powder. Texas chili powders, or simply "chili powder" as Texans call it, is a blend of powdered red chiles with the addition of cumin and occasionally other spices like garlic and Mexican oregano. In Texas most recipes calling for chili powder are referring to this blend, which always ends with an "i," not an "e."

It can be referred to in recipes as chili powder, Texas chili powder, or even Texas chile powder (though I would argue that the latter spelling reveals that the recipe author is not native to Texas and confused with the vernacular). The best Texas chili powders are the brands Gebhardt and Mexene, both boasting secret recipes deeply rooted in over a hundred years of Texas history.

NEW MEXICO CHILE POWDER: Straight from Hatch, New Mexico, the chile capital of the world, or the general region. New Mexico chile powder is usually mild with superb richness and flavor, and is readily available at the supermarket. When visiting the area, make sure to pick up the many other varieties, such as green chile powder and chimayo.

CHIPOTLE PEPPER POWDER: A rich, dark red powder made from ground chipotles. It is spicy and smoky. If you can't find it, just use any mild chile powder with a dash of cayenne for heat. But if you can find it, you really must try it for the unique, smoky essence.

LIQUID SMOKE: A seasoning ingredient infused with the fragrance of various smoked wood. Pecan, mesquite, hickory, and applewood are commonly available. About 1 teaspoon in a recipe is plenty and can be used to impart a whisper of smoke to sauces and marinades.

LARD: Lard is used in preparing tamales and in pastry recipes for a flaky crust. The best lard for tamales comes from Mexican butcher shops and grocery stores and is truly fresh rendered pork fat with a slightly rich pork flavor. It is best kept in the freezer. For baking sweets, I use flavorless grocery store lard, which comes in small boxes and also makes a decadent, creamy homemade soap.

FRESNO PEPPERS: Fresno peppers are a small red chile that looks so similar to a red jalapeño they are often confused for each other. In this book either one will do. The heat levels are about the same, and it's usually the stunning red color that is desired.

INSTANT ESPRESSO POWDER: Instant espresso powder is not really ground coffee beans as you would imagine but crystalized coffee that will dissolve in water. Look for espresso powder, which is concentrated in flavor compared to instant coffee. It's right next to the other bagged coffees on the aisle. In Urban Cowgirl Country we don't usually drink it, but use it in various rubs and baking.

PACKAGED CUPS OF DEMI-GLACE: Unless you have access to veal and beef bones, packaged demi-glace is going to be essential for high-end steak sauces, but only the pricey brands are an adequate substitute. More Than Gourmet is my favorite brand and it carries a staggering assortment of classic French reduced stocks and sauces. I have also been highly impressed with William Sonoma glaces, which are sold in tiny 1 1/2-ounce cups and are highly concentrated. Purchase in gourmet markets and online.

PEPPER JELLY: A jelly made from red bell peppers or jalapeños. It comes mild or spicy, but even the spicy versions aren't that hot. It's excellent in any recipe with cream cheese. If you can't find it, experiment with spicy chutneys. Although pepper jelly isn't tangy like a chutney, it's the interplay of sweet and hot that makes it so addictive.

KOSHER SALT: Keep it in a little bowl next to your stove and learn to measure with your fingers, like a chef.

FINE SALT: I recommend also having a salt grinder available for finely grinding salt onto fried foods. Kosher salt is just too large to melt into hot, freshly fried foods.

FRESHLY CRACKED BLACK PEPPER: The best gift you can give your kitchen is a battery-operated pepper grinder and some beautiful fresh black peppercorns. The pre-ground dust sold as pepper is a glimmer of its former beauty and robust flavor. I have always felt that pepper was the most abused ingredient by manufacturers.

MEXICAN CHEESES 101

HERE IS A PLAY BY PLAY OF THE CHEESES you've been curiously eyeing in the dairy section of the supermarket. Now, I am certainly no Rick Bayless, and I haven't studied in Mexico, although I have drunk a lot of margaritas there! Even so, the discussion of Mexican cheese making is an in-depth, regionally diverse science made even more difficult by the variation in common names from village to village. Simply put, it's as complex as discussing French cheeses.

Here is my guidance on the offerings that are available in most American grocery stores.

CREMA Crema is a light cream-based condiment in Mexican, Southwestern, and Tex-Mex cooking similar to sour cream and very close to crème fraîche. In fact, either is an adequate substitute if you can't find it.

Crema is drizzled on dishes as a garnish and cuts through rich and spicy flavors with a cooling flavor and refreshing sensation. Simply put, it cuts the heat. And it's cool! Quite literally, to the touch.

You can find crema in the Mexican cheese section of the dairy aisle in plastic screw-top bottles, or you can make a simple alternative with the recipe below and store it in the refrigerator.

1 cup sour cream

1 cup heavy cream

Whisk well in a small bowl and chill.

Keeps for 7–10 days.

ASADERO CHEESE A white, semi-firm cheese that melts like mozzarella but with a richer, buttery flavor and smooth mouthfeel. It melts into a luxurious, velvety filling that *runs* more than quesadilla or Oaxaca cheese.

It's perfect for enchiladas and chile rellenos, but due to the slightly nutty flavor that lingers on the palate, it really shines in red chile sauces and chile gravy far more than pairing it with a cream sauce.

It also combines great with cheddar as a dynamic cheese filling. I often find myself running to the Mexican grocery store to find it, and it's well worth the trip.

QUESADILLA CHEESE A happy, melty, buttery cheese. Quesadilla strings when it melts, giving it high marks in the ooey-gooey factor. As its name conveys, it's an excellent choice for quesadillas.

COTIJA CHEESE: A robustly flavored, salty cheese that crumbles when pressed and is used to accent dishes (sort of like sprinkling on parsley). It's tangier, dryer, and sharper than queso fresca but not as pungently flavored as feta.

FETA CHEESE: I know, it's not Mexican. But it is showing up everywhere because frankly it's perfect for topping a taco. It's robust, salty, and it melts like a dream.

QUESO FRESCA: Another "sprinkley" cheese that crumbles well for topping dishes. It is extra moist, with a milder flavor then Cotija, and a bit milkier than the other cheeses; when squeezed it springs back like a sponge.

OAXACA CHEESE: Oaxaca is the great Mexican melting cheese responsible for queso flameado (the appetizer dip restaurants light on fire tableside!). It's also great for melting on top of enchiladas or baked Tex-Mex dishes. Unmelted Oaxaca is a little rubbery like mozzarella. Pleasantly nutty flavors emerge when it is heated.

TO ORGANIC OR NOT TO ORGANIC? Are Pesticides the Only Question?

I'm going to go out on a limb here and suggest that many people believe the main reason to buy organic is to avoid pesticides in their food. I agree, and that's a dang good reason! But in this book you'll find instructions to "buy organic" for random ingredients, and it may feel like an arbitrary suggestion.

It's not. In taste tests we thought "organic" tasted and performed better with that particular ingredient. When I specifically note it, you will want to take heed!

Our generation has been raised on processed convenience foods like cake mixes and packaged biscuit dough for so long that we think that is what a biscuit should taste like. But why doesn't it taste like Grandma's?

These food products started out in the 1950s as a true convenience product (e.g., a frozen pie dough containing flour, butter or lard, and salt), with the convenience that some little factory in some little town rolled the dough out, placed it in a pan, and sent it to the grocery store to be sold to our grandparents. Our grandparents were delighted by the convenience, and at that time the ingredients were basically the same as homemade, lacking preservatives and extra chemicals.

Fast forward sixty-five years: I flip one of these products over and can't recognize the ingredients listed. But words like cellulose, artificial colors, and preservatives are more than familiar, and are the reason these products are shelf stable for a year or more. I'm not here to argue that these ingredients are safe or unsafe. I am here to tell you that they do not always taste as great as organic brands that are still creating true convenience products based on a simple, straightforward pie dough recipe.

Sometimes organic just tastes better. For the recipes in this book containing pumpkin puree, I suggest organic because during taste tests we preferred the organic canned pumpkin puree, which seemed to be bursting with slap-yo'-grandma pumpkin goodness, to the grocery store pumpkin puree, which was the equivalent of flavorless orange mush.

Bottom line, if I buy a convenience product (which I do, I'm so down for skipping a step), I will buy organic because in my experience it tastes fresher, has more flavor, and is closer to homemade. I make it easy for you by specifically noting organic in the recipes when I think it significantly enhances the dish.

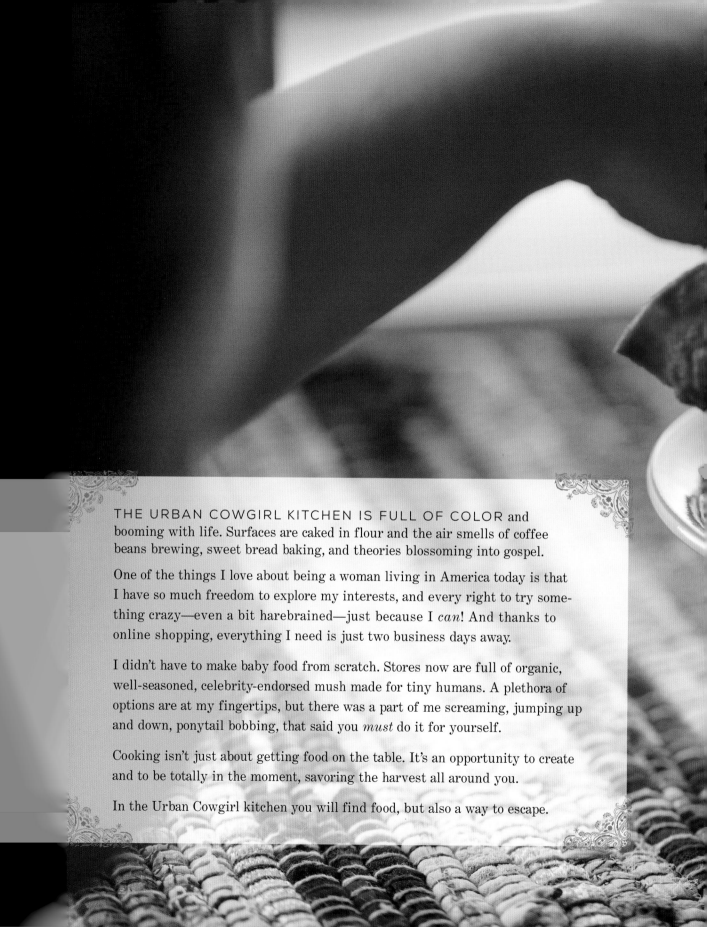

THE URBAN COWGIRL KITCHEN IS FULL OF COLOR and booming with life. Surfaces are caked in flour and the air smells of coffee beans brewing, sweet bread baking, and theories blossoming into gospel.

One of the things I love about being a woman living in America today is that I have so much freedom to explore my interests, and every right to try something crazy—even a bit harebrained—just because I *can*! And thanks to online shopping, everything I need is just two business days away.

I didn't have to make baby food from scratch. Stores now are full of organic, well-seasoned, celebrity-endorsed mush made for tiny humans. A plethora of options are at my fingertips, but there was a part of me screaming, jumping up and down, ponytail bobbing, that said you *must* do it for yourself.

Cooking isn't just about getting food on the table. It's an opportunity to create and to be totally in the moment, savoring the harvest all around you.

In the Urban Cowgirl kitchen you will find food, but also a way to escape.

RECIPES FOR THE
Urban Cowgirl
Kitchen

Urban Cowgirl Fuel

THE BEVERAGES IN THIS CHAPTER are as varied and useful as the food in the chapters that follow. In Urban Cowgirl land, we live dynamic and busy lives. We are moms powered by caffeine and kombucha. We are women who enjoy iced tea and margaritas (sometimes simultaneously). Staying hydrated keeps us moving. This chapter will not only teach you how to make delicious cocktails, but also give you the tools to fuel your body with healthy herbal teas, glorious coffee creations, and even low-calorie fancy dry sodas. Because, to Urban Cowgirls, what you're drinking is as hot a topic as who you're wearing.

HOW TO BUILD AN URBAN COWGIRL BARISTA STATION

COFFEE IS THE KEY TO SURVIVAL. One of my strongest memories as a girl was sneaking into my Aunt LeAnn's kitchen with my cousin Randi to investigate a seductive scent reserved only for grown-ups. Dark and brooding like a mysterious stranger slipping in to steal us away, it mingled with the decadent, sharp chocolate, floated up to her room like an apparition, and curled its finger, beckoning us to follow. It was an allure we didn't yet understand, but could never ignore. When LeAnn finally gave us our own tiny cups, topped with whipped cream and cocoa powder, we felt sure we were getting in on a secret.

It was a treat to any kid, but a lifeline to my Aunt LeAnn. Now I'm the cafe mocha ninja making little cups of chocolate salvation for anyone—Urban Cowgirl or Cowboy—who might find their way to my kitchen. With this list of essential tools, you can be too!

ESPRESSO MACHINE You really only need one basic espresso machine, and it doesn't have to cost more than your first car. I avoid anything with pods or a digital screen, and I always buy a good, heavy espresso tamper for making dense, compact espresso pucks. Start with a bag of espresso ground coffee, which you can get freshly ground at your favorite coffee shop. Fancy people like to grind their own beans, which works great, but you have to have an expensive espresso grinder. (No, a coffee grinder is not the same thing.)

FLAVORED SYRUP All of those syrups at the coffee shop can be purchased online, at restaurant supply stores, or at gourmet specialty shops like World Market and Whole Foods. Start with four flavors and get one sugar-free option for your skinny friends! The little toppers on the syrups the baristas use are available at the liquor store or restaurant supply.

SIMPLE SYRUP Homemade simple syrups need to be refrigerated but stay good for 4-6 months. These are going to be used for dry sodas, sweetening tea and coffee, and on the weekends boot the coffee and usher in the vodka. You're going to learn to make your own flavor combinations in this chapter. Score!

JOE GLO You need to flush your coffee maker and espresso maker with a citric acid based cleaner every once in a while. Soaking the portafilter in Joe Glo keeps the fresh coffee from getting that old coffee funk.

COFFEE MAKER You might as well keep it nearby because your coffee purists like it and iced coffee is a very good thing.

FRENCH PRESS Some people use it for coffee, I use it for making loose-leaf teas.

LOOSE-LEAF TEAS Find the loose leaf tea station at the natural food store and GO NUTS! (It's with the scoopable herbs and spices.)

PERSONALIZE FOR YOUR TRIBE This can include milk, half and half, flavored coffee creamer, Stevia, my recipe for Coffee Shop Caramel Sauce, hot water for tea (we have a cold water machine with a hot spout), coconut milk, almond milk, and sparkling water or soda stream machine for the bubble lovers (like me!).

MEXICAN CHOCOLATE LATTE WITH COFFEE SHOP CARAMEL SAUCE AND COCONUT CREAM

DESSERT COMES IN MANY MAGICAL FORMS in this book. This recipe for my Mexican Chocolate Latte is your first taste of pure decadence, but don't feel bad, it's really just coffee in a fancy dress. When my Urban Cowgirl tribe gets together for dinners now, we usually have kiddos to wrangle and figures to watch. This drink is a perfect way to top off a delicious dinner when dessert really doesn't need to be on the menu. Lighter, thanks to the coconut milk, and sweet and aromatic due to the addition of Mexican chocolate, it will quickly satisfy a sweet tooth or have you jumping out of bed in the morning. **YIELD: 1 LATTE**

FOR THE COCONUT CREAM:

1 (13.5-ounce) can full-fat coconut milk, refrigerated overnight

1 1/2 teaspoons coconut sugar or regular sugar

YIELD: 3/4 CUP

COFFEE SHOP CARAMEL SAUCE

1 cup sugar

1/4 cup water

1 cup heavy cream

4 tablespoons unsalted butter

Pinch of salt

Vanilla bean* or vanilla extract

FOR THE COFFEE:

2 triangles (2 ounces) Abuelita Mexican chocolate

2 tablespoons espresso coffee made into about 3/4 cup espresso via machine or French press coffeemaker

Cinnamon for sprinkling

STEP 1: For the coconut cream, remove the chilled can of coconut milk from the refrigerator and open gently. The coconut butter will have separated from the coconut water and will be floating on the top. Spoon the coconut butter off the top and into a medium bowl, avoiding the water as much as possible.

Beat the coconut butter with electric beaters for about a minute, just until it starts to look like thin whipped cream. Sprinkle in the coconut sugar and continue beating until thick. It's done when it looks like fluffy whipped cream. Refrigerate until needed.

STEP 2: For the Coffee Shop Caramel Sauce, combine the sugar and water in a sauecpan over medium-low heat until the sugar dissolves. Increase the heat and bring to a boil, without stirring. Boil until the syrup is a deep amber color, about 5–6 minutes.

Remove the sugar from the heat and carefully whisk in the heavy cream. The mixture will bubble madly! Stir in the unsalted butter, salt, and vanilla. When cool, transfer the caramel to a squeeze bottle.

STEP 3: To make the latte, chop two triangles of Mexican chocolate with a knife until finely crushed. Place in the bottom of your coffee cup. Pour 3/4 cup hot French press coffee or freshly drawn espresso over the crushed chocolate. (I draw the espresso directly into my chocolate-filled coffee cup!) Stir well until the chocolate is completely melted into the coffee.

Top the coffee with two heaping spoonfuls of coconut cream and caramel sauce, and sprinkle with cinnamon.

 PRO TIP

*TO USE A WHOLE VANILLA BEAN, pierce the bean with a sharp knife and drag the knife down, splitting the bean in two. Scrape out the fragrant black insides and add them to the caramel. The empty pods can be used to make vanilla-scented sugar!

REFRESHING GEORGIA STRAWBERRY PEACH TEA

AS A CHEF, I SEE THINGS IN COOKING CLASSIFICATIONS. When people make sweet tea, they are really making simple syrup. Simple syrup is equal parts water and sugar, so with tea you are essentially adding additional tea-infused water. When you begin to divide your cooking into categories and understand the reason why you do a thing rather than just doing it, the entire way you approach food changes. So instead of using simple syrup to sweeten my tea, I look to my fridge for homemade jams and jellies, which are just fruit-based simple syrups that turn to liquid when heated. They are just as effective as sugar for sweetening tea, and infuse the tea with refreshing fruity flavor. **YIELD: 1 QUART**

1^1/$_2$ cups water

^{1}/$_2$ cup strawberry jam or jelly (not preserves)

Peach tea bags—either 1 large family tea bag (makes 1 quart) or 4 small tea bags

3 cups ice water

In a small saucepan combine the 1^1/$_2$ cups water, strawberry jam, and large tea bag and bring to a boil. Boil for 1 minute. Remove from heat and let the tea steep for 10 minutes. Remove the tea bag if you wish (peach tea is usually an herbal tea, so it is not necessary to remove from the pitcher and will continue to infuse as it sits) and pour the contents of the saucepan into a pitcher. Pour in 3 cups ice water. Fill tall glasses with additional ice and serve.

NOTE: This recipe can be doubled to make 2 quarts of tea for large gatherings.

HEARTLAND BLACKBERRY MINT SWEET TEA

BLACKBERRIES GROW WILD IN TEXAS AND OKLAHOMA. They are everywhere—curling around barbed-wire fences, invading our cultivated gardens, and causing trouble for cattle ranchers when they attempt to take over pastures. As tiny tots we grow up picking them for our mothers to turn into jam, cobbler, wine, and pie. They are truly a gift from the heartland that we learn to appreciate as a child—years before we master pulling the black, glistening berries from the bush without the nick of a thorn. **YIELD: 2 QUARTS**

2 cups water

1 family-size black tea bag or 5 little tea bags

1–2 mint tea bags

1/2 cup seedless blackberry jam

3 cups cold water

In a small saucepan combine water, tea bags, and blackberry jam. Bring to a boil and boil just until the jam begins to break apart and melt. Remove from the heat and steep for 15 minutes. Pour the contents into a pitcher and add 1 cup ice and 3 cups cold water. Stir and enjoy!

HOW TO MAKE YOUR OWN DRY SODA

WANTED TO CUT SOME OF THE UNNECESSARY SUGAR

my diet, something that can get tricky when you are an Urban Cowgirl who loves an ice-cold Dr Pepper. I decided try dry sodas, which are low-sugar, bubbly drinks that come in an array of glorious gourmet flavors like blood orange and vanilla bean. I quickly fell madly in love, ready to embark on a whirlwind romance, when my wallet began to protest. So, I learned how dry sodas are made. I could save money create flavors—two of my favorites are Lemoncello and Lavender Vanilla. Lots extracts work, such as orange, coconut, pineapple, and apricot. I do not recommend vanilla extract, but the recipe for Lavender Vanilla Dry Soda Syrup can made without the lavender.

To make a dry soda using homemade extract, fill a tall glass full of ice and in about 2 tablespoons dry soda syrup. the glass with sparkling water from a bottle or soda stream, and be refreshed!

LEMONCELLO DRY SODA SYRUP

LEMONCELLO IS A SWEET ITALIAN LEMON LIQUEUR that we like to make from scratch every summer using fresh lemons and vodka. This recipe makes a similar syrup but without any alcohol, for a light, refreshing tonic. **YIELD: 2½ CUPS SYRUP**

2 cups water

2 cups sugar

2 tablespoons lemon extract

In a small pot bring the water and sugar to a boil, stirring occasionally. When the sugar fully dissolves in the water, add the lemon extract. Cool and pour into tall glass jars or containers with a spout.

LAVENDER VANILLA DRY SODA SYRUP

Lavender Vanilla is my guilty little pleasure. When I first discovered these light soft drinks, this was the flavor that hooked me and subsequently emptied my wallet! I showed them who was boss by re-creating the flavor infusion in this simple, homemade syrup. **YIELD: 2½ CUPS SYRUP**

2 cups water

1½ tablespoons dried lavender buds

1 cup sugar

½ fresh vanilla bean

Combine water, lavender buds, and sugar into a medium saucepan and bring to a simmer. Cut the full vanilla bean in half with a sharp knife (store the other half for another recipe). Split the remaining bean in half top to bottom. Scrape out the insides with the blade of the knife and add to the pot.

Boil the ingredients for 10 minutes or until reduced to about 1½ cups. Strain the mixture through a sieve or strainer and discard the used buds. Allow the syrup to cool and then pour into glass jars or containers with a spout.

★ ★

HOW TO MAKE HOMEMADE KOMBUCHA

SWEET, TANGY, FRUITY, EFFERVESCENT KOMBUCHA, how I love thee . . .

My acupuncturist actually introduced me to kombucha. She saw me walk in with my Dr Pepper and poured me a little cup of what looked like grape soda. She explained to me—in that gentle, angelic voice that natural, light-filled homeopathic people always have—that it was low in sugar, fizzy, and made from *sweet tea*.

What? I was not aware of any undocumented sweet teas in my greater metropolitan area.

I was apprehensive, but took a sip anyway—just to be nice—and praise the heavens, I was ready to get my "booch" on for good!

Kombucha is loaded with probiotics and antioxidants from the tea, and at about 60 calories per serving, it's less than half the calories of a soda (with no artificial flavors, colorings, or high-fructose corn syrup). I found it in the produce section of the health food store in flavors like ginger berry and grape.

I walked in the next week, smiling from ear to ear, with my kombucha in hand, waiting for her to beam with pride at my willingness to grow and embrace health. She did . . . and then suggested that I try brewing it in my own kitchen, which became my immediate quest for the day.

After a previous weeklong beer brewing adventure with my husband, I found brewing kombucha to be a complete walk in the park, and I know you will too. So let's get brewing!

FIRST, WE NEED A SCOBY

Sweet Tea + SCOBY = Fizzy Kombucha Tea

WHAT THE HECK IS A SCOBY?

The first step in making kombucha is brewing your very own SCOBY—the name is an acronym for symbiotic culture of bacteria and yeast. It's the jellyfish-looking mass that grows on top of the tea, transforming your brew into kombucha and sealing it off from the air. It is totally normal for it to get bumpy from rising carbon dioxide bubbles, stringy wisps from the natural yeasts, and little brown specks, and it has a tendency to fan out into layers if you nudge it.

The squishy little raft that will eventually begin growing on the tea is not actually alive, but merely a harbor for the good bacteria and yeast that create kombucha. It will always grow wide enough to cover the surface of the tea, and eventually it will grow thick as well. The SCOBY growing and changing is just a part of making kombucha, and is similar to working with live cultures in other foodie hobbies like cheese and yogurt making.

★ ★ ★ ★ ★ ★ ★ ★ ★ ★ ★ ★ ★ ★ ★ ★ ★ ★ ★ ★

If you live near a natural grocer, you may be able to pick one up, or you can easily make your own from a bottle of kombucha that contains the remnant of the SCOBY it was made from. Look in the refrigerated section for glass kombucha bottles, peer in the bottom, and look for a wispy little mass or globule. That's your new friend, aka the kombucha "mother," as it's sometimes referred to.

Now we have to make her grow! And lucky for us she must be a Texan, because her drink of choice is sweet tea.

TO MAKE YOUR OWN YOU WILL NEED:

2 quarts water

1 cup sugar (pure cane sugar or coconut sugar works great)

4 bags black tea (nothing fancy, it grows really well in plain black tea)

A large glass jar, clean and sterilized (I just send mine through the dishwasher with the heated dry setting on)

1 bottle unflavored kombucha, with the mother in the bottom (the wisp), as well as the contents of the bottle

Several coffee filters or a couple of paper towels and a rubber band or kitchen twine

In a large stockpot bring the water and sugar to a boil. When it comes to a full boil, turn off the heat and add the tea bags. Let it steep and cool completely. *This is really important because if the tea is too hot it will kill the kombucha mother.*

When the sweet tea is at room temperature, remove and discard the tea bags and pour the tea into the glass jar. Then pour in the whole bottle of store-bought kombucha including all the wispy stuff in the bottom of the bottle (I pour in half the bottle, swirl it around really well, and then pour the rest in).

Clean up any spills and cover the mouth of the jar with a stack of paper towels or a couple of stacked coffee filters and secure with a large

rubber band or kitchen twine. The jar will sit out on the countertop for 10–14 days as the SCOBY grows.

First you will notice bubbles, and then one day you will wake up to a film across the surface of the kombucha. Now we're in business. That film will grow across the surface, sealing the kombucha from the air, and after 2 weeks it will grow thick. I begin using mine to brew kombucha when it is $1/4$–$1/2$ inch thick. You can allow it to keep going for 4 weeks if you get busy or want to grow a large SCOBY to share with friends.

HOW TO MAKE HOMEMADE KOMBUCHA (CONTINUED)

SOME EXTRA TIPS YOU'LL WANT TO KEEP IN MIND:

- The fragrance of the kombucha is alkaline and reminiscent of apple cider vinegar. You won't be able to smell it unless you bend down to sniff it, but, boy howdy, the fruit flies will! Keep it well covered but not sealed, as it needs to have air circulation. Paper towels or a stack of coffee filters sealed with a rubber band work great.

- You cannot use a metal stockpot; it will make the kombucha taste metallic and weaken the SCOBY. The best choice is a large glass jar from a craft or home supply store.

- Avoid going tea crazy just yet; get the SCOBY growing nice and vigorously in a robust blend of plain black tea, and then we'll start experimenting with a rainbow of tea flavors in the next step.

CARING FOR THE SCOBY:

Once you have your SCOBY, you're ready to proceed immediately with brewing kombucha. You can store your SCOBY in Tupperware or glass in the refrigerator covered in the tea that it was brewed in.

NOTE: You will always need about 2 cups of this established kombucha tea to start a new batch of kombucha, so make sure you save it!

I have held mine for up to six months in this dormant stage, and many kombucha brewers agree that older SCOBYs make the best kombucha.

IF YOU PREFER CARBONATED KOMBUCHA, transfer the tea to the flip-top bottles using a funnel at about 7–10 days.

First remove the SCOBY to a clean Tupperware container and pour 2–3 cups of the liquid on top of the SCOBY. This will save the SCOBY until you are ready to brew again. Refrigerate the SCOBY until you're ready or brew your next batch of tea.

Stir the tea well before pouring into bottles, to make sure a bit of wisp gets into every bottle.

Pour the kombucha into flip-top bottles, leaving about 1 inch of space at the top. For a while I had trouble achieving carbonation until I took test sips and exposed a small pocket of air in every bottle, then the carbonation came! Seal the bottles and leave them at room temperature for 2–4 days to start the carbonation. Then refrigerate and enjoy! Don't forget about the bottles or they could pop. Check at least every 2 days until you determine how long they take to carbonate in your home.

COCONUT GREEN TEA KOMBUCHA

NOW YOU ARE READY TO PUT THAT SCOBY TO WORK. I recommend experimenting with a variety of different teas, but always obey the rules of kombucha! Anything naturally antiseptic will kill the kombucha, so honey, cinnamon, clove oil (yes, that means chai tea is out), Earl Grey tea (which is enhanced with bergamot oil), strong sunlight, and cigarette smoke are also no-nos!

Good teas to try are flavored or plain green teas, black teas, oolong (my favorite), and gentle white teas, which are often flavored with fruit flavors. Jasmine is an extremely fragrant floral tea. Herbal teas like hibiscus and yerba mate have been used in combination with real tea leaves for a flavored kombucha.

Kombucha can also be flavored after the SCOBY has been removed to a new batch of tea. You can add fresh fruit juices, ginger root, citrus, honey, mint, fresh fruit and berries, and even vanilla bean once the SCOBY has been removed. **YIELD: 4 QUARTS**

---

3 quarts plus 1 cup water
(filtered preferred)

2 tablespoons loose-leaf coconut green tea

1 cup sugar

2 cups kombucha tea
(you can take this from the batch the SCOBY has been growing in)

1 kombucha SCOBY

1 large glass jar
(gallon size or more)

Optional: flip-top bottles to make the kombucha fizzy, one funnel

STEP 1: In a large stockpot bring the water to a boil and add the tea and the sugar. Boil for 1 minute. Turn off the heat and let steep and cool. When the tea has completely cooled to room temperature, remove the tea bags or loose-leaf tea. Pour into a sterilized large jar. Pour in the kombucha and, with freshly washed hands, add your SCOBY. Try not to get your fingers in the tea.

STEP 2: Cover the jar just the way you did when brewing the SCOBY and place it in a warm corner of the kitchen or pantry. You want the SCOBY to stay around 70–75°F. Do not place it in direct sunlight.

This batch will only brew for 7–10 days. At 7 days you want to begin tasting it with a sterilized, clean spoon every day until you find the right balance of sweetness and acidity. As time passes, the SCOBY will process more and more of the sugar, and the mixture will taste less sweet and more tart. The happy place is somewhere in the middle!

HOMEMADE SODAS IN FLIP-TOP BOTTLES

THE FIRST TIME I MADE SODA AT HOME was for a dinner with a childhood friend and his family. They ended up having to delay the dinner a few days, and because it was my first time making soda with champagne yeast, I didn't know I couldn't just leave it in the bottle until we were ready to drink. By the time we cracked them open, the sodas were horribly inappropriate to serve children. They tasted more like Boone's Farm, the sickly sweet and slightly syrupy malt liquor popular with teenagers and grandmas the world over! I had accidentally made a long beer, when I intended to make short.

This formula will help you come up with many different soda recipes—or as we say in Texas, *a coke*, no matter what the flavor is!

Extracts are found in the baking section of most supermarkets in flavors like root beer, strawberry, and coconut. Traditional cola flavors can be found online and in home brewing shops for a very reasonable price. Look for them when you purchase your champagne yeast. **YIELD: 1 GALLON**

FOR THE CHAMPAGNE YEAST SLURRY:

1 package champagne yeast

1/2 teaspoon sugar

1/4 cup warm water

FOR THE SODA:

1 gallon water

2 cups sugar

2 teaspoons flavored extract

1/2 teaspoon champagne yeast slurry

3–5 flip-top bottles depending on the size, 2 growlers, or 4-liter plastic bottles with lids, sterilized

FOR THE CHAMPAGNE YEAST SLURRY: Combine the ingredients and wait at least 20 minutes until the yeast becomes activated and begins creating bubbles.

FOR THE SODA: In a large stockpot heat the water and sugar over medium heat until the sugar dissolves. Turn off the heat and pour in the extract. Make the yeast slurry while you wait for the water to cool. When the water is just warm to the touch, you can pitch the yeast (that's brew language for pour it in!). Stir well and then pour into the sterile bottles with a funnel or, if you have a steady hand, pour from any pitcher with a spout.

Twist or flip on the lids, and store in a cool, dry place for 24–32 hours. After this time test one bottle for carbonation. Open a bottle and give the soda a taste. If it is sufficiently carbonated, refrigerate all the bottles immediately. If not, wait 8 hours and try again.

A NOTE ABOUT BOTTLE SAFETY

SODA IS READY TO DRINK VERY QUICKLY COMPARED TO OTHER BREWING PROJECTS, and so it escapes much of the contamination dangers faced with brewing beverages for weeks at a time. That being said, with soda the problem becomes ensuring the bottles do not over-carbonate and burst. You can ensure this will not happen by purchasing fine-quality bottles from a homebrew supply shop, checking them every 8 hours, and refrigerating them as soon as they are sufficiently carbonated. I use a plastic 1-liter bottle when bottling every brew to gauge how carbonated the bottles are becoming without having to open one. With a plastic bottle you can press the plastic with a finger to see if it is hard from the creation of CO_2 gas during the carbonation process and therefore know how far along all the bottles have been carbonated.

PRO TIP

WHY CHAMPAGNE YEAST? Champagne yeast will not taint the flavor of your sodas, whereas common bread yeast leaves a yeasty, occasionally boozy aftertaste. Champagne yeast is very reasonably priced (about 50 cents a package) and stores well in the refrigerator or freezer.

TIP FROM MOM

I LIKE TO KEEP DRY SODAS IN TALL BOTTLES WITH POUR SPOUTS, found in liquor stores and kitchen stores. The best spouts have a little lid that flips back when you pour and keeps the fruit flies out. Dry sodas keep up to six months in the refrigerator in a glass container, which makes them even more appealing to busy moms! Champagne yeast goes dormant in cold temperatures, but be aware that if you remove the bottles from the refrigerator the yeast will eventually wake up and begin producing bubbles again.

NEVERLAND TEA

A PART OF ME IS STILL VERY MUCH THE LITTLE GIRL that believes "A Dream Is a Wish Your Heart Makes." And whenever I need to reconnect with that quiet part of myself, to find peace and enter into a restful sleep, I drink this tea. Calming chamomile is known for helping you remember dreams, and sometimes that's exactly what you need to do.

You can mix and match your own garden herbs such as sage leaves, basil, peppermint, and pineapple and chocolate sage. Any fresh edible herbs from the garden produce a delightful, mellow tea.
YIELD: 2 SERVINGS

1 handful lemon basil

1 handful lemon verbena

1 handful chamomile flowers, fresh or dried

1 teaspoon dried lavender buds

2 cups boiling water

In a pot or French press, combine your herbs and pour hot water over them. Steep 10–15 minutes and serve before bedtime with honey or lemon if desired.

TIPSY TEXAN

THIS IS A HOT TODDY MADE FROM HERBAL TEA and local honey from backyard bees. It will heal everything from your sniffles to your grumpy days. **YIELD: 1 SERVING**

1 tablespoon dried chamomile tea or 2 tablespoons fresh chamomile flowers and buds

$3/4$ cup hot water

1 ($1/4$-ounce) shot bourbon (from the big side of the jigger!)

1 tablespoon honey

Juice of $1/2$ a lemon

Steep chamomile tea with the hot water for 4–8 minutes. The longer it steeps the stronger the flavor. In a large coffee or tea cup, pour the shot of bourbon, honey, and lemon juice. Pour the brewed tea over the bourbon mixture and stir. Enjoy piping hot!

SPARKLING MANGO MINT AGUA FRESCA

AGUA FRESCAS, OR "FRESH WATERS" IN SPANISH, are iconic in San Antonio where I worked for years as a professional chef. Broken down to the basics, they are deconstructed fruit steeped in cold water that come in a variety of bright, refreshing flavor combinations. And that's wonderful, but I like bubbles—especially after a workout. When lounging in my yoga pants, calculating how many downward dogs it will take to burn off the calories in my Chocolate Caramel Decadence coffee creamer, the promise of a Sparkling Mango Mint Agua Fresca after my sweat-session spurs me to action. Agua frescas are a unique, deliciously tropical way to replenish your electrolytes and meet your goals. Because some days you drink agua frescas and run a 5K, and some days you binge Netflix and eat a pint of coffee ice cream. The Urban Cowgirl life is truly all about balance. **YIELD: 2 CUPS OF FRUIT BASE**

---

2 mangos

1/4 cup orange juice

Juice of 1 lemon

2 sprigs of mint

Sparkling water

Using a vegetable peeler, peel the green peel off the mangos. Cut the fruit up and add to a blender or food processor.

Add the orange and lemon juice and blend to a sauce consistency. Add mint leaves and pulse until they are chopped up and distributed throughout. Pour into a container with a lid and chill.

Combine 1 1/2 tablespoons puree in a small glass. Add ice to the rim. Top with 1/2 cup sparkling water and enjoy! The fruit base can be refrigerated and used for several days.

HOW TO INFUSE HOOCH

WHATEVER YOU CALL IT IN YOUR NECK OF THE WOODS . . . moonshine, white lightning, white whiskey, Mountain Dew, corn squeezins, or even kickapoo, hooch is back and more fashionable than ever! Of course for our tribe of Urban Cowgirls, born into a long pedigree of bootleggers and East Texas moonshiners, it never really went out of style. Uptown cocktail bars may be strewn with black pepper–infused moonshine martinis now, but the heart of the art lies in the country.

Texans trading candy apple white lightning for Georgia peach moonshine when we let loose with our Urban Cowgirl sisters is as old as the South itself. It really is an art form—infusing hooch takes finesse to get the right balance of flavors that enhance your liquor selection. It takes patience and a few batches to master, but the result is enough to warm your heart on a cold winter night, to give you courage to face a crowd of people, and to make friends of bitter enemies.

FORMULA

1 part shine: 4 parts liquid

FLAVOR INSPIRATION

Fresh and frozen juices

Cocktail mixes
(hurricane mix, daiquiri mix)

Flavored teas
(coconut, peach, chamomile)

Herbs and spices
(pumpkin pie spice,
cinnamon sugar, piloncillo)

Any flavor of soda
(orange, cream soda, cherry cola)

Fresh or frozen fruit
(peaches, sour cherries,
watermelon)

Frozen fruit purees
(guava, dragon fruit, mango)

In a large pot heat your liquid and add any fruit, flavorings, or spices to the infusion. Bring to a simmer and reduce by one-third. Cool thoroughly and pour in the moonshine. Add a tablespoon or so of sugar if needed. It should be strong. Pour into jars and seal or refrigerate.

NOTE: Do not reduce the mixture with the alcohol; it must be poured in after or it will cook off.

PRO TIP

I "ICEBOX INFUSE" MINE by keeping them sealed in our garage refrigerator, chilled until we're ready to drink them! This is best served straight from the jar.

CANDY APPLE MOONSHINE
(FOR THE BOLD AND ADVENTURESOME)

THIS RECIPE WAS GIVEN TO ME BY A BONA FIDE TEXAS MOONSHINER, and we fall in love with it every October when the leaves begin to fall and the promise of a chilly Friday night in front of the fire pit is guaranteed! **YIELD: 1½ GALLONS**

½ gallon apple juice

½ gallon apple cider
(best quality you can find!)

15 cinnamon sticks

1 quart moonshine

7 pint-size mason jars

In a large stockpot combine the apple juice, apple cider, and cinnamon sticks. Bring to a simmer and reduce by one-third. Turn off the heat and cool to room temperature. Add 1 quart moonshine. In pint-size mason jars place a couple of the steeped cinnamon sticks and fill with the mixture. These can be jarred traditionally by sterilizing the jars, filling with moonshine, and sealing.

CREAMSICLE MOONSHINE

THERE'S JUST SOMETHING ABOUT A GUY IN A TRUCK that makes me smile. Throw in a creek bottom, cut-off shorts, a couple fishing poles, and a cooler full of creamsicle moonshine and you're officially ready for a romantic summer tryst. This is a refreshing take on infused hooch that's not quite as strong as our standard recipe but will still sneak up on ya. So put the tailgate down, curl up on a quilt, and surrender to summertime. **YIELD: 4 TO 5 PINTS**

---

3 (12-ounce) bottles vanilla cream soda

12 ounces orange juice

24 ounces moonshine

A couple tablespoons of sugar, to taste if needed

4–5 pint-size mason jars

In a large stockpot combine the cream soda and orange juice. Bring to a low boil and simmer for 1 minute to blend the flavors. Turn off the heat and let sit for 5–10 minutes to cool, then add the moonshine. Sample a taste and add a couple spoonfuls of sugar if necessary while the mixture is still warm. Pour into four or five pint-size mason jars and seal if preferred or refrigerate.

BRISKET-INFUSED BOURBON

IN MY EARLY CHEF LIFE, I WORKED AS A LINE CHEF in a four-star restaurant on the San Antonio Riverwalk. After hours I'd pack my knives up in a weathered leather shoulder bag and head into the balmy night. I'd listen to the sound of my boots clicking against the cobblestones as I walked and plot the next day's line adventure like I was Buffy the Vampire Slayer on a mission to carve the perfect fillet. Then I'd find my way to this classy little bar where I'd find my line chef compatriots in a booth near the back wearing splatter-stained clothes and the look of blissful accomplishment. Together we would save San Antonio from mediocre cuisine.

This is for the chefs still working the line, for the ones about to begin, and for the bourbon-sipping Buffy in all of us. Raise a glass! **YIELD: 1 LITER**

---

1 tall jar (big enough to fit a liter of bourbon and the brisket fully submerged)

A piece of freshly smoked brisket about 2–3 inches x 4 inches, both meat and marbling, homemade or store bought from your favorite barbecue joint (tell them to leave it whole, unsliced!)

1 liter bourbon

1 long piece of cheesecloth

1 piece of butchers twine

Saran Wrap and foil or a lid for the jar

Lay the cheesecloth out on a clean countertop and cut enough fabric that your brisket can comfortably sit in the middle while gathering the sides at the top for tying. (Cheesecloth is designed with several layers so that no small pieces escape the cheesecloth bag.)

Place the brisket in the middle, gather the top of the fabric, and secure with butchers twine.

Fill your clean jar with the entire bottle of bourbon and, using tongs, gently place the brisket in the bourbon. It must be fully submerged under the surface of the bourbon.

Cover with Saran Wrap securely and then foil. (This keeps the fruit flies out, who love bourbon as much as any of us do.) Store at room temperature for 1 month.

To remove the brisket, freeze the jug for 6 hours, which will cause the fat to solidify. Remove the brisket with tongs. Pour the cold bourbon through a fresh layer of cheesecloth into another container. All the cold fat will be caught in the cheesecloth and you can discard it. Repeat the straining if desired.

PRO TIP

MAKE SURE TO CUT OFF THE BRISKET'S BARK if it is very salty. If it's just a rich, well-flavored bark, then it can stay. Also, make sure that you really like the combination of wood that the meat has been smoked on. The flavor of the brisket will infuse the bourbon, but the aroma of the smoke is much more pronounced.

BLACK LEMONADE FOR DETOX

URBAN COWGIRLS LIVE A LIFE OF FULL-FLAVOR, decadent dishes and the occasional Friday night jar of Candy Apple Moonshine. Sometimes our bodies need to get rid of unwanted toxins from all that glorious livin'. Google search "ways to detox" and you will find a mixed bag of options, from chile powder and lemon juice to green tea supplements with tons of fillers, but Urban Cowgirls know activated charcoal is the real secret cure. This Black Lemonade is great for starting your detox off right. After a few servings of this, you'll be fit as a fiddle and ready to fly! **YIELD: 1 LARGE GLASS**

1/4 teaspoon activated charcoal

3 juicy lemons, cut in half and juiced

1 cup cold filtered water

2 tablespoons honey (plus more to taste if needed)

1/2 cup ice

PRO TIP

ACTIVATED CHARCOAL can be purchased online and in your local vitamin shop. Make sure it is made for oral consumption and food grade. Always consult a physician to ensure this is a healthy plan of action for you.

I make this drink in my trusty protein shaker bottle with the little ball inside that mixes everything up! You can also use a mason jar with a lid, a blender, or a tall pitcher and a whisk.

Add all the ingredients to the jar and shake like the dickens! Give it a taste and add more honey if necessary.

ESPRESSO ICED TEA: AKA BLACK GOLD

By this point in the book, you probably know that I am in a long-term relationship with coffee, but honestly it's a little dehydrating for days when you have to go, go, go. The black tea in this concoction keeps me feeling light on my feet and hydrated, while the boost of espresso makes me invigorated and motivated. Don't feel like making it yourself? Hit up the local barista with this recipe and tell them the Urban Cowgirl sent you. **YIELD: 2-4 SERVINGS**

1 large family-size tea bag or
4 small black tea bags

2 cups boiling water

2 large shots of espresso or 1 cup
extremely strong coffee, cooled

2 cups ice

1–2 cups additional cold water
for diluting the tea if desired

In a pitcher place the large family-size tea bag and pour the boiling water over it. Allow it to steep 10 minutes. Remove the tea bag and squeeze it well.

Add the 2 shots espresso or 1 cup strong coffee and the ice. Taste and dilute with 1–2 cups cold water if desired.

Breakfasting

IN URBAN COWGIRL COUNTRY, BREAKFAST IS NOT A MEAL, IT'S AN EVENT. We don't always get to have a leisurely morning soiree, but when we do you better believe we do it right. That means elegant recipes and long morning chats, the scent of chicory coffee and applewood-smoked bacon dancing in the air, and friendly debates on philosophy and spirituality followed by comfortable moments of introspection with mouths full of buttermilk biscuits. The art of breakfast isn't food and drinks consumed in haste but not really savored, it's discussions of family history and last night's dreams, planning gardens and home projects and plots to take over the world while relishing a bite of sausage you just soaked in maple syrup. Breakfasting with the Urban Cowgirls is more than eggs and toast.

It's a meal served with a world of possibilities.

PUMPKIN SOUFFLE PANCAKES
WITH HOT CINNAMON SYRUP

PUMPKIN SPICE MAY BE EVERY *BASIC* GIRL'S GO-TO FLAVOR, but for me it's a way to infuse fall flavor into my food year-round. However, it's not the star of this recipe. The flavor I'm truly obsessed with is cinnamon. Cinnamon toothpaste, cinnamon chewing gum, and cinnamon candy at the bottom of my hot wassail—I even make a cinnamon soap! Once you've tried this syrup, you will find it hard to ever go back. It's good on everything, and keeps for ages. **YIELD: 8-10 PANCAKES**

2 cups all-purpose flour

1/4 cup brown sugar

1/2 teaspoon salt

1/4 teaspoon cinnamon

1/4 teaspoon ground cloves

1/4 teaspoon freshly shaved nutmeg

2 teaspoons baking powder

1 3/4 cups milk

1 teaspoon vanilla extract

1/3 cup organic canned pumpkin puree*

2 tablespoons butter, melted

4 large eggs, separated

Extra butter or coconut oil for frying pancakes

STEP 1: Prepare three bowls: one for dry ingredients, one for wet ingredients, and one for whipping the egg whites (preferably glass, metal, or ceramic), and a hand mixer or stand mixer equipped with the whisk attachment.

Dry bowl: Combine the flour, sugar, salt, spices, and baking powder. Whisk well.

Wet bowl: Combine the milk, vanilla extract, pumpkin puree, butter, and the yolks of the four eggs. Whisk well.

Egg whites bowl: Separate the egg whites by cracking an egg and, with clean, freshly washed hands, passing the egg back and forth between your hands, letting the whites run into the egg white bowl underneath. Drop the intact egg yolk into the "wet" bowl. Be sure to keep the egg whites pure; do not allow any yolk to be present in the mixture when you begin to whip them.

STEP 2: Pour the wet ingredients into the dry ingredients bowl a little at a time, whisking until the mixture is well mixed. Reserve.

Beat the egg whites to stiff peaks (mixture should be white and fluffy and stand straight up in peaks when you remove the whisk from the egg white foam).

PRO TIP

*AFTER TRYING EVERY PUMPKIN PUREE I could get my hands on, I can tell you my favorites for big pumpkin flavor are the classic Libby's brand or the various organic brands. I find generic pumpkin puree to be flavorless mush. You'll enjoy this dish so much more by spending an extra couple of dimes for a full-flavored pumpkin puree.

FOR THE CINNAMON SYRUP:

1¹/₂ cups maple syrup

¹/₄ cup water

2–3 tablespoons ground cinnamon (depending on the type of cinnamon and how fresh it is; I recommend organic cinnamon)

NOTE: This recipe can be doubled, but 2–3 tablespoons cinnamon is usually sufficient even for a double batch.

Gradually fold the egg whites into the pancake batter. For high-top airy pancakes do not overmix, but only fold until the mixture is just incorporated into the batter.

Heat a sauté pan or cast-iron skillet to medium heat. Add 1 tablespoon butter or coconut oil to the pan and pour in the batter. Cook for 2 minutes, watching for the edges of the pancake to turn golden brown and the wet batter on the top to begin to thicken and show air bubbles. Using a spatula, flip the pancake and cook an additional 1–2 minutes. Remove pancake to a warm dish and repeat until the batter is gone.

Serve pancakes drizzled with cinnamon syrup and dotted with a good-quality butter.

For the syrup: In a small saucepan pour in the maple syrup followed by the water (which helps to grab the cinnamon). Add the cinnamon and whisk well. Turn on the heat and bring just to a boil. Turn off the heat, stir, and allow the syrup to infuse with the cinnamon while you complete the rest of the recipe.

EXTRA PANCAKES CAN BE FROZEN in a freezer bag for lightning-fast breakfasts! As for the cinnamon syrup, well, there won't be any left . . . but it will keep refrigerated for a week or more.

SAUSAGE EGGS BENEDICT WITH CHEESE
SAUCE AND CANDIED TOMATOES

THE LASKER INN IN GALVESTON, TEXAS, is bursting with 150 years of Gulf Coast charm. The white columned, two-story wraparound porch was made for drinking iced tea and telling stories. I love the Lasker Inn, and when I was living in Galveston, I was their first chef when the bed-and-breakfast opened in 2012. I still visit the Lasker kitchen whenever I'm in Galveston and looking for a little class with my morning coffee. One of the recipes I created for the Lasker menu was this cheesy sausage eggs Benedict with candied tomatoes, and it is still my favorite way to start a relaxing morning. **YIELD: 12 HALVED MUFFINS TOPPED WITH EGGS**

FOR THE EGGS BENEDICT:

1 pound breakfast sausage

6 English muffins

6 tablespoons butter

1 dozen very fresh eggs

12 candied tomato slices, fresh or from the olive bar at your local grocery store

Fresh chives, for garnish

FOR THE CHEESE SAUCE:

6 ounces sharp cheddar cheese ($3/4$ of an 8-ounce block)

3 cups milk

$1/4$ cup butter

$1/4$ cup flour

5–7 dashes of Tabasco

Juice of $1/4$ a small lemon

1 teaspoon salt

Freshly cracked black pepper

Optional: fresh thyme

STEP 1: Remove sausage from wrapper and slice into $1/2$-inch circles. Place four or five sausage patties in a cast-iron skillet and turn the heat to medium. As the heat rises, some fat will render off the sausage and help lubricate the pan. Cook 3–4 minutes per side and drain on paper towels. Reserve and repeat with the rest of the sausage.

STEP 2: Preheat the oven to 350°F and slice each English muffin in half (if they aren't already split) with a serrated knife. Lay them out on a cookie sheet and butter each half with a dollop of butter. Sprinkle with salt and bake 10–12 minutes, until toasted.

STEP 3: Make the cheese sauce: Grate the cheddar cheese on a box grater and reserve in a bowl. If the milk is cold (straight from the refrigerator), pour it into a glass measuring cup with a pour spout and microwave just until warm, about $1^1/2$ minutes.

In a medium saucepan melt the butter and sprinkle in the flour, whisking well to make a roux. Cook for 1 minute and then begin adding in the milk a bit at a time, whisking and incorporating it in slowly to form the sauce. When the milk has all been poured in, turn up the heat until the mixture just begins to simmer and thicken. Simmer 2–3 minutes, whisking to ensure the bottom does not scorch.

Sprinkle in the cheese and whisk to incorporate. Add the tabasco, lemon, salt, and pepper. Season to taste. Finish with fresh thyme if desired.

STEP 4: Fill a medium pot with water, cover, and bring to a rolling boil. Add a dash of salt. Remove the cover and turn the water down to a slow simmer (an old French chef once told me the right bubbles wouldn't wake a sleeping baby, meaning slow, gentle bubbles). Crack a fresh egg into a small bowl, then pour the egg into the water gently but swiftly. It will sink to the bottom and immediately begin cooking.

Poached eggs take 3–4 minutes. Scoop them out with a slotted spoon and drain on a small paper towel before placing on the English muffins. Repeat.

STEP 5: On every plate place one or two English muffins. Top each with a slice of seared sausage and a poached egg. Top with cheese sauce and finish with one candied tomato, chopped well, and a sprinkling of chives.

COZY FIREPLACE CHAT

THE FIRST TIME I EVER POACHED AN EGG WAS RIGHT IN FRONT OF BOBBY FLAY.

I'm not much of a poached egg kinda girl, unless eggs Benny is on the menu. But for my audition in front of Bobby Flay for Food Network, I decided to brave the boiling waters and give it a go. I stood there with the same dumbfounded apprehension everyone feels when they look at a pan of hot boiling water and consider dropping a raw egg into it—even though we are told it will emerge as a lovely, tender, light, and wispy satchel of gooey egg goodness! I mean, even the mere idea sounds like something out of an egg-obsessed fairy tale.

Bobby is firing off questions at me and I'm smiling, trying to answer with wit and wisdom while also attempting to look like I've been poaching eggs since I could walk when really I had never tried it in my life. And guess what? It worked!

★ ★

BUTTER BREAD

FIVE YEARS AGO I SAT AT A DIMLY LIT DINING ROOM TABLE in West Texas, shuffling through a garbage sack full of recipe clippings and handwritten scribbles. With my two cousins by my side, we meticulously read through each scrap of paper, softly murmuring to each other when we thought we had found a good one. There may have been the occasional sneeze and eye-watering knuckle rub thanks to the sixty years of dust we were shaking off our great-grandmother's recipe collection.

We were looking for one particular recipe that had become legend in our family, lovingly referred to as "butter bread." Loaded with butter, this sweet, decadent dessert had been regularly devoured by my mother and auntie before returning to the sugarcane fields to "play pretend" like only little girls can do.

It sounded like a fantasy dessert, made even more interesting and provocative based on the fact that every time we asked our great-grandmother for the recipe she told us it was lost somewhere in the house, and she'd find it sooner or later. When she went on to that great bake shop in the sky, I had two missions:

• Liberate her cast-iron skillet from her stove.

• Find the recipe for butter bread somewhere in that little West Texas cottage.

Obtaining the skillet was easy; finding the recipe *was not*.

Just when we were getting to the bottom of her sack-o-recipes, and I was beginning to wonder if she had written the darn thing in invisible ink on the kitchen ceiling, there it was. *Butter Bread from Sweetwater, Texas*, shoved to the bottom of the sack and left to crinkle and discolor with time.

WEST TEXAS BUTTER BREAD

IF YOU'RE A BAKER, the first odd thing you'll notice about this old family recipe is that the dough is cooked raw in the icing. I know, I tried to "fix it" too. It doesn't work any other way than exactly as written. **YIELD: 1 JELLY ROLL STYLE PASTRY THAT SERVES FOUR TO SIX**

FOR THE DOUGH:

$1^{1}/_{2}$ cups flour

$^{1}/_{2}$ teaspoon salt

$^{1}/_{2}$ teaspoon baking powder

$^{1}/_{3}$ cup shortening

$^{1}/_{2}$ cup cold milk

FOR THE FILLING:

3 tablespoons softened butter

Sugar, sprinkled liberally

Cinnamon, sprinkled liberally

Nutmeg, sprinkled liberally

FOR THE ICING:

2 cups milk or water

$^{1}/_{2}$ cup butter

$^{3}/_{4}$ cup sugar

Pinch nutmeg and salt

Preheat the oven to 375°F.

In a bowl or standing mixture, mix the flour, salt, and baking powder. Cut in the shortening until it resembles little beads in the flour mixture. Continue kneading and pour in the milk a little at a time until the dough is stiff enough to handle. Divide the dough into four equal parts and roll out each part on a floured board until the dough is about $^{1}/_{8}$ inch thick. Dot each part with butter and sprinkle liberally with sugar, cinnamon, and nutmeg. Roll up each piece of dough like a jelly roll.

In a glass baking dish, combine the icing ingredients and microwave until liquid. Place the jelly rolls into the icing and drizzle with excess icing.

Place the baking dish into the oven and bake for 35–40 minutes. Cut into servable pieces and serve with hot coffee.

EIGHT-MINUTE CINNAMON SUGAR DOUGHNUT HOLES WITH STRAWBERRY LIME ICEBOX JAM

ARE THERE REALLY ANY MOTHERS OUT THERE WHO HAVE IT SO TOGETHER they remember to start a doughnut dough eight hours in advance? Show yourselves! I dare you.

Well, I've made a recipe for the rest of us, and you'll probably recognize it from the good ol' days before there was a cheap donut shop on every corner. Even though I coat these doughnut holes in cinnamon sugar, I still serve the kids a little bowl of homemade strawberry jam for dunkin' and a glass of ice-cold milk. In our house if it's homemade, it's healthier. **YIELD: 40–50 DOUGHNUT HOLES AND ABOUT A QUART OF JAM**

FOR THE DOUGHNUT HOLES:

1 quart oil for frying

1 cup sugar

1 1/2 tablespoons organic cinnamon

1-pound package organic biscuit dough (large can)

Optional: a little flour if the biscuit dough becomes tacky and won't release from your countertops

FOR THE STAWBERRY JAM:

2 pounds strawberries

1/4 cup lime juice (about 3–4 limes)

Zest of 2 limes

2 1/2 cups sugar

1/4 teaspoon kosher salt

FOR THE DONUTS: In a medium saucepan pour in the oil to about halfway and start heating the oil on medium high to about 375°F.

To make the cinnamon sugar, combine the sugar and cinnamon in a large bowl and mix well. Reserve.

Meanwhile, open the biscuit dough and remove three biscuits at a time. Press the pre-shaped biscuits down onto a clean countertop with the palm of your hand to flatten them out. You can also use a rolling pin to roll them out to about 1/4 inch thickness. Using your small cookie cutters, cut rounds, hearts, or other shapes. Peel the excess dough off the shapes and reserve that dough for rolling out last. Repeat with the remaining biscuits until you have used all the dough.

When the oil reaches the proper temperature, scoop up the shapes with a spatula and one by one drop them into the oil. The little shapes will immediately begin to puff up and turn golden brown. Fry them for about 30–60 seconds.

Using a fry skimmer or a slotted spoon, remove the doughnut holes, making sure to drain the excess oil back into the pan. Transfer them into the cinnamon sugar bowl and toss well to coat. Use tongs to remove them from the cinnamon sugar and serve immediately with a little bowl of strawberry jam for dunking.

FOR THE JAM: Wash the strawberries well and dice them into small pieces.

In a large saucepan combine strawberries, lime juice, lime zest, sugar, and salt. Bring to a rolling boil and stir to incorporate. Turn the heat down to a simmer for 10 minutes, mashing the strawberry mixture with a potato masher if desired. Let the mixture cool, transfer to Tupperware or glass jars, and refrigerate. This jam can also be frozen and transferred to the refrigerator when ready to consume.

PRO TIP

THIS ENTIRE PROCESS WORKS BEST IF YOU cut the doughnut holes and fry in batches so the dough stays chilled. If it becomes warm and tacky, you can dust the dough and the countertop with a little bit of flour to help keep the dough workable. Keep the dough you are not currently working with refrigerated.

HILL COUNTRY BUTTERMILK PEACH
MUFFINS WITH WHITE CHOCOLATE GLAZE

A FEW YEARS AGO, before I had my babies, my husband, Dereck, and I rented a sweet little cabin right on the banks of the Frio River, near a town called Utopia. We spent our evenings fishing, cooking s'mores on a bonfire, and dreaming of the life we would have and the children we would raise together. In the daytime we'd venture into the town, antiquing and eating at the local diners, walking past B&Bs and reading the menus posted outside. We promised ourselves that someday we'd go back and stay at the bed-and-breakfast with the white chocolate peach muffins and the wraparound porch. I created this recipe as a reminder. **YIELD: ABOUT 2 DOZEN**

FOR THE DRY INGREDIENTS:

$2^1/_2$ cups flour

1 cup sugar

1 teaspoon kosher salt

$2^1/_2$ teaspoons baking powder

FOR THE WET INGREDIENTS:

$1^1/_4$ cups buttermilk

2 eggs

$1^1/_2$ teaspoons vanilla extract

$^1/_4$ cup butter, melted

$^1/_4$ cup fresh oil or melted lard

1 (4-ounce) bar white baking chocolate

$1^1/_2$ cups frozen or fresh diced peaches

1 cup turbinado sugar

1 package muffin liners

Spray oil

Preheat the oven to 400°F. Spray a muffin tin with spray oil and line each cup with a muffin liner. Spray with spray oil again.

Combine the dry ingredients in one large bowl and the wet ingredients in another large bowl. Whisk the dry ingredients together well, and then whisk the wet ingredients. Chop half the bar of white chocolate into small pieces, about a $^1/_2$ cup. Reserve the rest for the glaze.

Pour the wet ingredients into the dry ingredients and whisk to combine. Fold in the peaches and white chocolate. Using a meatball or ice cream scoop, fill the muffin tins to the rim with batter. Sprinkle liberally with turbinado sugar.

Bake for 20 minutes. Remove the muffin tin from the oven and allow to cool slightly. When they are cool enough to handle, remove the muffins to a cooling rack and repeat baking muffins with any remaining batter.

To glaze the muffins, place the remaining half of the white chocolate bar in a glass bowl and melt it by microwaving in short blasts, stirring frequently with a fork. Brush the liquid white chocolate onto the tops of the cooled muffins. The chocolate will firm up as it dries, creating a sweet chocolate glaze.

JALAPEÑO CINNAMON ROLLS
WITH BROWN BUTTER FROSTING

JALAPEÑO CINNAMON ROLLS ARE ALWAYS A TREAT for out-of-town guests staying the night in our home. What better way to start a vacation in Texas than with a hot, buttery, jalapeño-infused cinnamon roll on the porch with friends? These sweet rolls are not spicy, but subtly infused with the aroma of pickled jalapeños. They are adored by toddlers and grandparents alike! For extra brownie points, sprinkle the whole pan with chopped crispy bacon, because, hey, you only live once.
YIELD: 12 ROLLS

SWEET DOUGH

1 cup milk

1/2 cup butter

1 tablespoon instant yeast

1/2 cup sugar

1 teaspoon salt

1 large egg

1/4 cup diced, pickled jalapeño peppers from a jar

4 1/2 cups all-purpose flour

FILLING

1/3 cup butter, softened

1 cup brown sugar

3 tablespoons cinnamon

FOR THE DOUGH: Set up your stand mixer with the dough hook or prepare your bread machine to knead dough. In a microwave-safe bowl combine the milk and butter. Microwave in 30-second bursts until the butter is melted into the milk. Pour the mixture into the bowl of the bread maker or stand mixer and allow it to cool while you gather and measure the dry ingredients.

When the milk and butter mixture is just warm to the touch, add the instant yeast, sugar, salt, egg, and diced pickled jalapeños. Turn the machine on to begin mixing the wet ingredients. A cup at a time, add in the flour until a solid ball of dough forms and pulls away from the bowl. (If you're using a bread machine, follow the manufacturer's instructions with this recipe.)

When the dough is formed, detach it from the dough hook, cover the bowl with plastic wrap or a kitchen towel, and put it in a warm location to rise. Allow the dough to double in size before proceeding, about 4–6 hours, or longer in cool weather.

When the dough has doubled in size, place it on a lightly floured surface and roll it out into a large rectangle, about 14 x 24 inches. For the filling spread the softened butter over the surface of the dough and sprinkle with brown sugar and cinnamon. Peel up the edge of dough closest to you and roll it up jelly roll–style into a little log. Cut the dough into twelve rolls.

PRO TIP

THE SECRET INGREDIENT to all those designer cupcake bakeries is copious mountains of brown butter icing. After all, it's all about the icing! Browning your butter before adding the powdered sugar brings out subtle aromas, toasty notes, and complex flavor profiles. It's a technique used in professional kitchens and referred to as a beurre noisette, or "brown butter." You can use this technique every time you make icing, if you like, and incorporate it into your own icing recipes.

ICING

1 stick butter

2 cups powdered sugar

1/4 cup milk

1 teaspoon vanilla extract

1/8 teaspoon kosher salt

Grease a 9 x 13-inch baking pan with butter or coconut oil and place the rolls inside. It is fine if they are lightly spaced out because they will continue to rise. Cover and let rise a second time until they fill the baking pan, about 30 minutes.

Preheat the oven to 400°F. When the rolls have doubled in size, remove the cover and bake for 20–25 minutes. While they are baking, prepare the brown butter icing.

FOR THE ICING: In a saucepan melt the butter and cook on low heat until the milk solids foam, then turn dark and fall to the bottom (they will look like little specks). After this occurs the scent of the butter will turn nutty, and the color will begin to turn golden brown. The entire process takes 3–4 minutes. Transfer the butter to a bowl and either whisk in the other icing ingredients or beat them in using electric beaters for a fluffier consistency. Finish with just enough kosher salt to enhance the roasted flavors of the brown butter, about 1/8–1/4 teaspoon. Set aside while the rolls finish baking.

To finish the rolls, remove them from the oven and allow them to cool until they are just warm to the touch, about 8 minutes. Then smear them with the brown butter icing and serve. The rolls will keep for a day on the countertop or longer if refrigerated.

COZY FIREPLACE CHAT

CARING FOR OUR FRIEND YEAST: IT'S ALIVE!

(Insert scary monster voice here.)

Have you ever used yeast in a recipe and the dough just didn't want to rise? It may be because the yeast needed to be activated. When making a dough, you have two main choices of yeast: instant yeast and activated dry yeast. In any recipe you can use them interchangeably, but active dry yeast requires a wake-up call!

Dissolve the dry yeast in a little warm water and sprinkle with a teaspoon or so of sugar from the recipe you'll be working with. This causes the yeast to foam and bubble after a few minutes. The yeast is now "activated," which means it has awakened, had a cup of coffee, and is now ready to work!

Instant yeast can go right into the recipe without activating it. It goes by many names, including bread machine yeast, fast rising, and rapid rise yeast. It works in half the time of plain activated dry yeast, which is why I like it. (I am impatient. Carbs excite me.) Store yeast in the refrigerator or the freezer and toss it after it has expired.

You can test to see if the yeast is still good by trying to activate it using the procedure above. If it foams, it is still fresh; if not, it's time to replace it!

BANANA NUT CORNBREAD

THIS IS A LOVE STORY between those forgotten ripe bananas sitting on your kitchen counter and grandma's sweet cake cornbread. It's baked in the oven and served with a hefty helping of smooth butter. **YIELD: 1 LOAF**

3 bananas (soft and overripe is best)

1 large egg

1 teaspoon vanilla extract

1/2 cup butter, melted

1/2 cup cornmeal

1 cup flour

1 cup sugar

1 teaspoon baking soda

1/2 teaspoon cinnamon

1/4 teaspoon nutmeg

1/4 teaspoon kosher salt

1 cup walnuts

Preheat the oven to 325°F.

In a stand mixer or bowl, mash the bananas using beaters. Add the egg, vanilla extract, and butter. Mix well.

In another bowl combine the cornmeal, flour, sugar, baking soda, cinnamon, nutmeg, and salt. Mix well.

Pour the dry ingredients into the wet ingredients and beat until just combined. Fold in the walnuts.

Pour into a greased bread pan and bake for 1 hour.

PRO TIP

OVER-RIPE BANANAS make the best banana bread!

Starters

WHEN DINING AT HOME, ONE DOES NOT ALWAYS HAVE A FIRST COURSE to one's meal. This is not 1912, and we do not, unfortunately, sup with Lord Grantham in Downton Abbey. In our daily life there is rarely the occasion for multiple courses to our family dinners. Yet, when gathered around a table at our favorite restaurant, we will undoubtedly order wings, or eggrolls, or a plate of cheese fries.

Despite their existence being optional, let's face it, appetizers are *everyone's* favorite. Chips and queso, beef nachos, bacon-wrapped shrimp, and other dinner darlings tend to be ambassadors in defining a culture in one bite, and routinely end up on the most loved dish list. They say life is short so eat dessert first, but I say appetizers prove we're already putting our heart where our mouth is.

A TALE OF THREE QUESOS

I've had my fair share of star-crossed love affairs, destined to end in disaster—only not with men! My love affairs have been with the varied personalities of the warm, gooey goodness we all know as *queso*. To save you from my fitful fate, I remove the veil of mystery and present to you one girl's guide to navigating the decadent and deceptive "Bowl of Melted Mexican Cheese." Arm yourselves with tortillas and chips, ladies, you're in for a sensational ride.

BÉCHAMEL QUESO The sexy French guy you meet on your summer study abroad. He seems wildly unattainable, mysterious, and complicated, with all the sophistication and class you think you need, but once you get to know him he's not any more magnificent than the cowboy you left back home. Once you figure him out, you can go back to what you love best.

VELVEETA This is your boy next door. You grew up together, saw each other at every neighborhood pool party or birthday. You always liked him, but you also wondered if there was something more exciting out there. He's practical, he never lets you down, and you know, after you try all the others, he is the one you'll be spending Christmas Eve with, especially if your mother has anything to say about it.

CANNED CHEESE He's the bad boy that drives into town on a motorcycle, buys you strawberry wine coolers, and makes you do things you'd blush to admit. He's a little dirty and sort of dangerous, and all your friends warn you that he's bad for you. But you don't care, you're gonna let him take you for a ride. You only live once!

CANTINA QUESO

SO WHICH QUESO IS MY ALL-TIME FAVORITE? YOU GUESSED IT. I'm a believer that canned cheese is the most misunderstood, but secretly exceptional, ingredient in the culinary arsenal. Even right here in the heart of Dallas, Texas.

The truth is, a hybrid approach to preparing queso is probably the best choice for flavor *and* texture. It's about starting with a good base and building flavor from there by adding various cheeses for complexity (if desired, but not required). The béchamel-based queso, in true French mother–sauce fashion, is always going to be lovely on upscale chicken dishes and seafood enchiladas, but it's heavier and almost too rich for many more familiar and practical uses like drizzling on nachos or smothering Texas soft cheese tacos.

Bench the béchamel base and, for heaven's sake, save the Velveeta for some righteous mac and cheese, and start your queso dip with canned queso blanco. Don't believe me? Here, hold my purse... **YIELD: SERVES 6-8**

---

6 Roma tomatoes

2–3 jalapeños

6 garlic cloves

Olive oil

Kosher salt

2 (15-ounce) cans Rico's Queso Blanco

2 cups whole milk

1 1/2 teaspoons kosher salt

Juice of 1/2 a lemon

PRO TIP

ADD LITTLE BITS

of robust cheeses left over from other projects to this base if you like. Shredded Monterey Jack, sharp cheddar, Parmesan, or many of the Mexican cheeses work great.

Preheat your oven to 450°F and line a baking sheet with foil.

Place the tomatoes, jalapeños, and six peeled, whole garlic cloves on the baking sheet. Drizzle with oil and salt lightly with kosher salt. Toss well and roast for 12–14 minutes. Remove to a counter-top and cool.

Meanwhile, in a medium saucepan pour in the two cans of Queso Blanco. Use one of the empty cans to measure out 1 can of whole milk, which is about 2 cups. Add the salt and lemon juice.

Dice the tomatoes and add them to the pot, including the juices. Dice the jalapeño and add it to the queso (including the seeds, don't be shy you can add them all!). Mince up the garlic and really try to mash it into a paste, as it is basically roasted garlic at this point. Add to the pot and stir well. Bring to a simmer and taste for seasoning.

I doubt you need any suggestions on how to serve queso, but if you've been trying to re-create restaurant-style soft cheese tacos, they are simply corn tortillas filled with a little cheese and smothered in this exact sauce. No Velveeta needed, cowgirl.

FANCY PANTS GUACAMOLE

BECAUSE IF YOU HAVEN'T HAD GUACAMOLE IN AN EVENING GOWN, you're doing something wrong!

Down here in the Tex-Mex capital of the known universe, we have a variety for almost every occasion. There's clean and fresh-mashed avocado guacamole, garlic guacamole, loaded guacamole, spicy and thin guacamole sauces for drizzling on tacos, guacamole–sour cream hybrids, and even vinegar-based guacamole (which is the subject of many a debate with Yankees who don't have it in their paradigm that guacamole makes a great salad dressing).

Whatever your mood, we have a "guac" for that. This guacamole is a showstopper appropriate for the Cattle Baron's Ball, but if you're feeling fancy and don't want to wear an evening gown to watch Netflix, it's easy to put together and tastes just as good in sweatpants as it does in sequins.

This recipe starts out with my "go to" guac! You don't really need a recipe, and it goes with everything! It's a basic formula I use: one garlic clove per avocado, a little lemon and salt, and always quartered cherry tomatoes. Why cherry? They have less water and juicy pulp than a regular tomato, and quartering them makes the perfect uniform-size pieces for guacamole. **YIELD: 4-6 SERVINGS**

---

4 Haas avocados
(the big avocados)

2 large garlic cloves

1/2 teaspoon kosher salt

Juice of 1/2 a lemon

1 ear of corn

1/4 small red onion

Cilantro

10 cherry tomatoes

2 Fresno peppers

Cotija or feta cheese, crumbled

1 cup pomegranate arils (if out of season, use fresh or frozen (and thawed) diced cherries)

FOR SARAH'S BASIC GUAC: Cut the avocados in half and remove the pits as described in the "Urban Cowgirl Cooking School" chapter. Scoop out the soft green flesh and place on a large, flat plate. Press two garlic cloves through a garlic press. Sprinkle on the avocado. Sprinkle with the 1/2 teaspoon salt and 1–2 teaspoons lemon juice from the halved lemon. Reserve the rest of the lemon in case you need to add more at the end.

Using a large fork, mash the avocado with the other ingredients, creating a smooth, flavorful mixture about the thickness of sour cream.

FOR THE FANCY GUAC: As described in the "Urban Cowgirl Cooking School" chapter, oven-char the corn, slice the corn off the cob, and reserve.

On a cutting board dice up about one-quarter of a small red onion and a small handful of cilantro. Using a serrated knife, cut the cherry tomatoes into quarters (halve them and then halve them again). Cut one fresno pepper in half and remove the seeds. Mince the Fresno pepper and reserve the other pepper for garnishing the dish.

Add the roasted corn, tomatoes, fresno pepper, onion, and cilantro to the prepared guacamole. Sprinkle in a little of the Cotija or feta cheese and reserve the rest for topping. Mix and mash the ingredients together to create a loaded guacamole.

Spoon onto a dish you would like to serve it on. I prefer a large dinner plate for scoopability!

Take the remaining Fresno pepper and slice rings (with the seeds intact) off the pepper to garnish all around the guacamole (for those who like it hot!). Finish the presentation with a sprinkling of cheese and additional cilantro. Top with the pomegranate arils and serve with tortilla chips.

Good grief, that's fancy!

CREAMY PARMESAN AND CHIVE
SHRIMP EMPANADAS

WHEN I LIVED IN SAN ANTONIO, I was part of a competition cooking team (which I cover in great detail in the "Urban Cowgirl Traditions" section of this book) that was really more like a family. This recipe won an award for the best shrimp at the Shrimp Festival in Galveston, but this story is actually about a young chef named Ally, who I met at a party thrown by my former boss, San Antonio Spurs player Tony Parker. At the time, Ally was still in high school. In a room full of celebrities, she picked me out and bent my ear about cooking and culinary school. I encouraged her to go to school, promised her it would be worth it, and years later reconnected with her when I moved to Houston, where she was working as a chef.

We both submitted dishes into the competition, but it wasn't mine that won. Ally, the young chef with a heart of gold, took the honors. **YIELD: 12 EMPANADAS**

$1/2$ small red onion

1 tablespoon fresh parsley or cilantro

1 teaspoon chives

1 pound shrimp, without shells and cleaned

2 tablespoons butter

1 teaspoon salt

$1/2$ teaspoon pepper

2 garlic cloves

$1/2$ teaspoon red pepper flakes

1 cup heavy cream

$1/2$ cup freshly grated Parmesan cheese

FOR THE FILLING On a cutting board dice the onion, chop the fresh cilantro or parsley, and mince the chives. Reserve.

Cut the clean and deshelled shrimp in half and reserve for use in the filling.

In a large sauté pan, heat the butter, pour in the shrimp, and cook 1–2 minutes. Add the diced red onion and continue to sauté and toss the ingredients around with a spatula. Add the salt and pepper and cook 1 minute. Add the two garlic cloves (pressed through a garlic press or minced well with a sharp knife). Add the red pepper flakes. Cook another 2 minutes or until the vegetables are softened.

Add the heavy cream and stir well to incorporate. Turn up the heat until the cream begins to boil. Boil 45 seconds, then stir in the freshly grated Parmesan cheese and lemon juice. Stir well. Cook another minute or so and add the fresh herbs. Taste the mixture for seasoning and let cool.

Juice of $1/2$ a lemon

1 package empanada dough (from the freezer section, defrosted)

1 egg plus a little water

1 quart high smoke-point oil (grapeseed, peanut, etc.)

Optional: jalapeño jelly or red pepper jelly, for dipping

PRO TIP

AN ENAMELED OR PORCELAIN DUTCH OVEN works great for frying,
comes in many colors (fuchsia, teal, purple), and holds in heat well! It's the workhorse in our kitchen, from frying empanadas and flautas to making gumbo, and it adds a pop of color to your kitchen!

FOR THE EMPANADAS Arrange a space where you can fill four empanadas at once, such as a clean countertop or large cutting board. In a little bowl crack the egg and whisk in a little water. This will be the "glue" used to seal the empanadas.

Open the package of empanadas and pull out four at a time. Using a small kitchen pastry brush, coat the edges of each dough circle with egg wash. Put a spoonful of the filling mixture in the center of each empanada—enough to fill the empanada completely when it closes but not so much as to seep out of the seal. A slotted spoon works well to drain out a little of the sauce while ensuring that the most shrimp get inside the empanada!

After filling an empanada, pull one side of the dough circle over the filling to create a half circle and press the two dough edges together. Crimp the dough edges with the bottom of a fork to make a ruffled seal. Place the empanada aside while you finish the others. It's helpful to keep them chilled in the refrigerator or freezer so they are firm to handle.

In a heavy-bottomed, large stockpot, begin heating the oil to 340–350°F. When the oil reaches the correct temperature zone, gently place an empanada in the oil. I like to fry about three at a time, monitoring their progress with some heat-safe tongs so that I can flip them often. With empanadas, if one side cooks faster than the other side, the crispier side will gravitate up! There is nothing you can do but hold them down with tongs if this happens, so stick close by and turn them every minute. They are done when they are a deep golden brown. Remove them gently to a cookie sheet lined with paper towels or a cooling rack.

I serve these hot with a little bowl of red pepper jelly thinned with 2 tablespoons hot water and mixed up with a fork. It's purely optional, as the empanadas are hot, creamy, and rich all by themselves, but they are terrific with a zing of spicy sweet glaze.

GULF COAST BAR TRASH

DON'T ASK ME HOW SOMETHING AS ELEGANT and fun as bar trash ever earned the name "bar trash." This prime seafood and wine sauce–soaked dish is served all throughout coastal Texas as a shareable feast on a plate. It's friendly and fun—like chips and dip (if chips and dip put on panty hose and went to the opera). It's the quintessential Gulf Coast dish for a small gathering of friends, perfect with a great bottle of Chardonnay. **YIELD: 4 SERVINGS (OVER COCKTAILS)**

FOR THE BREAD:

French Bread or Baguette, sliced into ¼-inch slices

Olive oil or butter, for toasting the bread

Salt and pepper

Pinch of fresh parsley

1 lemon, for squeezing on the final dish

FOR THE SAUCE:

1 tablespoon butter

1 shallot, diced

⅓ cup dry white wine

½ teaspoon salt

½ teaspoon red pepper flakes

1 cup cream

¼ cup parmesan cheese

1 stick unsalted butter, cut into pea-size cubes

1 tablespoon lemon juice

FOR THE BAGUETTE: Preheat the oven to 400°F. On a baking sheet, lay out the slices of bread, brushing them with butter or olive oil, then sprinkling them with salt, pepper, and a pinch of parsley for color. Bake 8 to 10 minutes. Remove the bread slices from the sheet and reserve.

FOR THE SAUCE: In a sauté pan, heat the butter over medium heat. Add the shallot and cook for 1 minute. Add the wine and cook until the wine has reduced to about 1 tablespoon of juice. Add the salt, red pepper flakes, and cream. Whisk well and bring up to a simmer. Simmer until the cream begins to thicken, about 1–2 minutes. Pour in the parmesan cheese and whisk. Begin to add in the butter cubes a little at a time. Whisk well to incorporate, lowering the heat if necessary to keep the sauce warm but not boiling.

When all the butter is whisked in, add the lemon juice. Taste for seasoning. Keep the sauce in a warm place on the back of the stove while you sauté the seafood.

TO FINISH: In a sauté pan, melt the butter and add in the olive oil. Bring the pan up to medium-high heat. Pat the scallops dry and place in the hot skillet. Sear approximately 2–3 minutes on each side. Remove and place on a plate. Add more butter or oil to the sauté pan if necessary.

1 tablespoon butter

1 tablespoon olive oil

4 scallops

8 jumbo shrimp, deshelled, tails on

Salt and pepper

4 ounces fresh crab meat

Next add the shrimp to the pan and sauté for 1–2 minutes, until they turn pink and curl. Salt and pepper them and remove them to the plate with the scallops. Repeat with the crab meat. The crab meat is already cooked, so it will just need a moment in the pan to get hot.

To plate, take a large plate or platter and spoon down a large ladle of the wine sauce. Place the crab meat directly on top of this. Decorate the plate with the scallops and shrimp in a pleasing arrangement. Sprinkle with parsley and serve with fresh lemon, baguette slices, and chilled cocktails!

PIMENTO CHEESE-STUFFED JALAPEÑOS
AND CHUTNEY

MY FAVORITE TREAT AT DINERS AND CAFES IN THE SOUTH is pimento cheese–stuffed jalapeños.

While dreaming of my own version for a fancy South Texas party I was catering, I tested a batch of pimento cheese using cream cheese as the base instead of gobs of mayo. And then I confirmed my own status as a Southern Cheese Queen.

Using cream cheese works like a charm! It reminded me of another popular Texas snack, cream cheese topped with spicy red pepper jelly, something popular at almost every casual family gathering you will ever attend in the Panhandle State. Because of the fluffy, smooth mouthfeel that cream cheese provides, it pairs great with that sweet-hot jelly. I decided to swap the flavors in this dish, making the pimento cheese spicy and using chutney to stand up to the bold, robust flavor of sharp cheddar and fruity habaneros.

This showstopper will go great with a glass of chilled white wine as an appetizer at your next barbecue! **YIELD: 12-15 STUFFED PEPPERS**

---

5 ounces sharp cheddar from the block

5 ounces Monterey Jack from the block

8 ounces cream cheese, softened

1/2 cup mayonnaise

1 teaspoon Worcestershire (optional)

1 small garlic clove

8-10 roasted jarred piquillo peppers (about 1 jar)

1 habanero pepper, seeds and ribs removed

1 jar Major Grey's Chutney or your favorite local chutney

1 (10-ounce) jar or can pickled whole jalapeños for stuffing

Using a food processor, shred the cheddar and Monterey Jack cheeses with the shredding attachment (or shred by hand). Switch to the blade attachment of the food processor and place the cheeses, including the cream cheese, into the food processor. If the cream cheese is chilled, just microwave it for 20–30 seconds to soften. Add the mayo and Worcestershire.

Mince the garlic and add to the bowl.

Remove eight piquillo peppers from the jar, drain, dice them up, and add to the bowl. Carefully slice the habanero in half. Remove and discard the seeds and any ribs from the pepper. Finely mince the habanero and add to the bowl.

Turn the food processor on and "pulse" the mixture a few times to get it going. You may even want to use a spatula to mix everything well within the bowl. Create a smooth, spreadable consistency. Season to taste and chill, or begin stuffing the jarred jalapeño peppers with a small spoon. When ready to serve, top with chutney.

GREEN BEAN CASSEROLE SOUP

THIS RECIPE WAS CREATED THANKS TO MY SWEET BUT SPOILED HUSBAND who begged me to make green bean casserole from scratch for Thanksgiving. I had done it once, and he felt certain that I would do it every year, forevermore. I joked with him that the only thing he even liked about green bean casserole was the creamy sauce and the crunchy onions, and I may as well make him a soup instead.

I didn't make green bean casserole from scratch for Thanksgiving, but a few weeks later, on a blustery fall day while rain pounded outside, I decided to try making it as a soup to surprise him for Date Night. I broke it down into the parts he loved best: creamy green bean goo and crunchy onion goodness. It was the holidays sloshing in your mouth, the onions crunching like leaves beneath booted feet.

YIELD: 4 APPETIZER PORTIONS OR 2 HEARTY DINNER PORTIONS

---

3 tablespoons butter

2 tablespoons extra-virgin olive oil or coconut oil

1 (8-ounce) package fresh mushrooms (shiitake and chanterelle are best; button mushrooms will work, but the flavor won't be as intense)

1/2 teaspoon salt

1/2 teaspoon pepper

1 cup chopped onion (about 1/2 a small onion)

1 garlic clove, minced

1/4 cup flour

1 quart good-quality chicken stock (room temperature from the pantry or heated gently in the microwave if using fresh stock that has been refrigerated)

FOR THE HOMEMADE CREAM OF MUSHROOM SOUP: In a large stockpot melt the butter and olive oil or coconut oil. Toss in the mushrooms and brown well over medium to high heat. Add the salt and pepper. Cook 3–5 minutes, turning and stirring to keep the mushrooms from burning, but also trying to get them as brown as possible.

Add the onion and sweat 2–3 minutes. Add the garlic and cook just until fragrant.

Using a whisk, whisk in the flour, creating a roux. When the flour is incorporated into the butter and vegetable mixture, begin slowly adding in the chicken stock, whisking well after each addition. When all the stock is incorporated, raise the heat to high and let the mixture come to a boil. Boil for 1–2 minutes, allowing the mixture to thicken. Turn the heat off and set up your blender. Allow the soup to cool slightly while you prepare the green beans.

FOR THE GREEN BEANS: On a cutting board slice both ends off the green beans and cut off and remove any stems or wilted beans. It is easy to do this by collecting a handful of beans and lining them up in one hand while slicing the tips off all in one stroke. I like to slice the ends off both sides of the green bean. Repeat with the entire three handfuls. In a colander wash the beans well and then dice them up into bite-size pieces.

3 big handfuls (about 3 cups) bulk green beans (you can use frozen green beans on lazy days, but you already figured that out, didn't you?)

1/2 cup heavy cream

Juice of 1/2 a lemon

1 (6-ounce) container French fried onions for topping

Note: For this recipe you will need a blender.

In a microwave steamer or glass bowl with a lid, add the green beans, a little water (about 3 tablespoons), and a pinch of salt and microwave, covered, for 7 minutes.

FINISHING THE SOUP: Very carefully pour the soup into the blender pitcher. Place the blender onto the base and put the lid on, but vent the top by removing the plastic feeding tube and covering the little hole with a kitchen towel. This helps so the pressure of the steam does not launch the lid off and soak your clothes in hot soup!

Pulse the blender slowly at first, allowing the hot steam to rise (and also making sure you've rigged the lid correctly). Work up to turning the blender on low and letting it run for 30 seconds, then blast it on high for another 10 seconds. Turn the blender off, remove the pitcher, and pour the soup back into the stockpot. Do I need to remind you to be careful again? It's so hot!

Heat the soup once more on medium and pour in the heavy cream. Bring to a boil. Season with salt, pepper, and a good squeeze of lemon juice.

Remove the green beans from the microwave and drain out any excess water. Try a green bean to make sure they are cooked enough for you! I like them crisp-tender. You can microwave them for an extra couple of minutes if you like really well-done vegetables.

Pour the drained green beans into the mushroom soup and stir well. Ladle into bowls and top with French fried onions and extra black pepper!

TEXAS FARMER'S SALAD WITH BLACKBERRY LAVENDER VINAIGRETTE

THERE ARE SO MANY PICK-YOUR-OWN FARMS throughout Texas, and one in particular in Galveston that I love to visit with my boys. It's a blackberry farm that reminds me of the farm my grandparents used to own in Hillsboro, a little bit wild and woolly, filled with the sounds of chickens and the smell of fruit ripening on the bush. The produce you get from a local farm is better—like you can taste the actual sunshine that made it grow. Since I don't have my own sprawling farm, I love to support these working farms whenever I can. This recipe reminds me to slow down, put my hands in some soil, and connect with the blessing of harvest. **YIELD: 4 APPETIZER SALADS OR 2 DINNER SALADS**

---

1 package spring mix or other tender local greens

1 (4-ounce) package goat cheese

1¹/₂ cups local nuts (candied pecans for a sweeter salad and shelled pistachios for a savory salad)

1 container or bundle of fresh chives

¹/₂ pint blackberries

1 Haas avocado (the big avocados)

BLACKBERRY LAVENDER VINAIGRETTE

¹/₃ cup balsamic vinegar

¹/₂ pint blackberries

³/₄ teaspoon salt

Dash of freshly cracked black pepper

¹/₂ teaspoon lavender buds

1 tablespoon minced shallot

1 small garlic clove, minced

1 tablespoon honey

Juice of ¹/₂ a small lemon

¹/₂ cup oil

FOR THE VINAIGRETTE: In a small saucepan combine the balsamic vinegar, blackberries, salt, pepper, lavender, and minced shallot. Bring to a simmer and cook 3–4 minutes. Turn down the heat and pour into a blender. Add the minced garlic, honey, and lemon juice. Put the top on and turn the blender on low. Slowly drizzle in the oil. Turn the blender up to high for 20 seconds. Use a spoon to sample the dressing and season to taste.

FOR THE SALAD: Place the cleaned spring mix on four plates and sprinkle with crumbled goat cheese, nuts, and freshly minced or snipped chives. Sprinkle the remaining 1/2 pint of blackberries on top. Remove the skin from the avocado, dice into bite-size chunks, and add to the salads.

Drizzle with vinaigrette and serve!

PRO TIP

BALSAMIC AND CINNAMON CANDIED PECANS: My favorite way to candy pecans is to toast them in a 325°F oven just until fragrant on a buttered foil-lined baking sheet. When they start to become fragrant (about 5–10 minutes), I microwave 1/3 cup of brown sugar and a few tablespoons of balsamic vinegar until warm and saucy, then drizzle the pecans with the mixture, tossing well, then bake an additional 15–20 minutes at 350°F. I finish by sprinkling with sea salt and cinnamon and put them in a child-free area to cool. Yum!

ROASTED TEXAS CAVIAR WITH SMOKED JALAPEÑO HONEY VINAIGRETTE

TEXAS "CAVIAR" IS A SOUTHERN RECIPE that is so popular you'll see it at most family gatherings, bridal showers, fancy teas, and somber wakes. One summer evening, I was asked to bring this salad to my best friend's bridal shower. It was her mother's and aunt's and sister's favorite thing since all-you-can-drink brunch mimosas.

The problem with being a chef is you can never leave well enough alone. But usually your experiments make good things better. (And when they don't, they make for great stories!) This is one of my winners! The Smoked Jalapeño Honey Vinaigrette makes it fabulous, dressing it up just enough that you could serve the Queen of England and she'd ask for seconds. **YIELD: 5 CUPS**

---

1 large red pepper

3 ears of corn

1/4 small red onion

1 (15 1/2-ounce) can black-eyed peas (plain, no bacon)

Cilantro

1 (10-ounce) container red grape tomatoes, rinsed well

SMOKED JALAPEÑO HONEY VINAIGRETTE

1 cup rice wine vinegar

1/3 cup honey

1 jalapeño, minced, seeds removed

2 teaspoons sriracha sauce

2 teaspoons liquid smoke (I prefer mesquite flavor)

1 tablespoon salt

1 teaspoon pepper

1/2 cup oil (fresh, please)

FOR THE VINAIGRETTE: Add all the ingredients (except the oil) to a blender or small food processor. Blend well and drizzle in the oil slowly. Stop, scrape the bottom, and blend again thoroughly. Season to taste. Transfer to a small container with a lid and chill.

FOR THE RED BELL PEPPER: Roast the bell pepper following the instructions in the "Urban Cowgirl Cooking School," page 22. Once the pepper is cool, cut the roasted pepper into manageable slices and dice to about 1/4-inch squares (about the size of an M&M's candy). Add to a large bowl.

FOR THE CORN: Prepare the corn following the instructions in the "Urban Cowgirl Cooking School," page 23. Then place on a cutting board to cool. Cut the corn off the stalks by standing the corn up on one end. Using a very sharp knife, slice from the top down, against the base of the corn kernels. Rotate and repeat. Scoop up the corn and place it in the bowl.

On a cutting board small dice the onion and add to the large bowl.

Drain the can of black-eyed peas and rinse them under cold water, drain again, and add to the bowl.

Roughly chop 2 tablespoons cilantro and add to the bowl. Cut the grape tomatoes in half and add them to the bowl.

Starting with about 1/2 cup at a time, add the vinaigrette to the vegetables and toss well. Taste for seasoning. Serve fresh and chilled with tortilla chips.

AHI TUNA SALAD WITH SALTED
MARGARITA VINAIGRETTE

SEDONA, ARIZONA, WHERE I LIVED WHEN I WENT TO CULINARY SCHOOL, has a pretty amazing food scene. You wouldn't think that in a landlocked state like Arizona, you could get "slap your grandma fresh" ahi tuna. But it happened. My time in Sedona inspired me to combine Southwestern flavors like the margarita with something decidedly coastal, seared ahi tuna. The key to living an Urban Cowgirl life is to stay open to inspiration, even at the oddest times. **YIELD: 2 DINNER-SIZE SALADS**

SALTED MARGARITA VINAIGRETTE

$^1/_4$ cup lime juice (2–3 plump limes)

Zest of 1 lime

2 tablespoons honey

$^1/_4$ teaspoon kosher salt

$1^1/_2$ tablespoon mayonnaise

2 sushi-grade tuna steaks

2–3 tablespoons (plus extra) high smoke-point oil such as coconut oil

Paprika

Onion powder

Kosher salt

Pepper

Mexican oregano

3–4 cups washed greens such as spring mix, baby kale, or freshly chopped romaine

$^1/_2$ cup julienned jicama

FOR THE VINAIGRETTE: Blend lime juice and zest, honey, salt, and mayo in a small bowl with a whisk. Season to taste. Chill. This dressing tastes best after chilling for 1–2 hours. It tastes just like a salted margarita!

FOR THE TUNA: Take the tuna steaks and dry them off well with a paper towel. Coat the tuna in just enough oil that the spices will stick to the fish. Sprinkle the tuna steaks with a good dusting of each of the spices starting with onion powder, which helps develop a nice crust. There is no need to measure, just dust the tuna steaks right from the container. Flip the tuna steaks and repeat on the opposite side.

Heat a heavy sauté pan or cast-iron skillet on high heat. Pour in 2–3 tablespoons high smoke-point oil and bring the heat up until the oil just begins to smoke lightly. Place one tuna steak in the pan, searing for about 30 seconds on each side. Let the pan heat come back up and repeat with the other tuna steak. Dry any excess oil off the cooked tuna steaks and place in the refrigerator while you make the salad.

½ cup diced fresh mango

½ cup blueberries

1 avocado

Pepitas (pumpkin seeds), toasted (see the "Urban Cowgirl Cooking School" chapter)

Optional: crispy tortilla strips, cilantro, sliced Fresno peppers, or sprouts, for garnish

FOR THE SALAD: **Prepare each plate with a serving of washed greens of your choice. On top add julienned jicama slices, diced mango, and blueberries.**

Split the avocado and remove the seed and skin. Place the avocado on a cutting board, curved side up, and cut slices. Top the salad with avocado and lay on the seared, sliced tuna.

Top with toasted pumpkin seeds and any of the optional garnishes. Serve with the dressing on the side, or toss the salad with the chilled dressing in a large bowl if desired.

PRO TIP

IF YOU'VE EVER WONDERED HOW THE RESTAURANTS get perfect slices of tuna, it's all in the chill! If you cut the tuna right after you sear it, it will always tear on you and look generally pretty amateur. Throw it in the refrigerator and chill it well before slicing for perfect sushi-esque slices.

BOILED SHRIMP SALAD WITH SOFT AND FLUFFY THOUSAND ISLAND DRESSING

DISCERNING SOUTHERN NOSES CAN PICK OUT A STORE-BOUGHT SALAD DRESSING by just a whiff from the bowl. In the South, dressings have to be handmade and fresh—just like Sunday suppers and homemade pie. You know the saying "the devil is in the details"? That holds for salad dressing, too. What makes this salad a winner is the secret ingredient mixed lovingly into the bowl. Airy light dressing comes from backing off the mayonnaise and substituting a spoonful of sour cream whipped in at the end. **YIELD: SERVES 4**

---

1 pound of the biggest fresh shrimp you can find, shell-on but deveined (for easy shell removal)

1 capful shrimp boil
(I use 2 capfuls—I'm a rebel!)

2 tablespoons salt

2 large eggs

1 head romaine, green leaf lettuce, or iceberg lettuce (or a combination)

1 cucumber

2 heirloom tomatoes

1/4 red onion

1 avocado, peeled

1 lemon

1 sleeve saltine-style crackers

FOR THE DRESSING: In a blender combine all the dressing ingredients except the sour cream. Blend until smooth. Pour into a bowl and whisk in the sour cream. Chill before use.

FOR THE SHRIMP BOIL: Fill a large stockpot halfway with water, cover, and bring to a boil. Pour in the shrimp boil and salt. Add the shrimp to the water and simmer 4–5 minutes or until the shrimp just begins to curl. Using a slotted spoon remove the shrimp to a colander sitting atop a bowl to catch any juices dripping from the shrimp. Spoon the shrimp into the colander and set aside to cool. After a few minutes peel the shrimp and reserve. Discard the bowl of drippings.

THIS DRESSING IS DELICIOUS FRESH, but a religious experience after marinating in the refrigerator overnight. It lasts 3–5 days before it's time for a new batch.

THOUSAND ISLAND DRESSING

1 cup mayonnaise

1/4 cup diced onion

1/3 cup ketchup

2 tablespoons sweet pickle relish

2 tablespoons freshly chopped parsley

Juice of 1/2 a lemon

1 teaspoon freshly cracked black pepper

1/4 teaspoon salt

2 tablespoons red wine vinegar

1 cup sour cream

FOR THE SALAD: In a small saucepan boil some water to cook the eggs. Add eggs and simmer for about 8–10 minutes; set aside to cool. Slice into rings.

Prepare the lettuce and place in a bowl in the refrigerator to chill. Using a vegetable peeler, peel the cucumber. Cut the cucumber in half down the middle, then cut the halves in half so you have four half-moon-shaped cucumber sticks. With the flat edge down, cut bite-size cubes of cucumber and add to the lettuce bowl.

Dice the tomatoes and add to the bowl. Fajita dice the red onion as thin as you can. Dice the avocado into bite-size pieces. Add all the veggies to the chilled salad bowl. Crush the package of saltine crackers into crouton-size pieces.

Right before serving squeeze a little lemon juice onto the shrimp and salt and pepper to taste.

To serve, toss the salad with the cooled shrimp, sliced soft-boiled eggs, and whipped dressing and top with crushed crackers.

THE SECRET TO WICKEDLY FRESH SALAD GREENS

Have you ever gone to a nice steak house, gotten your salad course, and noticed the salad is so fresh, crunchy, and ice cold?! That's because it's been soaked in ice water and then spun through a salad spinner. Soak the torn greens for about 30 minutes before mealtime, spin, and place in a large salad bowl covered with a damp cloth. It will be the most refreshing, crisp salad of your life. For extra points, serve on chilled plates.

Entrees

THE ENTREE IS THE MATRIARCH OF YOUR MEAL. It's grandma sitting at the head of the table saying grace and passing you the gravy. The Entree is not to be trifled with. She's serious. She looks you in the eyes and says, "Sit down and get off your phone." She forces you to focus on the moment, rather than the to-do list or that lingering e-mail you really should reply to. The Entree gives you an excuse to take a breath, sometimes unbutton your jeans, and lean back in the chair, sighing.

We treat entrees with such high regard in Urban Cowgirl Country because that's how we were raised. The table was set, the TV turned off, the meal and the conversation taking the focus. For some, sharing a meal is the only chance they have to pull together as a family, as friends, as human beings. In this world so completely scattered and full of unease, food can still connect us, giving us a moment in a hectic day to listen to each other face to face—not over text, not through social media.

So gather round, dig in, and let the Entree speak for you.

SEARED STEAKS WITH SWEET ONION MARMALADE

HOUSED IN THE THREE-STORY BOILER ROOM of the former Gruene, Texas, cotton gin is the Gristmill Restaurant and Bar. Nestled at the heart of the Texas Hill Country, on a bluff overlooking the Guadalupe River, the Gristmill has hosted celebrities, locals, and average travelers from far and wide. My first experience with the Gristmill was as a young chef with enough time on her hands to float the Guadalupe River all day, and enough money in her wallet to buy a juicy steak at the end of the day. Tired, but completely happy, I savored my first Gristmill steak in a pair of cowboy boots and freshly tanned thighs. This recipe is inspired by the bliss of that first bite after a long day on the river. **YIELD: 4 STEAKS AND 1 BATCH OF ONION MARMALADE**

---

4 of your favorite cut (rib-eye, strips, sirloin, filets, etc.)

2–3 tablespoons oil for coating the steaks, plus more for searing (I prefer coconut oil for searing)

Kosher salt or any great-quality salt

Freshly cracked black pepper

Onion powder, for dusting

Garlic powder, for dusting

Parsley, minced

Any great heavy-bottom sauté or fry pan (cast iron, all-clad, or copper)

FOR THE MARMALADE: In a large sauté pan melt the butter on medium heat, add the onions as you cut them, and sprinkle in the salt. Cook until wilted down and any water evaporates, about 15 minutes. You may have to lower the heat a little toward the end.

Add the chicken stock and red wine vinegar, and cook until the liquid is reduced by three-quarters. Add cream and bring to a boil just until the cream begins to thicken. Reduce heat and season to taste with freshly cracked black pepper. (It may need another tablespoon of red wine vinegar and another teaspoon of salt, depending on your tastes.) The flavors will really develop upon standing while you sear your steaks and set the table. I keep the pan on the back of the stove where it will keep warm while I finish dinner; leftovers keep well in the refrigerator for 4 days.

FOR THE STEAKS: Dry the steaks well with a paper towel and lay them out on a cookie sheet lined with foil. Preheat the oven to 450°F.

Coat the steaks with just enough oil that the seasonings will stick to the meat. Season all sides of the steaks liberally with salt and freshly cracked pepper. Dust all sides liberally with onion powder, then garlic powder and parsley.

PRO TIP

THE THICKER THE CUT THE MORE YOU WILL BE ABLE TO SEAR
the outside while keeping the inside a nice medium rare or medium. Thin steaks = overcooked, tough steaks.

SWEET ONION MARMALADE

2 tablespoons butter

2 sweet onions, fajita dice

1 red onion, fajita dice

1 teaspoon salt

1 cup chicken stock

1 tablespoon red wine vinegar

1 cup heavy cream

Cracked black pepper

Finish with an additional:

1 tablespoon red wine vinegar

1 teaspoon salt, if needed

In your heavy fry pan or cast-iron skillet, melt 3 tablespoons coconut oil on high heat. It will take a few minutes for the skillet to heat fully. When the oil just begins to smoke and you can tell the pan is roaring hot, place one steak into the center of the pan in the oil. It should begin searing and crackling! Fry the steak until you can see heavy browning on the edges of the steak, approximately 3–7 minutes on the first side, then flip. The second side will need less time.

Searing time will be different depending on how large a steak you chose and the temperature of the cold raw steak. Ultimately the biggest mistake people make when learning to sear a steak is flipping it too quickly or moving the steak before the sear gets substantial enough to stick to the steak and not to the pan! When you see the beautiful golden-brown stuff in the bottom of the pan, remember that if you had waited a little longer, that goodness would be sticking to your steak!

Line a baking sheet with foil for the hot steaks to finish on the oven. When a steak is done, transfer it to the cookie sheet in the oven and begin the next steak. I like to monitor the steaks in the oven by pressing gently on the meat to tell how done they are, then removing them to a nice platter or cooling rack to rest. A nice medium rare steak will seem soft to the touch, while a medium well to well done steak will push back on your fingertips. This is a technique that takes some time to master and you'll need to experiment and practice a few times to figure out how your perfect steak feels when it is ready.

NOTE: If you've never rested your meat, you don't know what you're missing! By giving the meat 10 minutes to relax, the moisture in the meat redistributes and the muscle fibers in the entire steak relax. The meat will be seared, tender, and bursting with juices and flavor. Never skip the rest, as it's the most important part after a good sear!

Top each plate with one steak and serve with the onion marmalade.

This dish pairs well with the Southwestern Cream Corn and the Boursin Cheese Whipped Mashed Potatoes in the "Sides" chapter.

COZY FIREPLACE CHAT

YOU CAN GET THE SAME EFFECT as a grill by using a cast-iron skillet or your best fry pan. I pour in plenty of coconut oil because it can get incredibly hot without smoking. And I dust my steak well with kosher salt, black pepper, parsley (just for a pop of color), and lots of onion powder. I feel like the onion powder makes a base for the crust you are working to develop on any well-seared steak. That and a very hot pan or charcoal grill will create the high heat needed for a heavy crust to develop. Don't worry about the inside of the steak getting cooked in the pan. In the professional kitchen we always finish the steaks off in the oven.

TEXICAN SHRIMP SCAMPI

AS A LITTLE GIRL, I HAD A SIMPLE—BUT SPECIFIC—MAN OF MY DREAMS. He had to love shrimp. Yes . . . I know, that's an odd requirement, and you could probably think of a lot better qualities to look for in a man, but that's what I wanted. Seafood is a huge part of my culture, and all the high-quality gentlemen in my life growing up were also seafood evangelists. I imagined shrimp boils and crab-stuffed mushrooms every weekend on the back porch with a tall, handsome someone who was as happy as I was to *Eat. All. The. Shrimp.*

Even as I grew up and met boys and men of all varieties, that guy sitting beside me in the daydream never changed. He still was a man who would roll up his sleeves and dig in to peel a bowl of shrimp with me. When I met my future husband, he did what he had to do to get me to the altar, taking me to seafood restaurants and cooking crabs with me in the kitchen whenever I had a craving. Once we were married, though, he confessed his deep, dark secret: He doesn't really love shrimp and he hates oysters. But he loves me. **YIELD: 1 POUND OF SHRIMP OF THE 21–25 SIZE WILL YIELD 21–25 SHRIMP, WHICH IS AT LEAST 10 SHRIMP FOR 2 PEOPLE, OR 5 SHRIMP FOR 4 PEOPLE. THIS RECIPE CAN BE DOUBLED AS YOU SEE FIT.**

---

1 jalapeño

1 green onion

2 tablespoons tomato paste

2 tablespoons chopped fresh cilantro

Zest and juice of 2 limes

1/4 cup high smoke-point oil (peanut, canola, safflower)

1 teaspoon salt

1/2 teaspoon pepper

1 pound shrimp (at least 21–25 size per pound or larger)

Skewers, soaked in a bowl full of water

For the jalapeño, cut the stem side off and slice the pepper in half. Using a spoon, scoop out the seeds and discard. Using a sharp knife, cut thin julienne slices of the jalapeño. Gathering them together horizontally, slice them again into a mince or very small, fine squares. Reserve.

Slice the green onion with a sharp knife left to right so you have both the green and white parts of the vegetable. Reserve.

To make a marinade for the shrimp, in a small food processor blend the onion, tomato paste, fresh cilantro, oil, both the juice and zest of the limes, the minced jalapeño, and salt and pepper. This can also be mixed in a bowl if a small food processor is not available.

FOR THE GARLIC BUTTER MOP SAUCE: The ingredients for this easy garlic butter can be microwaved in a small bowl until hot, or place a metal heat-safe bowl on your charcoal grill and melt the ingredients grill-side. Reserve to brush on during cooking.

FOR THE SHRIMP: If the shrimp has not been peeled, peel the shrimp under cold running water and discard the shells. Dry thoroughly with paper towels and thread onto the skewers,

Optional: ingredients to alternate on the skewers, such as fresh mango and avocado (which is fabulous grilled!), or your favorite kabob veggies

GARLIC BUTTER MOP SAUCE

$1/2$ cup good-quality butter

$1/2$ teaspoon kosher salt

3–5 garlic cloves, pressed through a garlic press

alternating avocado and mango, or your favorite kabob veggies. They are also terrific skewered on their own. In a large, shallow casserole dish, lay the shrimp skewers flat and pour the marinade over them.

Marinate 1–2 hours.

Start your grill or light your charcoal, making sure to clean the grates well and then oil them with fresh oil so the shrimp do not stick. The best way to do this is to let the grill get hot and burn off any old residue. Then saturate a paper towel with lots of your preferred cooking oil and use your long heat-safe tongs to paint the oil onto the grill grates.

When the charcoal has just turned gray (or your gas grill is clean and ready), place the skewers of shrimp on the grill. Place the lid on the grill just for a minute to help things get started nice and hot. Grill the shrimp until they just begin to curl, then flip and grill the other side. Mop with garlic butter during the last 2 minutes of cooking.

These shrimp are best with a little bit of char, which makes them look nice and rustic!

NOTE: This recipe also works great with jumbo shrimp. Just make sure to get extra because I've seen my two-year-old throw back six of these babies!

CHARCOAL BRICK CHICKEN
WITH PICO PANZANELLA

PANZANELLA IS JUST A FANCY WORD FOR BREAD SALAD. In this case, grilled buttered bread, juicy garden-ripe tomatoes, herbaceous cilantro, and a pop of lusty country vinegar are gently folded together and served alongside charcoal-grilled chicken with thin and crispy skin. It's sublime!

YIELD: SERVES 4

1 whole chicken

Olive oil

Kosher salt and black pepper

A sprinkling of any or all of these herbs and spices: paprika, Mexican oregano, garlic powder, onion powder

1 tablespoon brown sugar

PRO TIP

MY KITCHEN SHEARS cut through bone marvelously, but not through the skin very well, so I keep another small, sharp knife handy to slice through the skin if necessary.

FOR THE CHICKEN: To prepare the chicken to be butterflied and cooked whole, you need to remove the backbone. This is done by laying the whole chicken on a cutting board with legs closest to you (south), wings at the top of the cutting board (north), and backbone up. With kitchen shears, cut up the backbone through the ribs from top to bottom on either side of the backbone. Repeat with the other side and remove the backbone.

Now flip the chicken over and press down on the breast, flattening out the chicken. Terrific! All done, now time to season.

Coat the whole chicken well in olive oil. On both sides season with salt and pepper and rub with any of the seasonings listed and the brown sugar, which are all standard rotisserie flavorings that go great with chicken. Let the chicken rest while you start the charcoal; the seasonings will melt into the surface of the chicken.

Start the charcoal in the grill.

FOR THE PICO PANZANELLA: Cut the tomatoes in half, then in quarters, then dice and place them in the bowl. Add the minced garlic, red onion, cilantro, basil, lime juice, rice wine vinegar, extra-virgin olive oil, and salt. Stir and allow to marinate while you finish the chicken.

Slice the baguette diagonally to give each slice more surface area. Butter the bread and reserve for toasting over the fire.

FOR THE GRILLING: When the large flames have died down and the charcoal begins to gray, oil the grates using a paper towel drenched in oil with grill tongs to apply.

PICO PANZANELLA

6 Roma tomatoes

1 garlic clove, pressed through a garlic press

3 tablespoons minced red onion

1 tablespoon chopped fresh cilantro

1 teaspoon minced fresh basil

1 tablespoon lime juice (about 1 plump lime)

1 tablespoon rice wine vinegar

$1/4$ cup extra-virgin olive oil

$1/2$ teaspoon salt

1 baguette

$1/2$ stick butter, softened

2 bricks or large stones wrapped well in several layers of foil

Place the chicken skin side down and place the foil-lined bricks on top of the chicken. Place the lid on the grill and cook 15 minutes. After 15 minutes flip the chicken and adjust so it's over the hottest part of the coals. Replace the brick and cook an additional 15–20 minutes or until the instant-read thermometer registers 165°F.

When the chicken is done, remove it to a safe place in the kitchen and grill the buttered baguette slices over the hot coals until golden brown. Bring the toasted baguette slices inside, slice them in half, and then dice them up and fold into the pico panzanella to be served immediately.

Slice pieces off the chicken or remove breast and legs separately and serve according to your family's favorite cuts of meat. Make sure everyone gets a piece of that crispy skin! Serve with the freshly tossed panzanella.

This goes well with the Green Chile Corn Pudding in the "Sides" chapter.

PRO TIP

EVERY TIME YOU REMOVE THE LID, heat escapes and will tack a bit more time on to the cooking process—so try not to peek!

CATFISH DIABLO WITH BLISTERED TOMATO CREAM

WHILE MY HUSBAND AND I WERE EXPLORING the area around Lost Maples, Texas, we stumbled upon this roadside shack called Mac and Ernie's Roadside Eatery. It was a real shack, with dirt floors and no windowpanes. The menu changed daily and was written on a chalkboard next to a small window where a young cowpoke would stick out his head and take your order! I could actually hear goats bleating from somewhere nearby. We were on an adventure!

So we decided to take a chance and try something a little crazy. We didn't know that the cook was actually a gourmet chef in disguise, and the food, oh my stars, *The. Food!* It turned out to be one of the most memorable and delicious meals of my life, but it also sparked that curiosity that the Urban Cowgirl in me has learned never to ignore.

While sitting in that shack, eating a meal that was much more than meets the eye, I hatched the idea to create a gourmet recipe for a fish I'd always considered a little lowbrow. Catfish Diablo was born! **YIELD: 3 LARGE FILLETS AND SAUCE**

BLISTERED TOMATO CREAM

1 pound small, vine-on tomatoes

1 shallot

4 garlic cloves

2 red jalapeños

1 tablespoon butter

1 tablespoon extra-virgin olive oil

$1/2$ teaspoon salt

$1/4$ teaspoon pepper

3 tablespoons tomato paste

1 cup cream

$1/4$ cup Parmesan cheese

Juice of $1/2$ a small lemon

Optional: $1/4$ teaspoon cayenne

FOR THE SAUCE: Preheat the oven to 400°F. Line a cookie sheet with foil and coat with olive oil to prevent sticking.

Wash the tomatoes, remove the vine, and place whole on the cookie sheet. Drizzle with a bit of olive oil and toss well so they are lightly coated with oil. Season with salt and pepper. Place in the oven and roast 30–45 minutes, depending on size of the tomatoes. When done, the skins should be loosening up and wrinkled, and the tomatoes should be cooked through and roasted.

While tomatoes are roasting, on a cutting board mince the shallot and reserve. Peel the garlic cloves, squeeze through a press, and reserve. Cut the stems off the two jalapeños and cut each jalapeño in half. Mince each jalapeño, including the seeds, and place in a small bowl. Wash your hands and remove the cutting board and knife to a safe area.

In a large sauté pan, heat the butter and olive oil on medium heat until it bubbles. Add the minced shallot, salt, and pepper.

CATFISH

1 pound fresh catfish fillets
(3 fillets)

2 tablespoons favorite seasoning
blend (seasoning salt, Cajun
blend, seafood seasoning, etc.)

1 tablespoon minced fresh parsley

2 tablespoons olive oil

Optional: extra fresh parsley or
cilantro, for garnish

**JALAPEÑO PEPPERS
ARE AS FICKLE** as a small
child. They can be blazing hot one
day and mild the next! In the winter when peppers begin to cool off
in intensity, we use an extra dash
of cayenne pepper to keep things
nice and spicy. Urban Cowgirl folklore tells us that the runts of the
pepper harvest are hotter, as well
as peppers with a pointy tip!

Cook on low-medium for 2 minutes. Add the minced jalapeño and
cook another 2 minutes. Add the pressed garlic and cook until
fragrant.

Add tomato paste and combine with the other softened vegetables. Cook in the pan for about 1–2 minutes to bring out the
flavors in the tomato paste. Stir in the cream and incorporate by
whisking well.

Bring the sauce up to a boil slowly, whisking as you go to incorporate the veggies and cream with the tomato paste to become a
pink sauce. When the mixture begin to simmer, add the Parmesan cheese and lemon juice. Simmer for 30 seconds, allowing the
sauce to thicken, stirring continuously.

When the roasted tomatoes are done, use a metal spatula to chop
them into small chunks right there on the cookie sheet. Scoop the
tomatoes into the sauce and stir to combine. Heat on low as you
finish the sauce and catfish.

Taste for seasoning. It may need an extra 1/4 teaspoon salt
depending on how salty the Parmesan cheese is and 1/4 teaspoon
cayenne depending on the heat of the jalapeños.

FOR THE CATFISH: Lay the fillets out on a plate and sprinkle all
sides with the seasoning blend and minced parsley. Set aside.

In another sauté pan heat the olive oil on medium heat. When
hot, add the catfish fillets and cook 3–4 minutes on each side
until lightly seared and cooked through. Drain each fillet well
and plate immediately. Top with tomato cream sauce and finish
with a sprinkling of fresh parsley or cilantro.

SHRIMP AND POBLANO QUESADILLAS
WITH ROASTED GARLIC SRIRACHA CREAM

ONE OF MY VERY FAVORITE THINGS ABOUT THE SOUTH is that dining at a fancy restaurant or a five-star hotel doesn't remove you from the food culture, but presents that culture to you through an upscale lens. So whether you're throwing back quesadillas at a beach pub on Padre Island or having them delivered via fancy waiter to your own villa at the Four Seasons, you can bet that all of your favorite dishes will make an appearance on the menu—albeit gussied up in their best bib and tucker!

These shrimp quesadillas were inspired by our margarita and Mexican food–fueled honeymoon. For days we ate fancy shrimp quesadillas poolside, relaxing from wedding chaos and happy to finally be alone together. These are my own version, all dolled up with my favorite roasted garlic sriracha cream sauce. **YIELD: 2 LARGE QUESADILLAS (SERVES 4)**

---

10 large shrimp, peeled and deveined

2 tablespoons butter or extra-virgin olive oil

1 lime

4 giant flour tortillas (I love to use green spinach tortillas)

1 (4-ounce) can green chiles

2 cups quesadilla cheese (in the Mexican dairy section) or mozzarella

Oil, for frying

Garnish with cilantro, if desired

TO ROAST THE GARLIC: Preheat the oven to 400°F.

Take the entire head of garlic and, using a knife, slice vertically downward, trimming off all the tips of the garlic cloves. Place the trimmed head of garlic in the center of a small piece of foil, coat with olive oil, and sprinkle with salt. Close up the foil and place in the oven for 30 minutes. When it is done, carefully remove with tongs and allow to cool. Open up the foil and remove the garlic head. The roasted garlic cloves should be very easy to squeeze out into a bowl by simply pressing the root between your fingers. Mash or chop them up into a paste. Reserve for use in the sauce.

FOR THE SHRIMP: Cut the shrimp in half as you would if you were butterflying them, but make the cut all the way through, cutting each shrimp in half completely. They will cook faster and still be a nice bite in the quesadilla.

Heat the butter or olive oil in a medium skillet. When it begins bubbling, add the shrimp and sauté until the color changes from

IF YOU'RE A BUSY MOM LIKE ME herding two toddlers through every grocery store trip, I recommend asking the seafood department to steam the shrimp for you there in the store. It doesn't cost a nickel extra and will save you 20 minutes of prep time!

ROASTED GARLIC SRIRACHA CREAM

1 intact head of garlic

1 tablespoon olive oil

1 tablespoon butter

1 shallot, minced

$1/2$ teaspoon salt

1 teaspoon flour

$1/4$ cup dry white wine such as sauvignon blanc

1 cup heavy cream

1–2 teaspoons sriracha sauce

translucent to white and the shrimp curl slightly. Take the pan off the heat. Cut the lime in half and squeeze the juice over the shrimp. Pour the shrimp into a bowl and reserve.

FOR THE SAUCE: Heat the same skillet to about medium heat and add the butter. Add the minced shallot, sprinkle with the salt, and sweat until translucent. Add the flour and form a roux, and then stir in the wine, incorporating the ingredients together with a whisk to form a thick sauce. Cook the wine-flour mixture until it is reduced down by three-quarters.

Slowly add in the cream and stir. Add sriracha sauce and the roasted garlic mash. Stir well with a fork or small whisk until smooth. Season with salt and pepper.

TO MAKE THE QUESADILLAS: Fill a large sauté pan with 2 tablespoons oil and bring it to medium heat. Build the quesadilla by spreading one tortilla with the sauce, then sprinkle with cheese, half the green chiles, and half the shrimp. Spread sauce on the other tortilla and place on top. Take your uncooked quesadilla and place it into the hot pan. Cook until golden brown and then flip over with a long spatula and cook the other side. Remove to a cutting board and slice like a pizza. Repeat with the other quesadilla.

Serve on a platter with any extra sauce and garnish with cilantro if desired.

TEXAS CHICKEN SPAGHETTI
WITH FANCY MUSHROOMS

IT GENUINELY WORRIES ME THAT WHEN I EAT FOOD made by other cooks, there will simply not be enough cheese. Perhaps my mother gave me this paranoia as a young child. Her chicken spaghetti recipe only had cheese sprinkled on top. You know this dish is a winner because it is swimming in cheese sauce *and* topped with cheddar. I also add fancy seared mushrooms just for good measure. Checkmate, mom! **YIELD: SERVES 6-8**

1 rotisserie chicken with the juices/jelly reserved from the bottom of the container

3/4 pound spaghetti pasta (3/4 of a box)

3 tablespoons butter

1 (8-ounce) package exotic mushrooms (chanterelle, shiitake, or an exotic blend), sliced and chopped into medium-size bits

1 yellow bell pepper, small dice

1 poblano, seeded, small dice

1 jalapeño, seeded fully, small dice

1/2 onion, small dice

1 teaspoon salt

2 tablespoons flour

2 cups chicken stock

1 can mild Rotel tomatoes and green chiles or 1 can petite-diced tomatoes

Preheat the oven to 400°F and set aside a glass casserole dish.

Remove the chicken from the bone and shred into bite-size pieces. Reserve the juices (or jelly if it's still cold) from the bottom of the chicken container to add to the sauce later.

Boil a large pot of water for cooking the spaghetti. Cover the pot so it boils faster! Cook your spaghetti to al dente, or just a little firmer than usual.

In a skillet or cast-iron pan, melt the butter on medium-high heat and add the mushrooms. I like to cut up the rest of the vegetables while the mushrooms brown and caramelize, giving them plenty of time to develop a deep, rich flavor. Sprinkle with a pinch of salt.

Add in the yellow bell pepper, poblano, jalapeño, and onion. Stir to incorporate and add 1 teaspoon salt. Cook the vegetables until they begin to soften and wilt at medium heat, about 4–6 minutes.

Sprinkle in the flour, stir it into the mixture, and cook for 30 seconds. Add in the chicken stock and one can Rotel, or petite-diced tomatoes if Rotel is unavailable in your area. Stir and toss until the mixture begins to resemble a slightly thicker sauce. Add the juice from the rotisserie chicken and the Velveeta (cut along the lines on the package for easy measuring). Turn the heat down to low-medium and allow the Velveeta to melt, about 6–8 minutes. Stir in the cream and simmer a couple more minutes. Taste for seasoning.

8 ounces Velveeta cheese

$^1/_2$ cup cream

4 ounces cheddar cheese for sprinkling on top

Optional: fresh cilantro, for garnish

It should taste like heaven at this point, and you should have to restrain yourself from pouring it into a bread bowl and calling it soup night.

In the glass casserole dish place the drained, al dente spaghetti and the shredded chicken and give it a toss. Pour the sauce over the top. Give it another toss and sprinkle with cheddar cheese.

Bake for about 10–15 minutes, just to get it nice and bubbly and allow the cheese topping to melt. Garnish with cilantro if desired.

CHICKEN ENCHILADAS WITH BUTTERY JACK CREAM SAUCE

THE WORLD OF MEXICAN FUSION CUISINE is brimming with descriptive words and specific styles, and in my opinion anything covered in cheese is a holy creation, so I am not here to judge.

Except that I will. There is one Mex to rule them all. And that my friends, is Tex-Mex. This recipe epitomizes Tex-Mex goodness, and in the varied and vastly polarizing landscape of Mexican fusion, Tex-Mex will guide you to the light.

We are biased here in Texas, but the truth is, if you love one Mexican food, you will love all the Mexican food, and the ways it is fused with other regional styles. Texas does everything epic, and that's the difference you will experience when you bite into these enchiladas. Tex-Mex chicken enchiladas take an already good thing and make it great. **YIELD: SERVES 6**

---

1 whole chicken, uncooked, bone in, skin on

2 carrots, rough chop

2 stalks celery, rough chop

1/2 onion, rough chop

4 garlic cloves, crushed

2 teaspoons Mexican oregano

2 tablespoons kosher salt

1 tablespoon pepper

2 whole cloves

A small handful of cilantro (save a little for garnish if you like!)

Disposable gloves

In a large stockpot place the raw chicken, carrots, celery, onion, garlic, herbs, and spices. Fill with water to cover the chicken and place on the stove on high heat. Allow the stock to come to a boil (covering it will make this happen faster). When it comes to a boil, remove the lid and turn the heat down to medium-high, or just where the stock is simmering. Cook 25 minutes.

Remove the chicken with tongs by placing the bottom side of the tongs into the chicken cavity and the other side on the top of the chicken, pausing while lifting the chicken out to allow any hot liquid to run back into the stockpot. Remove to a cooling rack or large platter. Let cool while you make the sauce.

In a large saucepan or skillet, heat the butter over medium until melted. Sweat the onion about 2 minutes and add the salt. Add the garlic and sweat an additional 30 seconds. Sprinkle in the flour to create a roux. (It's helpful to switch to a whisk at this point.)

Slowly begin adding the half-and-half (1 cup portions), whisking briskly until the half-and-half is smoothly and entirely distributed into the roux. Bring the mixture up to a boil and allow it to thicken. Cook 1–2 minutes, then turn down the heat to medium. Whisk in the Monterey Jack cheese. Add a couple drops of lemon juice for

$^1/_4$ cup butter

$^1/_4$ small white onion, small dice

$1^1/_2$ teaspoons kosher salt

1 garlic clove, pressed through the garlic press

$^1/_4$ cup flour

1 quart half-and-half, warmed

3 ounces Monterey Jack cheese (a little less than $^1/_2$ an 8-ounce package) from the block, freshly grated

Juice of $^1/_2$ a lemon

1–2 cups reserved broth from the cooked chicken for thinning the sauce

Oil for frying tortillas (anything flavorless such as grapeseed or sunflower oil)

30 corn tortillas

1 cup shredded Monterey Jack cheese, for sprinkling on top

seasoning and 1/2 cup of the chicken stock juices. You will add more of the chicken stock to thin the sauce throughout cooking.

Allow the mixture to simmer very lightly while you pull the chicken meat. Whisk occasionally to avoid browning the bottom of the pot and thin with $^1/_2$ cup chicken stock when needed. Pull the chicken from the bone and shred in manageable pieces. Reserve.

Preheat the oven to 350°F.

Check the cream sauce and salt if needed; the sauce should be thick and rich but a pourable consistency.

In a sauté pan heat the oil to medium. Fry each tortilla for just a couple of seconds so that they are pliable and warm. Set each tortilla on a paper towel–lined plate to cool.

To form enchiladas, pour a little bit of sauce into the bottom of a large casserole dish. Fill a tortilla with a spoonful of pulled chicken and roll up. Place it seam side down in the casserole dish and repeat with remaining tortillas. This recipe will make enough filling to fill a large 9x13 casserole dish fully and with enough left over to fill a small half-size casserole dish. Just fill a few extra tortillas and then pop the smaller dish in the freezer or reserve the filling for another day. Top with extra cheese and bake for 20–25 minutes. Garnish with cilantro if desired.

EVERYBODY HATES PULLING THE CHICKEN MEAT—it gets under your fingernails, it's hot, and the dog looks at you with sad desperation the whole time. Pick up a pair of thin disposable gloves in the cleaning department of the grocery store (alongside the dishwashing gloves). They are intended for one use and usually come ten to a package. Gloves really make a tedious, messy job more pleasant, and you'll find yourself using them for everything from tossing salads to making meatloaf.

CAJUN BARBECUED SHRIMP WITH A FINE AMERICAN BLONDE (ALE!)

IN A PAST LIFE I THINK I LIVED IN THE GARDEN DISTRICT OF NEW ORLEANS, in a gabled mansion with a wraparound porch. I probably wore elaborate fascinators and fancy antebellum-style lace-up boots. Perhaps I carried a parasol everywhere that I went and had a line of suitors down the iron-fenced road. Maybe we were neighbors, and we'd sit sipping sweet tea and arguing about whose oleander garden was more divine.

After dark we'd slip away to a smoky cafe in the French Quarter, where we'd order Cajun Barbecued Shrimp and bootlegged prohibition ale, savoring it to the smooth groove of a Dixieland jazz band . . .
YIELD: 4 SERVINGS

---

1 baguette

2 tablespoons butter for the bread (if desired)

$1/2$ cup unsalted butter

2 teaspoons paprika

1 teaspoon black pepper

1 teaspoon kosher salt

$1/2$ teaspoon crushed red pepper

$1/2$ teaspoon Mexican oregano

2 teaspoons fresh thyme or
1 teaspoon dried thyme

1 teaspoon fresh rosemary

2 garlic cloves, freshly pressed through a garlic press

2 pounds shrimp (21–25 size per pound or larger)

Preheat the oven to 375°F. Toast the baguette either whole or sliced and buttered. Cook 10–12 minutes or until golden brown. Serve alongside the shrimp.

In a large cast-iron skillet, heat the butter until melted. Add all the herbs, spices, and garlic and cook 1 minute, allowing them to infuse the butter. Add the cleaned shrimp and toss well in the butter. Cook 2 minutes. Add the beer and bring the mixture to a boil. Boil 1 minute, then add the stock and simmer an additional 2–4 minutes. Whisk the cornstarch into a little bit of water or stock to make a slurry to thicken the broth.

Add the cornstarch slurry, cream, and lemon juice. Simmer until thick. Taste for seasoning. Serve in big bowls with freshly toasted baguette and sliced green onions as garnish.

1 bottle or can American Blonde Ale

1 cup seafood stock or chicken stock

2 tablespoons cornstarch whisked into a little water or stock

1/3 cup heavy cream

Juice of 1 lemon

1 green onion, sliced thin (green and white parts), for garnish

How to Spike the Stock: If you have a bit of extra time when making this blazingly fast recipe, you can always spike the stock! If you're using a canned or boxed stock, pour the stock into a small saucepan (2 cups is good) and place your reserved shrimp shells in with the stock. Fill the saucepan with a little water if need be, or add 1/2 cup water at a time while simmering to maintain the water level. Simmer 30 minutes to an hour, adding additional water as needed. Then just strain out the shells and use as planned. The leftover shrimp shells will infuse the stock with further flavor and richness.

OVEN BAKED CHIMICHANGAS

CHIMICHANGAS ARE ESSENTIALLY A FRIED BURRITO, and I can throw down on Tex-Mex and fried chicken with the best of them, but not even I can deal with a fried version of an already delectably decadent dish like the burrito. Oven-baked chimichangas are a cleaned-up version of the classic dish, and I like them better! They bake up fast and can be frozen and made into a grab-and-go snack for weeks, which makes them amazing for health-conscious moms on the go—and will make your life happier as well as healthier. This is skinny Southwest at its best. **YIELD: 12 CHIMICHANGAS**

---

1 pound ground sirloin

1/2 onion

1/2 cup salsa

1 (4-ounce) can mild green chiles

1 (16-ounce) can fat-free refried beans

1 (4-ounce) block Monterey Jack or Pepper Jack cheese

12 flour tortillas

Cooking spray

Toppings: jar of your favorite red enchilada sauce, tomatillo sauce, sour cream, or chili for the holidays!

Traditionally chimichangas can be topped with or laid upon a bed of thinly sliced lettuce, tomatoes, black olives, and extra cheese.

Preheat the oven to 425°F.

In a large skillet brown the ground sirloin, breaking up the larger chunks with a wooden spoon. On a cutting board dice up half an onion and shred the Monterey Jack cheese.

When the meat has browned and cooked, drain any excess grease, then return the skillet to the stove top and add the diced onion. Let the onion cook for about 2 minutes, tossing it as needed.

Add salsa, green chiles, beans, and cheese. Stir well to incorporate and turn the heat down to low until it all melts together.

On a plate microwave the flour tortillas in 30-second bursts until they are soft and pliable. Line a cookie sheet with foil and spray well with cooking spray.

Fill the tortillas and place on the cookie sheet. When the tray is full, spray the chimichangas with the spray oil and sprinkle with salt and pepper. Place in the preheated oven on the middle rack and bake for 15–20 minutes.

Bake the chimichangas until golden brown and crispy. Serve with sour cream, salsa, or your other favorite toppings.

BARBECUE CHICKEN FLAUTAS
WITH SHINER BOCK FONDUE

THE URBAN COWGIRL IS A NEW KIND OF MODERN WOMAN who will use craft beers in her cooking as frequently as she once used wine. She hosts beer and homemade pretzel tastings instead of wine and cheese. She can recommend obscure brews even your most manly man wouldn't know. And when she makes a beer cheese fondue, she calls the local microbrewery and has them handpick their best amber ale. Because that's how Urban Cowgirls roll on game day!

These flautas are *that dish* that everyone asks me to bring on game day. As if a crispy, hot flauta filled with juicy barbecue chicken wasn't enough, the Shiner Bock Fondue is rich and creamy with just a hint of sweetness! **YIELD: 20 FLAUTAS**

FONDUE

1 (8-ounce) block Pepper Jack cheese

4 ounces sharp white cheddar cheese

4 ounces Oaxaca cheese, for broiling on top

2 tablespoons butter

2 tablespoons flour

1 bottle Shiner Bock beer, room temperature

1 cup half-and-half

1 (4-ounce) can mild green chiles

1 lime

Using a cheese grater or the grater on your food processor, grate the Pepper Jack and sharp white cheddar into a bowl. Reserve. Grate the Oaxaca cheese into a separate bowl.

In a medium-size cast-iron skillet, melt the butter. Using a whisk to stir, sprinkle in the flour to create a roux. Whisk for about 30 seconds. Pour in the beer a little at a time until it gets thick and becomes fully incorporated into the roux. Stir in the half-and-half and continue to whisk, incorporating it all into the beer mixture. Bring to a simmer and cook 1–2 minutes. Add a handful of the Pepper Jack/white cheddar mixture. As it melts into the beer mixture, continue to add a little more until the cheese is all in the pot.

Add a can of green chiles and squeeze the juice of one lime into the mixture, mixing thoroughly with a large spoon. The fondue can be held warm until the flautas are almost ready to serve.

Toss the pulled chicken in the barbecue sauce. Heat the oil in an enamel dutch oven or stockpot to 350°F. Wrap the corn tortillas in a moist paper towel and microwave 30–60 seconds to increase their flexibility. Lay out several corn tortillas and fill each with two spoonfuls of the barbecue chicken mixture. The chicken mixture should run across the tortillas horizontally. Take the

FLAUTAS

3 cups pulled chicken (1 rotisserie chicken from the deli is perfect for this)

1 bottle of your favorite barbecue sauce

1 liter canola oil, for frying

20 corn tortillas

Box of toothpicks

bottom flap of the corn tortilla and tuck it up and over the chicken mixture. Roll it up and secure with two toothpicks on each side.

When the oil is ready, fry three to four flautas at a time until golden brown. Remove with tongs and immediately sprinkle each one with salt. Leave them to dry on a paper towel or cooling rack while you finish the remainder of the batch.

TO FINISH THE DISH: Top the fondue with the Oaxaca cheese and set under the broiler in your oven for about 1–2 minutes until the cheese gets thoroughly melted and bubbly. Be careful not to leave it unsupervised, as this happens quickly and can burn the top of the fondue.

Serve with the flautas immediately. Be careful not to touch the cast-iron skillet as it is very hot! I like to set it on a nice pot holder and stick a padded pot handle cover over the hot handle. The cast-iron skillet will keep the fondue piping hot and creamy as you serve your guests.

DR PEPPER TACO SOUP

"FRIDAY NIGHT LIGHTS" WAS A THING IN TEXAS long before it was a massive, critically acclaimed hit on television. It was about community coming together—scarves wrapped around necks, hands tucked into gloves, breath smoking in the cold air—to cheer the local football team to victory. After the game the community split off into families and close friends, little tribes gathering to bask in the glow of the high school stadium lights and the boys' win. Then it was time for dinner. Something warm, something savory, something simple, with ingredients you already had in your pantry. Something the rambunctious kids all hopped-up on adrenaline and hot cocoa, the dad who just opened a beer because it was finally Friday, and the starving teenage boy who just played a good game would all love equally.

Dr Pepper Taco Soup was born from those moments hollering with the cheerleaders in the cold. It's good no matter who wins, and can be eaten like soup or scooped onto Fritos like mini taco delights. And it always reminds me of home. **YIELD: 6-8 SERVINGS**

---

1 1/2 pounds ground beef

1/2 cup diced white onion

2 (14.5-ounce) cans tomato sauce

1 (14.5-ounce) can corn

1 (14.5-ounce) can ranch-style beans

1 (14.5-ounce) can diced tomatoes

1 1/2 ounces taco seasoning, about 1/2 a package

1 1/2 ounces (about 1/2 a package) ranch dressing mix

Cayenne pepper, to taste

1 can Dr Pepper cola

1 teaspoon garlic salt

Freshly grated cheddar cheese

Corn chips, such as Fritos

Optional: sour cream, for topping

Sear the ground beef and onions in a large stockpot. When the mixture is fully cooked, drain the grease. On low-medium heat, add the rest of the ingredients except the cheese and corn chips. Just dump them all in! How easy is that? Simmer 20–30 minutes with the lid on, letting the flavors blend.

Serve with cheese, Fritos, and your favorite taco toppers.

ULTIMATE TEXAS CHICKEN FRIED STEAK
WITH WEST TEXAS GRAVY

MY WEST TEXAS GRAVY BEAT GRADY SPEARS—cowboy food legend and my great friend—in the Golden Chile Awards, to come out on top as the definitive gravy king. The secret? Well, it's two-fold.

Like many girls, I was blessed with a grandmother I adored. I grew up listening to her stories and eating her homemade chocolate chip cookies while I watched her fry up dinner in her ancient cast-iron skillet. When my grandmother passed away, the entire family descended on the house to take care of my grandfather and help ourselves to a memento from her life. My grandfather leaned over, placing his calloused, life-weathered hand on my knee, and pinned me with his still sparkling blue eyes, "What do you want of hers, Sarah?" I swallowed back tears and said, "Her cast-iron skillet."

The day I beat Grady, I was using her skillet. I also used a secret ingredient my grandmother taught me: The key to simply perfect country gravy is a couple cans of evaporated milk. It's sweeter, warmer, and, though it might sound crazy, it's *almost* as good as being safely wrapped in your grand-ma's warm embrace. **YIELD: 4 SERVINGS**

---

4 (^{1}/2-inch-thick) steaks of eye of round

3 cups all-purpose flour

1 tablespoon seasoning salt

Freshly cracked black pepper

2 tablespoons cornstarch

3 eggs and a little milk for thinning

1 liter canola oil

FOR THE STEAKS: Pound out your steaks with a tenderizing mallet to thin ^{1}/4-inch slices. They will get bigger and wider as you go. I alternate between the spiky side and the flat side of the mallet as I go. This is really therapeutic. Pound the crap out of them!

Combine the flour, seasoning salt, black pepper, and cornstarch in a bowl and whisk it well, then place it on a large platter. In a glass dish (big enough to dunk a whole steak) combine the three eggs and a little milk and whisk into a thin mixture to make an egg wash.

Dip each steak into flour mixture, shake it off, then into egg wash, shake it off, then back into the flour. Place each steak on a nice big cookie sheet. Repeat with all the steaks, then transfer into the refrigerator for a half hour. Do not skip this step. This

PRO TIP

WATCH THE EDGES OF THE STEAK FOR A GOLDEN-BROWN COLOR. The edges will tell you what it looks like underneath!

WEST TEXAS GRAVY

3–4 tablespoons oil, reserved from the pan you cooked the steaks in

3–4 tablespoons flour (grab some of the seasoned flour from breading the steaks)

2 cans evaporated whole milk

1 1/2 teaspoons fresh lemon juice

1/2 teaspoon each garlic powder and onion powder

1 teaspoon salt

Freshly ground black pepper

Garnish: I don't think there is anything better than fresh thyme!

is giving the flour mixture time to bind and develop. Reserve 4 tablespoons of seasoned flour for the gravy.

TO COOK THE STEAKS: Fill your cast-iron skillet about half-way with canola oil. Heat the oil to 350°F on medium-high heat. (You can test the oil with the back of a wooden spoon. When it bubbles around the spoon, it's hot enough. That happens at about 350°F.)

Using tongs, place a steak in the oil. It should immediately start to bubble and cook, but not explode with activity. If it does, you will want to turn the heat down a nudge. Depending on the size of your skillet, you can cook two or more at the same time, especially if you preheated that cast-iron skillet. You may have to monitor the heat when adding new steaks. I think a good secret is to let the majority of the first steak get well fried on one side before adding another one.

As each steak is done, remove it from the pan and immediately salt it on each side. Hold on a cookie sheet in a preheated oven at about 225°F. This will keep them hot while you cook the other steaks, but they are best served quickly for maximum crispiness.

When all of the steaks are resting and toasting in the oven, pour all the grease out of the skillet except about 3–4 tablespoons and turn the heat down to low. Sprinkle in the reserved flour and whisk until a brown paste begins to form.

Slowly whisk in one can of milk and whisk until it is thoroughly combined. Turn the heat up to medium and whisk as the gravy begins to take form and thicken, which happens when the mixture starts to simmer. Little bubbles will begin to form. Keep the heat around medium.

I usually add another 1/2 can of milk as I decide how thin/thick I want my gravy . . . that's just a preference thing. Feel free to do what you like. Add the lemon juice, onion and garlic powder, and salt. We crack freshly ground pepper in just before serving and sprinkle on fresh thyme from our herb garden.

Top the chicken-fried steaks with gravy and serve with your favorite sides.

FANCY STEAKS WITH BLACKBERRY BORDELAISE

BORDELAISE IS A CLASSIC FRENCH SAUCE named after the Bordeaux region of France, famous for its renowned red wine. Dishes such as sauce bordelaise and coq au vin traditionally use this light-bodied red wine, similar to pinot noir, which reduces into a sauce or gravy and pairs well with meat. My favorite Bordeaux wines are often described as jammy, referring to a rich cooked berry flavor profile reminiscent of jam. For this particular bordelaise, I was inspired to try out the same technique with local blackberry jam, which creates a unique velvety sauce. **YIELD: 4 SERVINGS**

4 steaks, of your favorite cut

Kosher salt

Black pepper

Onion powder

Garlic powder

3 tablespoons coconut oil, for pan searing

Note: Garnish with sliced blackberries if desired.

SAUCE:

1 tablespoon butter, plus 1 tablespoon butter to finish sauce

1/4 cup shallots, minced

1 garlic clove, minced

1/4 teaspoon salt

1 tablespoon fresh thyme

1 tablespoon black pepper

1 cup demi-glace (made with a demi concentrate according to package instructions)

2 tablespoons seedless blackberry jam

A couple drops of lemon juice

FOR THE STEAKS: Preheat the oven to 500°F. Season the steaks on all sides with salt, pepper, onion powder, and garlic powder. Heat the coconut oil in a saute pan or cast-iron skillet over high heat. Sear the steaks one or two at a time for 4–5 minutes on each side (depending on the size of the steaks).

Transfer the skillet to the hot oven and roast to the desired degree of doneness. Medium rare takes about 4–5 minutes; increase the time by 2–3 minutes for larger steaks or for medium well steaks. Remove steaks to a plate and let rest for 8–10 minutes.

FOR THE SAUCE: Over medium heat, melt the butter into a small saucepan and add the shallots, stirring with a spatula. Cook 1 minute. Add the garlic and stir until fragrant. Add the salt, thyme, and pepper, stirring well. Pour in the demi-glace and bring the sauce up to a simmer. Whisk in the blackberry jam until melted throughout the sauce. Simmer 3–5 minutes, reducing the sauce and blending the flavors. Add a couple drops of lemon juice. Taste for seasoning. Finish by whisking in the last tablespoon of butter to finish the sauce. Keep warm and serve with the steaks.

This dish pairs well with the Boursin Cheese Whipped Mashed Potatoes (page 164) and the Rustic Potato Cake (page 175).

Photo on following page.

GOAT CHEESE CHILE RELLENOS
WITH TOMATILLO GRAVY

A CHILE RELLENO IS A GIANT PEPPER, usually a poblano or an Anaheim, roasted, stuffed full of white melty cheese or picadillo, then fried and blanketed with red or green sauce (sometimes both if you are lucky)! It's the quintessential dish to show that there is much more to appreciate from a pepper than a spicy bite. The flavor of a pepper blooms rich and mellow when roasted, and a perfectly executed chile relleno is your first stop down a highway of unquenchable pepper obsession.

Stewed tomatillo sauce paired with a filling of classic Monterey Jack cheese is a hard-to-beat combination, but after I left home to study cooking, I found a new cheese to use in combination with Monterey Jack. Goat cheese, which melts into a fluffy cream, working hand in hand with melt-o-licious Monterey Jack, just might make the chile relleno to rule them all.

YIELD: 4 CHILE RELLENOS

TOMATILLO GRAVY

10–12 tomatillos

1/2 large white onion, sliced into large wedges

2 small whole garlic cloves

1 jalapeño, sliced in half and deseeded

2 tablespoons fresh cilantro, chopped

1/8 teaspoon cayenne pepper

3/4 teaspoon kosher salt

1 teaspoon Mexican oregano

1/2 teaspoon sugar

1/3 cup water

1–2 tablespoons oil, for frying

Optional: feta or Cotija cheese, cilantro, balsamic glaze, for garnish

Turn on the broiler in the oven to 500°F.

Wash the tomatillos and remove their husks by gently peeling off and discarding.

On a cookie sheet lined with foil, place the tomatillos, the wedges of white onion, garlic cloves, and the jalapeño. Deseed the jalapeño and remove the light green ribs inside if you prefer a milder sauce. Toss the vegetables with a bit of oil to prevent them from sticking to the foil and sprinkle with salt. Place the sheet under the broiler and shut the oven door.

In about 10 minutes, when the vegetables are done roasting, let them cool to the touch, then remove the skins and any black skins or burned areas. Transfer to a blender. Add the herbs and spices, sugar, and water and blend well.

In a skillet heat the oil over medium-high heat. Pour in the sauce and pan-fry for about 10 minutes to enrich the flavors. Season to taste. Keep the sauce warm.

To make the goat cheese mixture, grate the Monterey Jack cheese on a cheese grater and place the cheese into a bowl. Stir in the goat cheese, cilantro, and salt to form the mixture that will fill the poblano cavity. Keep chilled.

ROASTING THE VEGETABLES IN MEXICAN SAUCES

COZY FIREPLACE CHAT

In Tex-Mex and Mexican cooking, one particular trick that I have come to love is roasting fresh vegetables before they go in a sauce or salsa. This is quite customary in Hispanic homes, but less known in our American kitchen. While in Mexican kitchens cooks may roast over an open fire or a comal, which is a smooth skillet similar to our cast-iron skillet, I find the broiler of my oven to be adequate and quite handy. All types of veggies can be roasted, from tomatillos and chiles to garlic and onions.

When roasting the vegetables, you should remain in the immediate area, as they will need to be turned every couple of minutes. As they roast and begin to brown, you can pull them out as they finish roasting, starting with the garlic cloves and ending with the onions, tomatoes, and tomatillos. The skins will turn black and peel away, leaving freshly roasted vegetable underneath. This intensifies the flavor and mellows the bite of the onions. It's just the thing to give your sauces the dynamic flavor of your favorite Mexican restaurant.

GOAT CHEESE CHILE RELLENOS

4 poblano peppers

5 ounces Monterey Jack cheese

7 ounces goat cheese

1 teaspoon salt

1 tablespoon chopped cilantro

1/2 cup flour

1/4 cup cornmeal

4 eggs, separated into whites and yolks

1 teaspoon baking powder

2-3 cups oil for pan frying (a large nonstick skillet is helpful for frying)

PRO TIP

DON'T TRY TO REMOVE ANY OF THE SKIN off the top of the chile relleno—the little "hat" where the stem is attached—you won't be eating that anyway and it helps to hold the whole thing intact.

Take the chilled goat cheese mixture and split it evenly among the four cleaned poblano chiles, placing the cheese inside and through the T-cut (see page 144). Tuck the cheese in tight, then allow the poblanos to chill in the freezer or refrigerator while you prepare the batter and begin the tomatillo gravy.

FOR THE BATTER: On a plate combine the flour and cornmeal and whisk together with a fork.

In two bowls, crack and separate the eggs into yolks and whites. The bowl for the whites must be squeaky clean and dry; you can use the bowl of your stand mixer if you have one. Beat the egg whites to stiff peaks using electric beaters or a stand mixer with the whisk attachment.

Gently whisk the yolks together with a fork and combine with the baking powder.

Using a spatula, fold the yolk and baking powder mixture into the stiff egg whites. Fold well until the yellow is dispersed into the egg whites. Heat the oil in a pan to about 350°F.

Using a silicone spatula, place a dollop of the batter about the size of the stuffed poblano into the hot oil. Take one goat cheese–stuffed pepper and place it in the flour mixture, dusting it well on all sides. Place the stuffed poblano directly on top of it. Use your spatula to smooth the batter up around it and spoon more on top until you have covered it 360 degrees with the batter. Fry the chile relleno for 4–5 minutes on each side. When it is done, remove the hot chile relleno carefully with a spatula and drain well of all grease.

Repeat with remaining peppers and then serve on a plate, topped with the tomatillo gravy. Garnish with cilantro, feta, or Cotija cheese or your choice of Mexican condiments.

MASTERING THE T-CUT

Chile rellenos might be the most intimidating dish in the Texas catalog, but there is a procedure that I call the T-cut, which I think will have you whipping up this restaurant favorite like a pro in no time. It goes like this:

On a cutting board lay down your poblano and, using a sharp knife, begin like you are cutting the top part of the chile off, including the stem. Sever it halfway through, but make sure to stop halfway. Remove your knife and cut another slice perpendicular from stem to tip, making a "T" shape. Put down the knife and use your hands to remove and pull out any seeds that are inside, but be careful not to open the chile up any more than necessary. Preserve the structure of the chile at all costs!

Lay your prepared chiles on a baking sheet lined with foil and greased with a little pan spray or oil. Turn the broiler to high and place the chiles right under the broiler. Shut the oven door but stay nearby to turn them occasionally as they roast and the skin blackens and bubbles. When the chiles have turned blackish-brown, the flesh has softened, and the skin is beginning to peel away, remove them from the oven and transfer to a heat-safe bowl. Cover the bowl tightly with Saran Wrap and leave the chiles to steam for 10–20 minutes. This technique will help to loosen the skin, making it easy to peel off.

Place the baking sheet near the kitchen sink so you can remove the skin by turning the cold water on low in the sink to use it to help wash the skins away and remove any residual heat from the chiles, but don't let the stream of water beat up the fragile chiles and cause them to fall apart.

FRIED CHICKEN WITH JALAPEÑO HONEY DRIZZLE

I'VE SPENT YEARS PERFECTING FRIED CHICKEN, and I assure you it has very little to do with a magic recipe and much more with excellent technique. So instead of the Ten Commandments for living a blessed life in the Lord, I give you my five commandments for restaurant-quality fried chicken. And you have my word that if you follow these commandments your fried chicken will have people shouting hallelujah!

This sweet honey glaze is rich, tangy, and loaded with the full-bodied flavor of sun-ripened tomatoes and fiery jalapeños! It's truly finger lickin' good. I find it hard not to just stand over the bowl and eat this with a spoon—but it's even better on the chicken, so let's use our self-control and save it for the main event. No need for a napkin, just lick your fingers. Fried chicken falls in the no-judgment zone!

YIELD: SERVES 4

FOR THE MARINADE:

1 cup half-and-half

1 bottle Tiger Sauce or $^1/_2$ cup of any sweet hot pepper sauce you like

3 large eggs

4 chicken thighs

2 chicken breasts, butterflied (you can also use chicken tenders)

5 chicken legs

HONEY JALAPEÑO DRIZZLE

2 garlic cloves

3 small jalapeños

$^1/_3$ cup extra-virgin olive oil

$^1/_3$ cup honey

$^1/_3$ cup red wine vinegar

3 cups diced tomatoes

FOR THE MARINADE: In a large bowl, blend the half-and-half, Tiger Sauce, and eggs with a whisk. Place the chicken pieces in to marinate overnight or at least 4 hours.

FOR THE DRIZZLE: Mince the garlic and cut the jalapeños in half. Using a teaspoon, scrape the insides of the jalapeños out, reserving the seeds and ribs of one of the jalapeño halves for the sauce; discard the rest of the ribs and seeds. Half of one of the jalapeños gives a nice medium-hot flavor, but fine-tune to your preference. Dice the seeded jalapeño peppers.

In a small saucepan, pour in the olive oil and honey. Bring it to a boil and let bubble for approximately 1 minute. Pour in the red wine vinegar and turn down the heat, as it will bubble and gush for a moment. Add the diced tomatoes, garlic, two sprigs of basil, diced jalapeño, salt, pepper, and the seeds and ribs of half of one jalapeño. Simmer for 15 minutes. Take the mixture off the heat and cool for several minutes. Transfer to a blender and blend for 1 minute. Season with salt and pepper and reserve for the chicken.

FOR FRYING THE CHICKEN: Mix all the dry batter ingredients in a deep casserole dish. Prepare a large platter or cookie sheet lined with foil to rest the chicken pieces on after they are battered. Using one hand for pulling the chicken out of the egg

5 COMMANDMENTS OF FRIED CHICKEN

Marinate the chicken in a brine, buttermilk, or other flavored wet batter to add flavor, moisture, and interest.

Use a self-rising flour in your batter for extra crunch and texture.

Always let the breading develop before frying. It should transform from looking like flour resting on the chicken to looking like the chicken has been dipped in a batter. This helps marry the flavors in the batter, helps the flour to adhere, and gives a more professional restaurant-style look to the fried chicken.

Fill the deep frying vessel with enough oil that the chicken is fully submerged.

Salt immediately upon taking the chicken out of the oil. Don't even wait one minute! Salt over the cooking oil as you pull the chicken out if you must!

2 sprigs of basil, leaves and stem

1 1/2 teaspoons kosher salt

1/2 teaspoon pepper

FOR THE CRISPY FRIED
BATTER:

2–3 cups self-rising flour

1/3 cup cornstarch

1 tablespoon salt

2 tablespoons freshly cracked
black pepper

1 teaspoon garlic powder

1 tablespoon onion powder

2 tablespoons dried parsley

2–3 liters canola or peanut oil,
for frying

mixture marinade and the other hand for coating the chicken in the seasoned flour mixture, batter each piece of chicken with a good coating of batter. Place them on the platter. Chill in the refrigerator for at least 30 minutes and up to a day ahead. (I batter them during the day for dinnertime.)

Fill a large, heavy-bottomed enamel dutch oven or wide stockpot half full with oil. You want the chicken to be completely submerged when frying. In my kitchen, this means two to four pieces at a time.

Heat the oil to 350°F. After resting the chicken, take it out of the refrigerator and check to see that the flour mixture has turned from white and powdery to looking like an opaque batter is coating the chicken. Bits of white may still be seen, but primarily the chicken should look coated in thick batter. This is the secret to a strong, crunchy crust that will adhere to the chicken.

When the oil has reached 350°F, begin placing the chicken into the pot, up to four pieces at a time. I always use a thermometer to check the temperature of the oil to make sure it's not rising too much (over 365°F) or dropping below 325°F. This recipe cooks in three or more batches depending on the size of your cooking pot.

The chicken takes 8–12 minutes per batch to cook, but you must turn the pieces while frying to avoid getting a burnt side on the chicken that is touching the bottom of the pan.

Kitchen lore says the chicken is done when it floats, but I find that to be unreliable. When the chicken is a deep golden brown, I begin using a digital thermometer inserted into the thickest part of the meat. Chicken is done at 165°F but will rise a few degrees from carryover heating when it is removed from the oil.

Salt the chicken with freshly cracked salt immediately after removing from the pan, then place on wire cooling racks.

The batter in this recipe is so crunchy there is no need to keep the chicken warm in the oven (where I find it tends to steam the breading off). Serve it fresh and hot drizzled with the sweet jalapeño glaze and served with an ice-cold glass of strawberry-peach sweet tea! Divine!

MOM'S SWEDISH MEATBALLS
AND HOT BUTTERED NOODLES

THIS RECIPE PERSONIFIES MY MOTHER. She made it every time I was sick, sad, or struggling to cope with growing up, and one of my favorite things about it is how completely countrified it is. As a trained chef and card-carrying IKEA fan, I will be the first to confess to you, these are not quite authentic. Still, I can still remember sitting on her countertop at the wee age of five, ponytail and all, dipping my finger in the sauce as she cooked (and getting my hand slapped away!).

These Southern Swedish meatballs will be your kid's new favorite dish!
YIELD: 4 LARGE SERVINGS

---

1 1/2 pounds ground beef, 90/10 preferred

1 egg

1/4 cup milk or cream

1/2 teaspoon salt

1/4 teaspoon pepper

Pinch of nutmeg

1/2 cup Ritz cracker crumbs

1/4 cup grated onion

2 cans cream of mushroom soup

1 (12-ounce) can evaporated milk

2 1/2 tablespoons butter

1 tablespoon lemon pepper

1 teaspoon salt

3 tablespoons sour cream

In a large bowl combine the ground beef, egg, milk or cream, seasonings, and the well-crushed Ritz crackers. (Crackers can be crushed with a food processor or placed in a ziplock bag and beaten with a kitchen mallet or rolling pin.) Grate the onion on a cheese grater to get fine ribbons of onion. This is always the best method for meatballs! Using your hands, combine the mixture well and then scoop out, and roll meatball-size balls in your palms and reserve.

Start a big pot of boiling water to cook the pasta. In a large saucepan combine the cream of mushroom soup, evaporated milk, butter, lemon pepper, and salt. Bring this mixture to a simmer and taste for seasoning. Turn off the heat and gently whisk in the sour cream. Cover the sauce with a lid and reserve.

In a frying pan heat about 1/4 cup oil over medium heat. When the pan is hot, add a round of meatballs. Do not overcrowd them, as you will need room to roll them with your tongs or spatula.

Sprinkle meatballs with a little salt and pepper. Turn them every 3 minutes as they crisp and brown on each side, until they are all brown and crusty and cooked through. Transfer to a holding

Oil, for lightly pan frying

1 package egg noodles

2 tablespoons butter

$1/2$ teaspoon salt

1 tablespoon minced fresh parsley

plate and repeat until all the meatballs are cooked. Or place the meatballs in the sauce if you like, and if you have room in the pot. That's what my mom always used to do!

When the pasta water begins to boil, salt the water well, and add the egg noodles. Boil them just until tender. Drain the pasta well and return to the pan. Add the butter, salt, and fresh parsley. Stir to combine.

To serve, fill a plate with hot buttered noodles and top with meatballs and sauce. Sprinkle with more parsley if desired.

HOMETOWN CHEESE ENCHILADAS
WITH DALLAS CHILI GRAVY

SOMETIMES I FEEL LIKE I'VE BEEN ON THE ENCHILADA WORLD TOUR. It seems like every region puts their own tasty spin on this sinfully delicious dish, and therefore you can think of enchiladas as a food compass of sorts.

Lost? Tell me what the enchiladas are like, and I will tell you where you are.

I was born just north of Dallas, where the decadent cheddar cheese enchiladas are smothered in beefy, robust chili gravy and diced white onion, an extension of chile con carne. I went to culinary school in Phoenix, where the Sonoran enchiladas are coated in red and green chile sauces and stuffed with creamy-white Mexican cheese (a newbie for my enchilada codex and a style I have grown to miss). Then I chef'd the Riverwalk in San Antonio, where the enchiladas are filled with gooey American cheese and smooth, red chili gravy.

Bonus: These are always accompanied by a live mariachi band!

Every single one has elements that I adore and memories of the path I've traveled, but of all the enchiladas in all the world, these that I grew up with are my favorite. There's no place like home y'all. **YIELD: 16 ENCHILADAS**

---

1 pound 80/20 ground beef, chili grind if available

1 tablespoon kosher salt

$1/2$ teaspoon black pepper

$1/3$ cup minced white onion

2 tablespoons Texas chili powder such as Mexene or Gebhardt

1 teaspoon powdered garlic

2 teaspoons cumin

$1/2$ teaspoon Mexican oregano

$1/4$ cup flour

$2 1/2$ cups beef stock

In a skillet on medium-high heat, sear the ground beef, breaking it up well with a wooden spatula. Sprinkle in the salt and pepper and let the meat sear well. The dark brown parts of the sear will dissolve and enrich the chili gravy later, adding to the flavor.

When the meat is well seared, add in the onion and cook 2 minutes, tossing frequently.

Add in the chili powder, powdered garlic, cumin, and Mexican oregano and let the spices brown and toast in the pan along with the beef. Finally, turn the heat down to medium and sprinkle in the flour. Toss the flour in the meat and incorporate into the fat and juices, creating a roux of sorts. When the flour dissolves into the mixture, pour in the beef stock and whisk it into the mixture.

½ teaspoon salt

1 teaspoon fresh lemon juice

1 cup oil, for frying

12–16 fresh corn tortillas

12 ounces medium cheddar
from the block, freshly grated

½ cup minced white onion

Turn the heat up and stir frequently, bringing the mixture to a boil. Lower the heat and cook for 15–20 minutes (or longer if desired); the longer the chili cooks, the more the flavors in the chili gravy will enhance and deepen. Finish the gravy with ½ teaspoon salt, if needed, and fresh lemon juice.

Preheat the oven to 400°F.

In a skillet heat the oil to medium-high heat and fry each corn tortilla for about 20 seconds to soften them. Drain on paper towels as they come out.

Fill the corn tortillas with 2 tablespoons or so of the cheddar cheese and a sprinkling of minced onion. Roll them into enchiladas with the seam on the bottom and place in a 9 x 13-inch baking dish. Fill the entire dish with enchiladas, tucked closely together. Ladle the hot chili gravy on top of the enchiladas.

Place in the oven and bake for 20 minutes or until hot and bubbly. Sprinkle extra cheese and white onion on top if desired.

These go well with Papa Wiggs' Mexican Rice with Crema and Bacon Fat Refried Beans (see the "Sides" chapter).

POBLANO PESTO GRILLED CHEESE SANDWICHES

NOW THAT I AM IN MY THIRTIES, I can finally admit in front of God and everyone:

I am a fanatical late-night snacker.

I know . . . *But your health! Carbs after six p.m. make you fat! You'll never be a size two again!*

Overrated. I like sandwiches more than I like abs. Adulting truly is about finding and accepting who you are deep down inside, and letting that person out to shine. I am just a girl who likes frying bread in butter at eleven o'clock at night.

It started when I was little. I wasn't a stellar eater when I was a wee one. So anytime I was willing to gobble a little snack, my adoring grandparents would *Jump. On. It.* Midnight and little Sarah wants cheese bread? My grandmother was like a mafia boss ordering around her goons: "Make it happen! No mistakes like last time, I want a clean job. Do *not* put *anything* green on that plate!" (I would end up taking two tiny caterpillar-size bites and move on with my life.)

Late-night snacking grew to be a favorite pastime on weekends when my family would stay up late watching movies. Midnight? What a great time for a round of eight grilled cheese sandwiches!

Tell me we weren't the only ones.

And now it's such an extravagant treat to steal a few moments to myself at the end of the night, once the kids are sleeping soundly and the hubs is passed out on the floor next to the toddler bed. Just me and the dog and a hot grilled cheese sammich. What a sinfully pleasant indulgence. How lavish a way for us mothers to end our most frantic days.

This recipe is from my catalog of pan-fried, late-night encounters. It's from the Urban Cowgirl college years, and the poblano pesto was inspired by a little bistro I used to frequent.

And when you're eating your grilled cheese sandwich while everyone else is snoozing, just remember that somewhere out there, I am too.

Know you aren't alone . . . We'll be like those mice in *An American Tail*. The league of late-night snackers. **YIELD: 2 SERVINGS, WITH EXTRA PESTO**

GRILLED CHEESE SANDWICHES are easier to make in a nonstick skillet.

4 tablespoons butter

4 pieces Texas toast (a white bread cut into double-thick slices)

Several 1/4-inch-thick slices quesadilla cheese (see the "Urban Cowgirl Ingredients" chapter)

Several 1/4-inch-thick slices medium sharp cheddar from the block

POBLANO PESTO

3 poblanos

1/2 cup pine nuts

3 small garlic cloves

1 cup Parmesan cheese

1/4 cup extra-virgin olive oil

1/2 teaspoon salt

3 heaping tablespoons chopped cilantro

Juice of 1 lemon

Roast the poblanos and deseed and skin them as described in the "Urban Cowgirl Cooking School" chapter.

In a food processor or blender, combine all the ingredients for the pesto. Turn the machine on and stir between pulses to help incorporate the ingredients and get a smooth puree. Reserve.

In a skillet over medium heat, melt 2 tablespoons butter. Put two slices of bread down in the melted butter to thoroughly coat in butter, then remove one slice and set it aside to be the top of the grilled cheese.

On the slice of bread in the pan, place slices of quesadilla cheese and cheddar until you cover the bread. Both cheeses will melt together when they cook. Shingle them if you like, depending on how much cheese you prefer!

Take the other piece of bread and slather it with pesto. Place it down on the cheese with the pesto facing the cheese and the buttered side of the bread facing up.

Fry the grilled cheese on medium heat for 2–3 minutes. Flip it with a spatula and fry an additional 2 minutes, adjusting the heat if necessary to not burn the bread.

Repeat with the remaining bread and cheese. Serve hot, with pickled green beans or cold grapes!

GULF COAST CRAB BALLS

My husband is truly my best friend, but because his favorite role to play is devil's advocate (in most every situation I get myself into), he's also my constant adversary. I think of it as a little game we play. He's a tough critic, ambitious, and smart, but I am creative and persistent. He understands my mind intimately, so he is continually calling me out on my schemes. And I am constantly and politely telling him to shove it.

I knew that picking out our little house in Galveston, Texas, would be no different. I anxiously watched him walk through the hundred-year-old house, silently inspecting the AC window units and floor heaters, the tiny kitchen, the complete absence of a dishwasher, the peeling paint, and the original (and totally) shabby wooden floors. Nervous, I lumbered out to the porch, because not only were we moving, but I was currently eight months pregnant. I perched on the cutest porch swing you've ever seen, utterly cheerful, content, determined that, finally, we had come home.

Dereck stepped out onto the porch, closed the door with a soft thud, and pinned me with his eyes. He began to roll up the sleeves on his Brooks Brothers button-down, wiping the sweat off his forehead. The humidity was thick, overwhelming the gentle breeze from the water, and it was clearly starting to take its toll on this city boy.

"You chose this house because it's next to Shrimp 'n Stuff."

My mouth dropped open, and I sputtered, feigning offense. I tried to think of a response that would eviscerate him. I managed a weak "Nuh-un," followed by a loving gaze past him toward the restaurant.

He gave me the side eye, not fooled, and peered across the little tangle of grass and palm trees that would become our front yard.

"You chose this house because Shrimp 'n Stuff is less than a block away, and you can waddle down and get crab balls anytime you want. Don't deny it, *you* would never choose *this* house."

He had a point, but it no longer mattered. I was consumed with the glorious knowledge that Gulf Coast crab balls were within a thousand feet of where I would be sleeping.

YIELD: 22–24 1-OUNCE BALLS

1 pound crab meat (8 ounces claw meat, 8 ounces back-fin)

1 egg

$^3/_4$ cup cream

2 cups crushed saltine cracker crumbs

1 tablespoon butter

$^1/_3$ cup finely diced white onion

$^1/_4$ cup finely diced green bell pepper

$^1/_4$ cup finely diced red bell pepper

$^1/_4$ cup finely diced celery (about 1 stalk)

$^1/_4$ teaspoon kosher salt

$^1/_4$ teaspoon black pepper

$^1/_2$ teaspoon garlic powder

1 tablespoon minced fresh parsley

BREADING STATION

$^1/_2$ cup flour

1 egg

$^1/_4$ cup water

2 cups panko bread crumbs

1 quart fresh oil, for frying

Extras: Lemons, tartar or cocktail sauce, for serving

In a large bowl combine the crab meat, egg, cream, and crushed saltine cracker crumbs.

Heat the butter in a small sauté pan. Add the onion, bell peppers, and celery and cook over medium heat for 4–5 minutes. Add the salt, pepper, and garlic powder. Continue to cook the veggies until they are soft and wilted. Turn off the heat and set them aside to cool slightly.

Add the vegetables and fresh parsley to the bowl of crab mixture. Use your hands to mix and fold the mixture together. Using a 1-ounce meatball scoop or your hands, scoop out balls of the mixture, roll between your palms until firm, and place on a lightly greased baking sheet. You should have 22–24 balls. Freeze for 30–60 minutes.

Meanwhile, pour the flour onto a plate, whisk the egg with the water in a bowl, and pour the bread crumbs onto another plate, creating a breading station for the crab balls. Pour the oil into a medium saucepan and heat to 350°F.

Slice lemons (if using) and pour tartar or cocktail sauce into small bowls.

When the balls are chilled solid, remove them from the freezer. Take a crab ball and roll it first in flour, then dunk it in egg wash, then roll it in panko bread crumbs. Set aside and repeat with the remaining balls.

Fry the balls, several at a time, for about 4–5 minutes at approximately 350°F. Remove the balls with tongs when they are golden brown. Drain over a cooling rack or on paper towels.

Salt and serve immediately with tartar or cocktail sauce.

PICNIC OVEN FRIED CHICKEN

ANY SOUTHERN BELLE KNOWS YOU CAN'T *KEEP* FRIED CHICKEN. The crust becomes soggy and falls clean off, just like Cinderella's dainty glass slipper when she stayed too long at the ball. Fried chicken is a dish with a time limit on the crunch factor. But I'm here to offer you a fried chicken recipe that breaks that rule, defying the pitfalls of frying, to stay good well past the stroke of midnight.

Like Sunday afternoon family picnics in the park beneath parasols, on checkered blankets while wearing our church-finest, this technique has largely been lost to our busy lives. Who needs picnic chicken when we can swing by McDonald's on the way to the park?

But picnic chicken is the stuff of dreams. A little girl running through the grass, pudgy hand clasping a chicken leg with crisp, flavorful skin; Mom lounging on a warm blanket under a tree pouring fresh iced tea; and Dad tossing the baseball with his son—his first catch, her first butterfly landing on her nose. Picnic chicken is a fairytale dream come true. **YIELD: 8 PIECES**

---

8 chicken thighs

1 stick butter

1 cup flour

2 teaspoons onion powder

1 teaspoon garlic powder

1 teaspoon kosher salt

1 teaspoon freshly cracked black pepper

1/2 teaspoon paprika

1/2 teaspoon Mexican oregano, basil, or dried parsley

5–6 sprigs of fresh thyme

Dash cayenne (optional)

Preheat the oven to 425°F.

In a glass casserole dish, place the stick of butter and put it in the oven for 10 minutes to melt while you prepare the chicken.

In another casserole dish place the flour and all the spices, and mix well with a whisk. Place a chicken thigh skin side down into the flour and dust all over with the flour mixture. Repeat with the other chicken thighs and reserve.

Using oven mitts, remove the hot casserole dish with the melted butter. Coat each chicken piece on both sides with butter and then place each piece skin side down in the dish.

Place in the oven and cook 35 minutes. Pull the dish out and flip the chicken pieces. Return to the oven for 20–25 minutes or until the juices run clear. Cool and chill overnight. The crust will not deteriorate in the refrigerator, and the entire dish will become more flavorful the next day.

Picnic chicken is best served cold! And preferably outdoors!

JALAPEÑO PICKLED SHRIMP
WITH SASSY SAUCE

I LIVED IN GALVESTON FOR YEARS, and what drew me there—besides the gorgeous water and the amazing Gulf Coast cuisine—was the proximity to my father's house. Now when I visit him, I can't seem to make it there without stopping to buy shrimp on 61st Street, headed to Seawall Boulevard. I buy mine shell and head on—ripping those off when I'm ready to prepare them, and believe me, it makes a difference. When you prepare shrimp this fresh, these little velvety ribbons of sweet white meat remain where you've removed the shell. It only happens when they are fresh from the water— if you're an islander, you know exactly what I am talking about!

If you've never had freshly caught, right out of the water Gulf brown shrimp, you haven't experienced shrimp properly. The next time you visit the coast, buy shrimp fresh and cook it up simple. You can thank me later!

I have two methods for cooking shrimp for my beloved dad, (aka Pop Pop to my kids)—sautéed shrimp with lemon sauce and linguine, or pickled shrimp with sassy sauce. Combining either of these preparations with shrimp plucked from the sea that day will spoil you (and your dad) for life.

YIELD: 2 LBS. SHRIMP

2 pounds peel and eat shrimp, raw, shell on

4–5 cups water (make sure the shrimp are covered in water)

2 tablespoons liquid shrimp boil

FOR THE PICKLE:

1 (12-ounce) jar sliced, pickled jalapeño peppers (you will use half the peppers and all the juice)

1/3 cup salad vinegar

TO MAKE THE PICKLE BRINE: For the jalapeño pickle brine, you will use half a jar of sliced jalapeños and all the juice. The remaining jalapeños can be refrigerated for another use. Add all the ingredients to a medium saucepan and heat on low until the sugar and salt have dissolved. Remove from the heat and place in a large bowl to cool. Add all of the nibbling veggies in bite-size pieces.

TO BOIL THE SHRIMP: In a large saucepan with a lid, heat the water on high heat and add the shrimp boil concentrate. When it comes to a simmer, add the shrimp and cover the pot. Cook for 4–6 minutes or until shrimp are cooked through. Small shrimp will need less time. Watch for the shrimp to turn opaque and

IF YOU'RE NOT NEAR THE OCEAN, the best shrimp for this dish are deveined but with the shell on. This allows you to have the best of both worlds: shell on (for the flavor!), but the process of deveining the shrimp leaves the shell on the shrimp very loose, which means it's easy for you to peel off later! Buy the largest shrimp you can afford when making "peel and eat" shrimp, to cut down on the labor!

1 tablespoon kosher salt

Juice of 1 lemon

$1^1/_2$ cups water

1 teaspoon sugar

1 tablespoon Mexican oregano

Nibbling veggies to pickle
(you can also add your favorites):

$^1/_2$ red bell pepper, medium dice

$^1/_2$ white onion, cut into small
wedges

2 stalks celery, medium dice

2 carrots, sliced into thin coins

SASSY SAUCE:

$^3/_4$ cup diced roasted piquillo
peppers from the jar

1 cup mayonnaise

$^1/_4$ cup onion, diced

2 small garlic cloves, minced

2 teaspoons horseradish

1 tablespoon fresh parsley

3 sprigs of thyme (leaves only)

2 tablespoons cider vinegar

1 teaspoon Tabasco

$^1/_2$ teaspoon salt

$^1/_2$ teaspoon pepper

2 teaspoon sugar

Juice of 1 lemon

curl into a soft "C" shape. Remove the shrimp with a slotted
spoon, drain well, and transfer directly into the pickle brine.

Pickle the shrimp and veggies $1^1/_2$–2 hours before serving for
best flavor.

THE INCREDIBLE SASSY SAUCE

Here is a sassy little sauce that everyone begs me to make.
It's sort of like a remoulade sauce kissed with the sweet and
smoky essence of piquillo peppers.

TO MAKE THE SASSY SAUCE: Combine all the ingredients
in a blender and blend well until pink. Taste for seasoning
and chill for $1^1/_2$–2 hours. Serve with the shrimp as a
dipping sauce.

Serve the shrimp on a platter chilled with a bowl of the sauce.
You can remove the pickled veggies to their own bowl or serve
them with the shrimp.

Sides

THE ENTREE MAY BE THE MATRIARCH OF THE MEAL, but Granny still needs some support to keep us all in line. Enter: side dishes. For some, sides are the best part of dinner, like that cool aunt who gives you cash every time you see her.

Side dishes are the stars of the potluck, the hero to a mediocre chicken breast. We get two at restaurants but four or five at any respectable Southern family supper! On the Urban Cowgirl table, they get just as much appreciation as the entree, so we give them just as much consideration!

BOURSIN CHEESE WHIPPED MASHED POTATOES

BOURSIN CHEESE IS THE QUEEN'S VERSION OF CREAM CHEESE. If you ever need a side for a dinner party that will feel fancy and taste fabulous, these potatoes will always come through.

YIELD: 4-6 SERVINGS

2 pounds red potatoes
(about 12 small to medium)

3 tablespoons unsalted butter

1/2 cup cream

1 (5-ounce) package boursin cheese

1 teaspoon salt

1 teaspoon freshly cracked pepper

Fresh herbs (such as parsley, chives, chervil)

PRO TIP

THE SECRET TO FEATHERY LIGHT POTATOES is to mash them first, then whip them with beaters or the paddle attachment to your stand mixer. To whip these mashed potatoes, add in the cream sauce and whip 2-4 minutes until airy light.

Peel the potatoes and place them in a large stockpot. Fill the stockpot with water and cover the pot. Bring the potatoes to a boil and cook for about 15 minutes or until the potatoes can be pierced easily with a fork and are cooked through. Drain the water from the potatoes and mash with a potato masher or press through a food mill.

Meanwhile, in a small saucepan melt the butter, cream, and three-quarters of the package of boursin cheese. Add the salt and pepper and whisk together. When the mixture has melted into a sauce, pour the hot mixture over the potatoes. Fold the sauce into the potatoes until smooth and fluffy.

Taste the mashed potatoes for seasoning and transfer to a serving platter. Serve the mashed potatoes hot, topped with the remaining bits of boursin cheese slowly melting on top.

Sprinkle with any fresh herbs and black pepper for a pop of color.

PAPA WIGGS' MEXICAN RICE WITH CREMA

THIS MEXICAN RICE IS A FAMILY FAVORITE taught to me by my sweet Papa Wiggs, who is one of the most authentic, well-versed Texas cooks I know. As a young man, he cooked his way through Dallas/Fort Worth's most iconic, historic institutions: the Six Flag's El Chico, Don Juan's Romantic Mexican Food; our family even owned one of the original Dairy Queens. Some nights we'll sit on the patio and drink a cold one, flipping through the worn pages of the old restaurant books his father kept, documenting the day-to-day orders—how many dip cones they made, how many burgers he flipped—even the paper still smells like French fries and a hot buttered skillet.

Through the years, Papa Wiggs has continued to teach me all of his tricks. His secret recipe for hearty Mexican rice is a family favorite that you're sure to pass on to the next generation.
YIELD: SERVES 4-6

---

1 1/2 pounds Angus ground sirloin

1/2 green bell pepper

1/2 large, white onion

1 jalapeño, seeds removed

3 garlic cloves, minced

2 cups long or medium grain rice (I recommend 1 1/2 cups regular long or medium grain rice and 1/2 cup wild rice for great chew and texture)

1 quart chicken stock

FIRST SEASONINGS:

1/2 teaspoon black pepper

1 teaspoon Texas chili powder

1/2 teaspoon powdered garlic

1 teaspoon onion powder

1 tablespoon kosher salt

In a large nonstick skillet with a lid, break up the hamburger meat with a wooden spoon over high heat. I do this as I dice up the bell pepper, onion, and jalapeño. The veggies can be any size that you like, but I prefer mine about the size of an M&Ms candy and my jalapeño diced as fine as possible.

Continue searing the meat; when it has some nice browning, add in all the vegetables, garlic, and the first set of seasoning spices.

Sauté the vegetables in the grease from the hamburger meat, incorporating them into the mixture. Cook about 3 minutes. Pour in the rice and allow it to toast with the meat and vegetables. Cook 2–3 minutes.

COZY FIREPLACE CHAT

A SECRET TECHNIQUE for competition cooking used by all the pros: add your seasonings in two portions of the recipe, for example, in chili. The first portion seasons the meat and builds depth of flavor. The second gives the chili a pop of pronounced flavor at the end. Long stewing can morph the flavors of the spices and mellow them. I use the same technique with my rice as competition cooks use with chili. While some Mexican rice can be flavorless mush, this one is loaded with flavor, texture, and fresh-seared Angus ground beef. It's dinner in a skillet.

SECOND SEASONINGS:

1/2 teaspoon garlic powder

2 teaspoons Texas chili powder

1 teaspoon kosher salt, if needed

Juice of 1 lemon

A couple shakes of hot pepper sauce, such as Tabasco

GARNISH WITH:

12 petite yellow tomatoes, washed and quartered

1/2 cup fresh crema

Snipped fresh chives

Start with 2 cups of the chicken broth, pouring it into the mixture and stirring the ingredients together. I like to add the chicken stock as I go (much like a risotto), placing the lid back on and cooking a bit, then coming back to add more. You will eventually use all the stock and perhaps even a little extra water.

Cook for about 20 minutes, until rice is tender. If using wild rice the mixture will cook for 40 minutes, as wild rice takes longer to become tender. During the last 5 minutes or so, add in the second set of seasonings, lemon juice, and Tabasco. Keep warm until serving.

On a cutting board cut the petite tomatoes carefully in half and then in half again. Top each plate with crema and a sprinkling of freshly diced tomatoes. Using kitchen shears or scissors, snip fresh chives onto the top of each plate.

NOTE: *Wait! Where's the tomato?!* I love fresh tomatoes diced on top of Mexican rice, but if you prefer roasted red tomatoes in the rice (you little Texican you!), you'll simply turn on the broiler and roast three tomatoes on a foil-lined cookie sheet for 5–7 minutes, turning once during cooking. The tomatoes will roast and the skin will turn black, wilt, and peel off easily. Give the tomatoes a dice and stir them into the rice, along with the spices, during the last 5 minutes.

TIP FROM MOM

THIS DISH WORKS GREAT IN AN ELECTRIC SKILLET with a temperature knob! You can walk away and leave it, kind of like crockpot cooking for rice. The bottom develops a slightly chewy crust but never burns. Naturally, the crunchy pieces are the best part! This dish is ready in 30 minutes or sits well for several hours on warm.

SOUTHWESTERN CREAM CORN
WITH LOBSTER TOPPING

THIS CREAMED CORN IS DREAMY, rich decadence plated up for your enjoyment. The green chiles add a roasted smoky essence that rounds out the sweet crunch of fresh corn and the zippy bite of jalapeño. It pairs perfectly with steaks, but can be eaten with all sorts of home-style fare—even fajitas and your favorite Mexican dish. **YIELD: 4-6 SERVINGS**

6 cobs fresh corn, uncooked

1 tablespoon butter

$1/2$ white onion, diced

1 (4-ounce) can green chiles

1 Fresno (red jalapeño) pepper, minced and seeded, or a 4-ounce jar pimentos

1 package cream cheese

$1/4$ cup milk

Cilantro, for garnish

Optional: butter-poached lobster

With a sharp knife slice the corn off the cob and reserve in a large bowl. Discard the cobs.

In a saucepan melt the butter and sweat the onion. Add the corn, green chiles, Fresno pepper (or pimentos for milder flavor), cream cheese, and milk. Cover with a lid and set to low-medium heat.

Let the cream cheese melt and form a sauce, about 12 minutes. Thin with water or milk if needed. Top with cilantro and serve.

To make a lobster topping, purchase two lobster tails. Remove the meat from the shells and cook the meat in 2 T. butter briefly just before serving. It will turn white and firm up. No need to add salt, but a little chopped cilantro for color is gorgeous. Spoon on top of the cream corn.

BACON FAT REFRIED BEANS

THERE WILL ALWAYS BE PEOPLE IN YOUR LIFE that just get things wrong. It's important never to seek out their counsel. It's especially important not to listen to those people when they advise against putting bacon fat in your refried beans. They are not living their best life possible, and Urban Cowgirls *always* strive for greatness. **YIELD: SERVES 4-6**

$^1/_3$ cup bacon fat

$^1/_2$ yellow onion, diced

1 garlic clove, minced

1 teaspoon salt

2 (16-ounce) cans refried beans

$^1/_2$ cup taco sauce (store bought or homemade)

$^1/_3$ cup freshly shredded medium sharp cheddar

3-4 tablespoons sour cream

In a medium saucepan heat the bacon fat at medium-high heat. Add the onion to the pot, stirring well. Add the the garlic to the pan along with the salt.

Cook for 4 minutes, then add both cans of beans and the taco sauce. Stir until the mixture is thoroughly combined. Add the freshly shredded cheddar to the pan and finish the dish by stirring in the sour cream.

We serve individual portions with extra cheese, taco sauce, and freshly minced onion.

GREEN CHILE CORN PUDDING
FROM THE LORD HIMSELF

I CAN TELL YOU WITH PERFECT CERTAINTY that no aroma will elicit a more neck-jerk reaction than the beckoning call of fresh green chiles roasting over an open fire. When summer hits its peak in early August and the Texas air is about as hot and thick as bonfire smoke, grocery stores set up green chile camps in their parking lots to taunt unwitting shoppers on their way through the doors. And no matter what you planned on cooking that night, the lure is impossible to ignore. It is primal, an urge from some long-dormant place, it whispers to buy a whole batch of chiles, maybe two, or you're sure to regret it. **YIELD: 6-8 SERVINGS**

1 stick butter

$^1/_2$ onion, diced

1 jalapeño, cut in half, deseeded, and minced

5 freshly roasted green chiles such as New Mexico, Hatch, or Anaheim, seeded and diced, or a 4-ounce can roasted green chiles if out of chile season

1 can corn, drained

1 can creamed corn

1 (8-ounce) container French onion dip

1 box corn bread mix

Preheat the oven to 350°F.

In a large skillet melt the butter and begin sweating the onion and jalapeño at medium heat. Cook 3 minutes and add the green chiles. Cook an additional 2–3 minutes and add both cans of corn, the French onion dip, and the box of corn bread mix.

Grease a small, half-size glass casserole dish with a little butter. Pour the mixture into the dish and bake for 30–40 minutes. Remove carefully with oven mitts and serve hot.

MEXI RANCH PASTA SALAD
WITH COTIJA AND CHEDDAR

THIS IS NOT YOUR AVERAGE, run-of-the-mill, can substitute with grocery store pasta salad, this is pasta salad hooked up to a Texas-size generator and lit up like a Christmas tree. But beyond bold flavors and festive ingredients, this recipe will teach you the key to great pasta salad: It's all about picking the right shells.

Pasta shells, that is. There are tiny shells used for macaroni and jumbo shells used for filled pasta dishes, but the large shells, or "seashells," are perfect for pasta salad because they stand up to all the other ingredients commonly found in pasta salad dishes, like chopped fresh veggies and mayonnaise-based dressings. Plus, they're a lot of fun to eat. And enjoying your meal is just as important as an adult as it is when you're a child. **YIELD: 6-8 SERVINGS**

MEXI RANCH DRESSING

4 cherry tomatoes

1/2 jalapeño

1 tablespoon diced red onion

1 cup mayonnaise

1/2 cup sour cream

1/2 teaspoon salt

1/2 teaspoon pepper

1 teaspoon Texas Chili Powder

1/2 teaspoon garlic powder

1 tablespoon water

2 teaspoons red wine vinegar

PASTA SALAD

8 ounces fun pasta such as fusilli, bowtie, rigatoni, or *my favorite* large shells (see intro)

On a cutting board halve the cherry tomatoes. Cut the jalapeño in half and deseed into the sink with a spoon. Give the jalapeño a rough chop and place in a blender with the tomatoes and red onion.

Add the mayonnaise, sour cream, spices, water, and red wine vinegar to the blender. Blend well into a sauce, making sure that no chunks of vegetable remain. Taste for seasoning and chill.

Fill a large stockpot with water and put on the stove to boil. Salt the water with about 3 tablespoons salt.

When the water comes to a boil, pour in 8 ounces of your pasta of choice. Cook to al dente (still firm but cooked through) and drain. Place the drained pasta in a large bowl and toss in the salt and red wine vinegar just to marinate the pasta. Chill.

On a cutting board slice the cherry tomatoes in half and then in half again so they are quartered; toss in the bowl with the pasta. Mince the red onion as fine as you can get it before adding to the bowl.

Cut each long stalk of celery in half so it is easier to handle. Slice each piece down the middle, dragging your knife from top to bottom. Collect all the pieces and chop finely into small dice. Add to the pasta salad bowl.

¹/₂ teaspoon salt and 2 teaspoons red wine vinegar to marinate the pasta salad

5 cherry tomatoes

2 tablespoons chopped red onion

2 stalks celery

¹/₂ yellow bell pepper
(about ¹/₂ cup)

1 green onion, white and green parts

1 carrot

1 cup freshly grated cheddar cheese from the block

¹/₂ cup Cotija cheese, for topping

Cut the yellow bell pepper in half, then cut slices from top to bottom about 1/4 inch thick. Gather them together, chop into a small dice, and add to the bowl.

Chop one green onion from right to left, slicing as thin as you can get it. Add to the bowl.

For the carrot I prefer peeling it and then using a julienne peeler to shave perfectly thin ribbons off the carrot. You can also small dice the carrot like the celery. Add to the bowl.

Grate the cheddar cheese fresh from the block on a traditional grater. Toss about a cup into the bowl.

This pasta salad is best served freshly tossed with the dressing. With a large spoon or salad tongs, toss the vegetables, cheddar cheese, and pasta and drizzle in the Mexi Ranch Dressing until it's as wet as you like it. I prefer a really well-dressed pasta salad, but you can eyeball how much dressing you like. Top with freshly crumbled Cotija cheese and enjoy fresh!

HONKY TONK, DIVE, HOME

IN ARLINGTON, TEXAS, THERE IS A TEENY HOLE-IN-THE-WALL restaurant with so much character you feel like it has to be some kind of fictional oasis . . . like that crazy bar in *Star Wars*.

Tables are snuggled close to one another, covered in red and white checkered cloths, dim multicolored Christmas lights hang from above, casting everything in a halo of shimmery light. Individual privacy booths boast tiny personal jukeboxes at each table. There is (of course) red glass, globe candleholders flickering and casting long, dramatic shadows around the place.

Privacy netting hangs on the booths where hundreds of couples have engraved their names with little hearts. If you know where to look you'll find a little D & S surrounded by a heart, marking a date and a love that blossomed into more.

It's a honky-tonk, and a dive.

It is home.

It's a funny place because they serve several types of fare. The meal always starts with chips and salsa. I order a Coke but the waitress always brings an RC cola. After that, all bets are off.

The Special Mexican Dinner is the house favorite. It wouldn't be out of the ordinary to have an entire 10 top come in and every single one of them order the Special Mexican. It's two courses, and the first starts off with a queso tostada, a beef taco, and *The Guacamole Salad*. Served as a salad dressing to thin-sliced ribbons of lettuce, this tangy and luscious avocado creation is unlike any guacamole I've ever had. And I've had All. The. Guacamole.

They also happen to cook Italian (usually pronounced "eye-talian" by the old-timers), and they don't mess around. The pizzas are thin and the dough is boozy. The cheese just runs—but in a good way. The spaghetti and meatballs are unlike anywhere else I have ever been—sweet, herbaceous, and addicting. Even the garlic bread is made with thick, buttery Texas Toast.

Every dish is euphoric. There's a reason the place has been here so long: It has a Texas soul.

ARLINGTON, TEXAS, GUACAMOLE SALAD

GUACAMOLE IS A LIFE-GIVING FORCE I have toyed with since I was a young girl. But the Guacamole Salad I'm referring to became legend in my home. I can close my eyes and go right back to that moment in my childhood kitchen with my mother hollering for me to try more lime juice, because we still hadn't quite managed it. We tried for years to figure out what made that Guacamole Salad so special. The flavor we sought was elusive...but I *would* discover it.

Then, working on the line in an upscale four-star hotel on the Riverwalk, I finally found a savior in the form of a Mexican cook named Jorge. While we made refried beans for the breakfast rush at Las Canarias, I shared my lifelong quest and subsequent misery with him. He chuckled at me and said, his eyes sparking with inspiration, "You don't cook the tomatillos, Sarah. That's where the bright flavor is coming from."

I didn't even know you could use raw tomatillos in anything. They are so *tart.* My mind was blown. So I went home that night, and after half a lifetime searching, I finally captured that flavor. **YIELD: DRESSES 2-4 SALADS, OR MAKES A LARGE BOWL OF GUACAMOLE TO SERVE WITH TORTILLA CHIPS**

---

3 large tomatillos

2 Haas avocados

1 teaspoon salt

1 teaspoon garlic powder

1 teaspoon onion powder

1 tablespoon plain white vinegar

1 tablespoon lemon juice

2 tablespoons water

1 tablespoon *fresh* flavorless oil (sunflower, canola, safflower)

3-4 cups freshly sliced iceberg lettuce, sliced thin in ribbons or chiffonade style

1 cup diced tomatoes

NOTE: In the restaurant they serve the salad topped with a green olive and a thick slice of white onion. We usually pick those off, but if you're a purist you must have them!

If the tomatillos still have the papery husky, remove it. Wash, roughly chop, and put the tomatillos in a food processor or blender. Process the three tomatillos until pureed. Measure out 1 cup of puree and discard the rest.

Remove the avocados from their skins and place them in the bowl of the food processor or blender. Pulse just until smooth along with the tomatillo puree, salt, garlic powder, onion powder, white vinegar, fresh lemon juice, water, and oil. Make sure not to pulse it too long or it will become mousse-like from whipping so much air into the avocados!

Serve like a salad dressing on top of the thinly shredded iceberg lettuce. Top with a sprinkling of diced tomato.

Simple, yet refreshing and delicious! It's easy to see why this is an infamous dish at this iconic Texas restaurant.

RUSTIC POTATO CAKE WITH CHIPOTLE CREMA

TEXANS LOVE THEIR HASHBROWNS—all day, always. I've eaten hashbrowns served in tiny cast-iron skillets at upscale steak houses from Amarillo to Houston, or fried up in the kitchen for Saturday morning brunch and served alongside a passion fruit mimosa, and once I saw them fashioned into tiny bird's nests for a country-chic wedding by the lake. All are wonderful ways to dress up a plain, but delicious dish, but one of my favorites is the potato cake. And for this classic French technique, I set out to enhance it in true Urban Cowgirl fashion. **YIELD: SERVES 4-6**

POTATO CAKE

6 russet potatoes (do not use red or golden potatoes for this dish)

2 blue potatoes (optional for color)

1 stick butter (you won't use it all but it's easier to handle as a stick)

Salt and pepper

3/4 cup grated Manchego cheese

Fresh chives

Preheat the oven to 450°F.

To prepare the potatoes, you need to either own a razor-sharp knife to slice as thin as possible or use a mandoline. Slice them into thin coins. Slice the blue potatoes in the same fashion.

On the stove top heat up a cast-iron skillet. I grease the whole thing with butter, including the sides, and then I cut the stick of butter in half (1/4 cup) and let that half melt into the pan.

Remove the pan from the heat and start placing slices of potato down, going around in a circle. I like to add in a blue potato here and there for color, but the majority of the potatoes need to be russet so the cake will form correctly.

After getting one to two layers down, salt and pepper the cake and sprinkle in the cheese. Add a couple knobs of butter about the size of a pea. Continue placing potatoes down in a circle for another two rotations. Salt and pepper lightly again.

Return the pan to the stove and heat on medium heat for about 4–5 minutes. You will be able to hear the butter sizzling and the potatoes on the bottom of the skillet cooking and getting golden brown.

Without moving anything in the pan, use an oven mitt to place the entire thing on the second rack of the oven, as far in the back as you can get it. Close the door and cook 40 minutes.

CHIPOTLE CREMA

Chipotle pepper powder
(found in the spice section
of the supermarket)

Crema or sour cream thinned
with a little milk

Lemon juice, just a squeeze

Pinch of salt

In a bowl whisk the ingredients
together and allow the mixture to
sit until it becomes pink. Chill.

Check the tenderness of the potatoes by inserting a knife to make sure they are soft; if they aren't, return to the oven for another 5–10 minutes.

When the potatoes are cooked, go around the edge of the "cake" with a knife to free it from the pan. Place a cutting board on top of the cast-iron skillet and flip the cake onto it. It should come out clean and easy.

Cut into slices like a pizza and serve with Chipotle Crema and minced fresh chives.

DRIED CHERRY AND LEMON ISRAELI COUSCOUS RISOTTO

ISRAELI COUSCOUS IS A LITTLE BALL-SHAPED PASTA perfect for toasting and cooking in flavorful broths. It is similar to a rice pilaf. As a family of four, not many dishes get a thumbs-up from everyone, but with this simple dish, what's not to love? For the adults it's a unique lemony risotto, and for the kids it's reminiscent of the little kid-size pasta they are so fond of in canned soups and SpaghettiOs. It's filling enough that you can eat it for a light dinner, or it works well with grilled salmon and chicken dishes as a tasty side. **YIELD: ABOUT 3 CUPS**

1 tablespoon extra-virgin olive oil

$1/2$ cup pine nuts

$1^1/2$ cups Israeli couscous

2 shallots, minced

$2^1/4$ cups good-quality chicken stock, plus extra $1/4$ cup

$1/2$ teaspoon salt

$1/4$ teaspoon pepper

2 large handfuls baby spinach

2 lemons, zested and juiced

$3/4$ cup dried cherries

In a large saucepan heat the olive oil to medium heat and add the pine nuts and couscous. Toast well until the pine nuts are golden and fragrant and the couscous smells toasty, about 4–5 minutes.

Add the shallots and cook for 1 minute.

Add in the $2^1/4$ cups chicken stock, salt, and pepper. Bring to a simmer, cover with a lid, and cook for 10 minutes, stirring halfway through to prevent the couscous from sticking. Meanwhile, slice the baby spinach into thin ribbons and reserve.

Remove the lid and add in the zest and juice of two lemons and the dried cherries.

Fold the sliced baby spinach into the couscous along with the extra $1/4$ cup chicken stock, which should loosen up the mixture to the consistency of a creamy risotto. Simmer for 1–2 minutes, stirring well. Season to taste with salt and pepper and serve immediately.

BLACK-EYED PEA CAKES WITH JEZEBEL JAM

ALMOST EVERY URBAN COWGIRL I KNOW WENT TO SUNDAY SCHOOL as a little girl. In fact, I met most of my tribe decked out in patterned pantyhose and oversize pastel bows, and the bonds we formed have carried us a lifetime. Every one of us remembers the biblical character Jezebel as both a cautionary tale and an example of a chick with a serious attitude problem. When I created this sassy little jam to accompany my black-eyed pea cakes, I thought of that biblical queen with a bad attitude. Eat this jam and go forth and sin no more. **YIELD: 10 LITTLE CAKES**

---

2 (10-ounce) cans black-eyed peas in water, drained

$1/4$ cup finely minced red onion

$1/4$ cup finely minced poblano pepper

$1/4$ cup finely minced red bell pepper

2–3 tablespoons finely chopped fresh cilantro

2 eggs

$1/2$ cup panko bread crumbs plus 2 cups for breading the cakes

$2^{1}/_{2}$ teaspoons kosher salt

$1^{1}/_{2}$ teaspoons black pepper

1 teaspoon cumin

$1/2$ teaspoon cayenne pepper

$1^{1}/_{2}$ teaspoons garlic powder

2 tablespoons lemon juice or red wine vinegar

$1/2$ cup oil, butter, or bacon fat, for frying the cakes

Extra salt and pepper, to taste for seasoning

Using a food processor or blender, puree the two cans of black-eyed peas to a rough mash. Use 1–2 tablespoons water to assist pureeing if needed. Pour the roughly mashed peas into a bowl and add the minced veggies. All the veggies must be minced very small, $1/8$ inch in size, to hold well in the cakes.

Add the cilantro to the bowl along with the eggs, $1/2$ cup panko bread crumbs, and all the seasonings. Mix well with your hands and drizzle in the lemon juice or vinegar. Form into ten little cakes.

Pour the additional 2 cups panko bread crumbs into a shallow bowl or plate and roll each cake in the bread crumbs. Reserve.

In a nonstick sauté pan, heat $1/4$ cup oil or butter over medium heat. Fry four to five cakes at a time for 2–3 minutes per side, or until golden brown and crunchy. Use more oil as needed. Season well with salt and pepper the minute they come out of the pan. Serve with Jezebel Jam.

JEZEBEL JAM

16 Roma tomatoes, quartered and chopped

1 jalapeño, destemmed and chopped

1 finger of fresh ginger root, small dice (about 2–3 tablespoons)

4 small garlic cloves, minced

1¼ cups sugar

2 tablespoons apple cider vinegar, plus 1 extra tablespoon

½ teaspoon kosher salt

Place the Roma tomatoes, jalapeño, ginger, and garlic into a food processor and blend until it resembles salsa and is totally chopped.

In a heavy-bottomed, large saucepan, pour the mixture in and add the sugar, 2 tablespoons vinegar, and salt. Bring to a boil. Boil the mixture for about 30 minutes or until it becomes less liquidy and closer to the consistency of jam. Stir with a spatula as needed. When it begins to appear more dry, turn the heat down to low and taste. Add the last 1 tablespoon apple cider vinegar if needed for bright flavor. Season to taste, cool, and serve with the black-eyed pea cakes.

RUSTIC HONEY ROSEMARY CARROTS

THIS IS A DISH THAT WILL GO DOWN IN THE "ETERNAL FAMILY FAVORITES FOREVER" section of your recipe box, just as it has in mine. I was taught the combination of honey and rosemary by an actual bona fide, swashbuckling, American five-star chef over seven years ago, and I've probably made it once a week since. When entertaining, this dish looks quite impressive made with baby heirloom carrots with the greens trimmed off—especially the little purple ones. It turns carrots into candy, so make sure to stock up! **YIELD: 2–3 SERVINGS**

1 tablespoon butter, plus
1 tablespoon for finishing glaze

10–15 small heirloom carrots, washed and greens removed

Salt and pepper, to taste

1 tablespoon finely chopped fresh rosemary

3 tablespoons honey

1 teaspoon fresh lemon juice

In a small sauté pan or omelet pan with a lid, heat the butter and carrots on medium heat. Season with salt and pepper. Toss well and sauté for 3 minutes. Turn the heat down to low, cover, and steam for an additional 4–5 minutes. Remove lid and add fresh rosemary and the honey.

To make the sauce, add the 1 tablespoon butter, swirling it slowly around the pan and into the honey mixture. Swirl the butter patiently on low heat until it melts thoroughly into the sauce, creating a glaze. Add lemon juice and taste. Season with salt and pepper if needed. The carrots can be heated gently on low and covered for an additional 1–2 minutes if they need additional time to cook to the desired tenderness.

TIP FROM MOM

SUBSTITUTE ½ POUND OF BABY CARROTS instead of the heirloom carrots if desired.

Desserts

THE INTERNET IS LITTERED WITH CHARMING QUOTES touting the merits of dessert.

"Dessert. Because no great love story began with salad."

"Life is uncertain. Eat dessert first."

"A party without cake is just a meeting."

That last one was said by Julia Child, and I have to say, she sounds like my kind of woman. Dessert is more than a way to end a meal; it's food you can eat just because you want to. It's not necessarily nutritious (though dark chocolate has loads of health benefits), and most of us can't eat dessert every day even if we wanted to. (We all want to. Don't lie.)

Laura Ingalls Wilder—who would have been an Urban Cowgirl were she born in this century—said this: "It is the sweet, simple things in life which are the real ones, after all."

Dessert can be complex by design, but nothing will make you feel more like a child again than a scoop of ice cream on a sweltering Southern day. Desserts require a little whimsy, and we could all use some of that.

MEXICAN AFFOGADO WITH SALTED CARAMEL SAUCE AND BLUE BELL

AFFOGADO IS AN ITALIAN DESSERT that has made its way to America but hasn't quite gained the notoriety of gelato. It's a coffee lover's dream: hot rich espresso poured over perfect vanilla ice cream. I put my own Southern spin on this classic by using Mexican espresso beans and using Blue Bell Ice Cream . . . since (like most card-carrying Southerners) I've always got about five gallons in my freezer. **YIELD: 2 SUNDAES**

1/2 cup salted caramel sauce

6 scoops of vanilla Blue Bell Ice Cream

Candy of your choice

4 shots of espresso (or 1 cup very strong coffee) made from 1/2 cup ground Mexican espresso beans

FOR THE SALTED CARAMEL SAUCE:

1 cup sugar

1/4 cup water

1 cup heavy cream

4 tablespoons unsalted butter

1 teaspoon vanilla extract

1/2 teaspoon good-quality salt (Himalayan pink salt, fleur de sel, sea salt, black salt)

In a saucepan combine the sugar and water over medium-low heat until the sugar dissolves. Increase the heat and bring to a boil, without stirring. Boil until the syrup is a deep amber color, about 5–6 minutes.

Remove the sugar from the heat and carefully whisk in the heavy cream. The mixture will bubble madly! Stir in the butter, vanilla extract, and salt. Add more salt if you like the combination! I always do.

Cool slightly before topping ice cream.

Prepare two parfait bowls and scoop the ice cream into them. Top with caramel sauce and candy. Right before serving, top each sundae with a double shot of hot espresso or coffee.

Die of happiness.

IN THE ICE CREAM SAUCE AND CONES SECTION of the supermarket, you can often find miniature versions of your favorite candy made to go on sundaes.

LUCKY HORSESHOE PIE

THE MAGIC OF THIS PIE IS WRAPPED UP IN THE MYSTERY of its make-up. Without seeing the recipe, casual observers can't discern what actually is in it, but can't stop nibbling once they start. It's like a giant cookie that's been engulfed in a cloud of decadence. It's won at least four competition titles for my stepfather, Ross, who created it, and it makes an appearance at every family gathering!

So, shhhh, this one's just between you and me. **YIELD: 1 PIE**

---

4 egg whites

1^1/$_3$ cups sugar

2 teaspoons vanilla extract

^{2}/$_3$ teaspoon baking powder

28 Ritz crackers, finely crushed to bread crumb size

1^1/$_2$ cups finely chopped pecans

1 (8-ounce) package cream cheese, softened and at room temperature

1 container Cool Whip

^{1}/$_4$ cup sugar

Pinch of salt

One milk chocolate bar for curls

Preheat the oven to 350°F and grease a 9-inch glass pie pan.

In a clean bowl or stand mixer, beat the egg whites to medium peaks. This means that when the whisk is removed and flipped right side up, the batter will just slightly curl over the tip of the whisk. At this point continue to whisk and add in the sugar. Continue beating the mixture to stiff peaks (which means the batter will stand straight up and not curl over the whisk). Add the vanilla extract and baking powder. Fold in the Ritz crackers and pecans.

Transfer this mixture to the pie pan and bake for 30–40 minutes. It should have a chewy cookie-like texture. Remove from the oven and cool fully.

For the topping, in a bowl combine the cream cheese, Cool Whip, sugar, and salt and beat the mixture until light and fluffy and thoroughly mixed. Top the pie with the cream cheese mixture, sculpting the top as you desire. Chill for 4 hours. Before serving use a vegetable peeler to slice the chocolate bar and create curls for decorating.

**PRO
TIP**

THE CRACKERS AND PECANS CAN BE FINELY CRUSHED in a food processor, chopped with a sharp knife, or beaten with a rolling pin in a secure plastic bag.

FRIED TEQUILA WITH CANDIED LIME

AT THE STATE FAIR OF TEXAS, for forty tickets and your dignity, you can stand in a line to receive any fried thing your heart can imagine. Including, Fried Tequila. This title is a bit deceptive; it's fried cake soaked in tequila, but we'll explain that in a minute.

Rebekah, my longtime bestie, and I wanted to figure out a way to make this little treasure available to people year-round. One warm and sunny spring afternoon, I called to tell her that Casamigos had sent me a few bottles of tequila and it was time to create a phenomenon. After hours in the kitchen testing out the recipe, our husbands came to retrieve us and found us giggling, covered in powdered sugar, surrounded by tequila bottles, and the joyful creators of a fried tequila recipe.

YIELD: THIS RECIPE SERVES TWO (WITH ONE GOING HOME IN A WHEELBARROW), BUT COULD SERVE UP TO TEN IF YOU'RE NOT TWO URBAN COWGIRLS ON A MISSION.

---

1 store-bought angel food cake

1 liter sunflower or grapeseed oil to fill a small pot halfway full, for frying

1–2 cups powdered sugar

Zest of 2 limes

1 cup tequila

Cut the angel food cake into 1-inch squares. Pour the oil into the fry pot and turn to medium-high heat. For rapid frying the oil should be heated to 380–400°F. In a small bowl, place the powdered sugar. Zest the limes directly into the powdered sugar and set aside. Pour the tequila into a bowl.

Once the oil is hot, dunk the cake squares in the bowl of tequila, soaking thoroughly, and place in the hot oil. Fry 45 seconds on each side, until the cake cube has turned a lovely golden brown.

Using a slotted metal spoon, remove the cakes from the oil and set aside to drain on paper towels or a cookie rack. Continue until all cakes are fried.

Once drained, coat with the powdered sugar and lime mixture.

Serve immediately lest you be tempted to eat them all yourself.

PAPAW'S RED PEANUT PATTIES

IF YOU WALK INTO A GAS STATION ALONG ANY HIGHWAY DOWN SOUTH, you'll see little cellophane-wrapped packages of red peanut patties. My Papaw would always buy me one whenever I was on the road with him, but he got his homemade by Oleta—a longtime family friend whose daughter married my uncle Lindy—whenever she'd come visit him and my Nanan.

In 2016 my Papaw went on his final journey to meet the Great Spirit in the Sky, and when Oleta walked by me at the funeral, she leaned over and whispered, "I almost brought him some red peanut patties to keep in his pocket, just in case he got hungry along the way."

This recipe is dedicated to him. I hope now he has an unlimited supply. **YIELD: ABOUT 20 PATTIES**

---

2 1/2 cups sugar

2/3 cup white corn syrup

1 cup whipping cream

3 cups raw peanuts

1 tablespoon butter

2-3 drops red food coloring (if desired)

1 teaspoon vanilla extract

In a medium saucepan combine the sugar, corn syrup, cream, peanuts, butter, and food coloring (if using) and let the mixture come to a simmer. Cook for 1 hour at a low simmer, stirring often. Remove from the heat, add vanilla extract, and whisk rapidly. Beat until it thickens and loses its shine. Drop on wax paper in circles about the size of a cookie and allow to cool and harden. (It can also be poured into a buttered 9 x 12-inch pan and allowed to cool, then broken into individual pieces.)

Store in a cool, dry place. If the air is humid, the peanut patties should be stored in Tupperware or a plastic bag.

WHITE CHOCOLATE PUMPKIN MOUSSE WITH
GINGER SNAPS AND SALTED VANILLA CARAMEL DRIZZLE

EVERY YEAR WHEN THE LEAVES BEGIN TO CHANGE from green to gold and brown, the entirety of female-kind collectively loses its mind for all things *pumpkin spice*. This recipe is a take on the pumpkin spice craze, but for me, it's my gift to all women who liken baking to science class and would rather skip. You too can master the dark arts of dessert. **YIELD: 4-6 SERVINGS**

1 bar Ghirardelli white chocolate

2 cups whipping cream, divided

3/4 can organic canned pumpkin (use the rest for building layers in the glass)

Tiny pinch of salt

Pumpkin pie spices (cinnamon, nutmeg, cloves)

1/2 cup powdered sugar

1 box Ginger Snap cookies

Vanilla Caramel Sauce or 1 bottle of your favorite caramel sauce

VANILLA CARAMEL SAUCE

1 cup sugar

1/4 cup water

1 cup heavy cream

4 tablespoons butter

Pinch of salt

Vanilla bean* or vanilla extract

In the microwave heat the bar of white chocolate with 1/4 cup of the cream in 30-second increments until melted. Stir very well to form a sauce consistency. Whisk in the pumpkin, salt, and pumpkin pie spices. Set aside to cool.

In a large bowl beat the rest of the cream (1 3/4 cups) and the powdered sugar to soft peaks. Fold half the cream into the pumpkin mixture and then fold the cream-pumpkin mixture back into the whipped cream. In dessert glasses spoon the mixture into individual portions and chill until ready. For a layered effect spoon in the remainder of the unsweetened canned pumpkin between the mousse layers for visual interest.

Top with crushed Ginger Snaps and a drizzle of caramel.

To make your own caramel sauce, in a saucepan, stir the sugar and water over medium-low heat until the sugar dissolves. Increase the heat and bring to a boil, without stirring. Boil until the syrup is a deep amber color, about 5–6 minutes.

Remove the sugar from the heat and carefully whisk in the heavy cream. The mixture will bubble madly! Stir in the butter, salt, and vanilla bean. Transfer the caramel to a squeeze bottle when cool.

CHERRY ICEBOX COOKIES

THESE LITTLE PINK GEMS ARE BASICALLY THE STATE COOKIE OF TEXAS. Collin Street Bakery has positioned themselves on I-35 and I-45 so that every road-tripper through Texas will become acquainted with their cookies. And it's maddening, because driving through these small Texas towns and stopping off for a restroom break—but really for cookies—is the only way to get them in your belly. This is my gift to every person who has driven south in Texas, stopped off at the bakery, and fallen madly in love with those tiny pink confections of chewy, gooey goodness.

YIELD: 24-30 COOKIES

---

1 cup butter

1¼ cups white sugar

2 eggs

1 teaspoon vanilla extract

1 (16-ounce) jar maraschino cherries, drained of all juice and roughly chopped

1 tablespoon fresh lemon juice

2¼ cups flour

1½ teaspoons baking powder

½ teaspoon salt

White sugar for sprinkling

Cream the butter and sugar in a stand mixer or bowl with beaters. Add in the eggs one at a time, then the vanilla extract, chopped cherries, and lemon juice. Blend well.

In another bowl combine the flour, baking powder, and salt and mix with a whisk. In two parts add the dry ingredients into the wet ingredients, mixing in between.

When the dough is formed, pour it onto two large sheets of parchment paper and roll it into a long cylinder (like you see cookie dough sold at the store). You will have two rolls of cookies. Chill overnight.

When you are ready to make cookies, preheat the oven to 375°F. Take the rolls of dough out and slice ¼-inch slices. Sprinkle cookie slices with sugar. Place onto a greased cookie sheet and bake for 8–10 minutes. Cool on cookie racks and serve.

TIP FROM MOM

THIS DOUGH CAN ALSO BE DROPPED ONTO THE COOKIE SHEET from a spoon (drop cookies), scooping about 1 ounce per cookie and baking at the same temperature and time. But keeping them in icebox form, ready to go at a moment's notice, is the definition of Southern hospitality! As Momma always said, "When opportunity comes, it's too late to prepare!"

WHITE CHOCOLATE AMARETTO TIPSY CAKE WITH BUTTERMILK GLAZE

I DON'T THINK I HOLD ANY MEMORY OF FOOD IN GREATER FAVOR than the church socials of my childhood.

I can remember sitting in the big wooden pew staring down at my white patent leather shoes and trying to ignore the aroma of fried chicken, taco salad, bacon creamed potatoes, and tipsy cake dancing through the sanctuary and curling in the blue light cast by the giant stained-glass windows. An apparition sent to taunt me into bad behavior.

When the sermon ended, I would dart through the adults to the feast of homemade goodness waiting in the back. My Nanan would make me a plate, and I'd burst through the back door into the sunshine to sit in the cool green grass and savor the best dishes offered up by the sweet church grandmas. No dining experience in the world can compare with the memory of my greasy little fingers pulling apart fried chicken and sipping real Coca-Cola with the other little girls in fluffy dresses and panty-hose, frolicking and giggling under an enormous oak tree. And once we were as stuffed as a bunch of little ticks, I'd go looking for the tipsy cake.

Culinary lore may have you believe that a tipsy cake is a trifle, but I've never seen it that way in Texas. To me it will always be the most succulent butter pound cake spiked with booze and dripping with buttermilk glaze. Although I can remember my family using bourbon, I prefer amaretto because it's simple and sweet, yet strong . . . just like my grandma.

---

1 package butter-flavored cake mix

1 package vanilla pudding

1/2 cup Disaronno Amaretto liqueur, plus 1/4 cup for soaking

1/2 cup buttermilk

1 stick butter (melted in the microwave)

4 large eggs

Juice of 1/2 a lemon

Preheat the oven to 350°F. Grease a standard sized bundt pan with butter and reserve.

In a stand mixer beat the cake mix, pudding mix, liqueur, buttermilk, and melted butter. Crack each egg into the mixer and squeeze in the juice of half a lemon. (It really brings out the flavor of the liqueur.) Mix for about 1–2 minutes, scraping the bowl halfway through with a spatula to release any batter stuck to the bottom.

Pour the batter into the bundt pan and place in the oven to bake for 30 minutes. When it is done, take it out and cool in the pan while you prepare the glaze.

FOR GLAZING:

2 tablespoons buttermilk

3 squares Ghiradelli white baking chocolate

3/4 cup powdered sugar

Squeeze of lemon

Microwave the buttermilk and white chocolate in short bursts until melted. Whisk in the powdered sugar and a small squeeze of lemon. Set aside.

While the cake is still warm, flip it out onto a plate and then over again to reveal the golden top (as it was in the pan). Take 1/4 cup amaretto liqueur and a pastry brush, and brush the top and sides of the cake until all the liqueur has been absorbed.

To glaze the cake, pour the warm white-chocolate glaze over the cake, allowing it to run down the sides.

Amen!

RASPBERRY WASABI FUDGE

A LIVELY URBAN COWGIRL ROAD TRIP down I-35 is not complete without a big hunk of gourmet fudge to boost your mood for the remaining stretch of glorious country exploring. Is it just me or are flavors getting more adventurous every season? Maple Chocolate Butternut, Sugar Lime Margarita, Coconut and Dewberry—I'll just take 40 pounds of fudge and a diet coke please! Not to be outdone by my fudge-creating brethren, I present to you Raspberry Wasabi Fudge. It's juicy raspberry and creamy white chocolate kissed with a dusting of wasabi! You're gonna dig it. **YIELD: ABOUT 3 POUNDS OF FUDGE**

2 cups sugar

1 cup seedless raspberry jam

3/4 cup butter

2/3 cup evaporated milk

12 ounces white chocolate

3/4 teaspoon wasabi powder

1/4 teaspoon salt

1 (7-ounce) jar marshmallow cream

1 cup pistachios, peanuts, or sliced almonds, shredded coconut, or sugar pearls

Line a 9-inch square pan with foil, allowing the ends of the foil to extend beyond the edges of the pan. Bring the sugar, jam, butter, and evaporated milk to a boil in a large saucepan over medium heat, stirring constantly. Cook 4 minutes, or until a candy thermometer reaches 234°F. Never stop stirring!

Remove from heat. Add marshmallow cream, white chocolate, wasabi powder, and salt; stir until melted. Pour into the pan and spread evenly. Top with nuts or toppings of your choice. Allow to cool completely before removing from the pan by the extra foil.

Dig in and experience bliss!

TEQUILA LIME AND TORTILLA CHIP PEPITA BRITTLE (PLUS HOW TO MAKE ALL THE OTHER GOURMET BRITTLES)

URBAN COWGIRLS ARE REQUIRED BY THE LAW of our people to take classics and revamp them for our modern life. For brittle, that meant adding lime and tequila—because anything that tastes like a margarita is a winner—to get a fresh take on an old familiar favorite. I spent two years hacking at the gourmet brittle equation until I beat it into submission, and here is the fruit of my labor.

YIELD: APPROXIMATELY 10 LARGE PIECES

TEQUILA LIME INFUSION

2 tablespoons tequila blanco

Zest of 2 limes

1 teaspoon lime juice

$1/2$ teaspoon salt

1 cup sugar

$1/2$ cup water

$1/2$ cup white corn syrup

1 cup raw, unsalted pepitas (pumpkin seeds)

2 tablespoons salted butter

$1/2$ teaspoon baking soda

1 cup crushed lime tortilla chips

STEP 1: Prepare the tequila infusion by combining the tequila, lime juice and zest, and salt and mixing well. Let this sit as you prepare the other ingredients, or infuse for up to a day.

STEP 2: Measure all the ingredients and put into small bowls. Place the sugar and water into a small saucepan. Measure the baking soda into a small bowl. Prepare a cookie sheet with a Silpat or parchment paper sprayed with kitchen spray to spread out the batter for cooling. As the syrup approaches 300°F (hard crack stage), the browning of the mixture happens very fast, and you will need everything close by and measured out so you can act quickly.

In the saucepan begin heating the sugar and water mixture on high. When it begins to boil and becomes a sugar syrup, add the corn syrup, scraping the pan well. Whisk briefly to combine. Clip a candy thermometer on the edge of the saucepan and bring the mixture up to 240°F (soft ball stage).

When the mixture hits 240°F, add in the pepitas and the butter, mixing with a wooden spoon. Do not stop stirring the candy until it is done, as the nuts will scorch on the bottom of the pan. Stir the mixture, including under the candy thermometer (wiggle around it if necessary), until the mixture approaches 300°F. Prepare for a flurry of activity!

At 305°F take the mixture off the heat and add the tequila infusion (scraping to make sure you get all the salt). Stir madly with the wooden spoon to get the tequila and lime zest evenly distributed into the brittle. Last, add the baking powder and stir. The mixture should foam. Pour the brittle onto the silpat or parchment and spread it out with a spoon.

Top with the crushed tortilla chips and set aside to cool. The brittle can harden overnight (traditionally) but is usually ready within an hour. Keep the brittle away from moisture; in humid environments store brittle in ziplock bags.

RULES OF GOURMET BRITTLE

Use a candy thermometer. Though it seems convenient, a laser thermometer can be off by more than 20°F compared to an inexpensive candy thermometer submerged in the syrup.

Use raw nuts only; the browning of the nuts flavors the brittle syrup.

Once you put the nuts in, stir continuously with a wooden spoon or the nuts will scorch.

Bring the mixture to 305°F if you prefer a non-sticky brittle with good snap.

Maintain a ratio of 1 cup sugar to 1 cup nuts when creating your own brittles.

Add toppings like chips, pretzels, or crisp bacon on top of the brittle batter as it is cooling.

Any liquor can be substituted for the tequila when creating your own recipes.

SPIKED BANANA PUDDING
WITH RUMCHATA AND CINNAMON

RUMCHATA IS A SEDUCTIVE LIQUEUR that gets its name from the combination of rum and Horchata. It is made from Caribbean rum and ingredients found in the Latin beverage Horchata, such as cinnamon, vanilla, sugar, and commonly a nut or seed milk. The name Horchata is derived from the Valencian word *orxata*, meaning "from barley," but modern Horchata is no longer made from barley seed. The drink itself is loud and balanced, creamy and sensual, evocative of warm nights spent dancing beneath starlight surrounded by palm trees. This dessert will transport you away from your kitchen to a world of mystery and romance. Though, thanks to the nice serving of alcohol, it's not a dessert for the whole family to enjoy. **YIELD: SERVES 6**

---

2 (3.4-ounce) boxes vanilla pudding mix

2 cups whole milk

$3/4$ cup rumchata

$1/4$ cup crème de banana

$1/4$ teaspoon cinnamon

$1/4$ teaspoon nutmeg

$1/8$ teaspoon kosher salt

2 (8-ounce) containers Cool Whip or 4 cups freshly whipped cream

1 (11-ounce) box vanilla wafers

5–6 bananas, sliced thin and reserved

A large glass bowl for displaying the layers

In a mixing bowl combine both packages of pudding mix, the milk, rumchata, and crème de banana. Whisk until smooth. Add the cinnamon, nutmeg, and kosher salt. Whisk well.

Fold in $1\frac{1}{4}$ cups Cool Whip and blend into the base. This will be the pudding layer.

In the glass bowl place about $1/3$ cup pudding. On top of the pudding make a layer of vanilla wafers, then a layer of Cool Whip, followed by a layer of bananas. Repeat four or more times until you have used all the pudding and Cool Whip. (You will want to end with a pretty white layer of Cool Whip topped with crushed cookies, so keep that in mind!)

Reserve the rest of the cookies for a final garnish.

Chill the banana pudding for 3–4 hours. Before serving, crush the remaining cookies and sprinkle the crunchy topping on top of the last layer. Serve immediately.

BUTTERMILK PIE BRÛLÉE

FRESH BUTTERMILK, SUGAR, AND EGGS IN A PIE CRUST? Well, if you ask me, that sounds like a giant buttermilk crème brûlée! This is my grandma's original recipe for buttermilk pie, but with a good dose of my meddling. By sprinkling sugar on the top of the pie (similar to the classic French technique for crème brûlée), a crispier, golden-brown layer of crunchy caramelized sugar develops. You might not want to boast of your enhancements of your grandma's dishes too loudly around her, though, or you might find yourself sitting at the kids' table next to me. **YIELD: 1 9-INCH PIE (8 SLICES)**

3 eggs

1 1/2 cups sugar, plus additional for sprinkling

4 tablespoons butter (half a stick), melted

1 cup buttermilk

1/4 teaspoon kosher salt

1 teaspoon vanilla extract

1 9-inch pie crust

Preheat the oven to 350°F.

In a bowl or stand mixer, cream the eggs and sugar by beating well. Add the butter, buttermilk, salt, and vanilla. Beat the mixture until smooth and pour into the pie pan. Sprinkle lightly with additional sugar.

Bake for 45 minutes. Remove from the oven and chill thoroughly. Slice and serve.

For additional brûléeing, sprinkle the top of the cooked and chilled pie with sugar and brûlée with a small kitchen brûlée torch until brown. Serve immediately.

IN THE FOLLOWING PAGES you're going to find an introduction into the world of homemade bath luxury. It's actually a lot like cooking: You'll use bowls and spoons, food processors and immersion blenders. You'll use things like coffee, green tea, cocoa butter, rose petals, and coconut oil. If you like piping icing and tiny pastries, you will love sculpting soap and decorating bath truffles.

Everything smells delicious and you will devour it, only not with your mouth, but with your skin and your nose and your heart. Instead of feeding your body, you'll be nurturing your spirit. You'll be removing filler ingredients that are in store-bought products. You'll be returning to recipes that were quite common in our great-grandparents' homes, like homemade soap and healing salves. You'll also get to make really fun new items, like bath fizzies, that you may never have even seen in stores.

You will find a simple handmade soap in this chapter as well as some of my favorite handmade spa products, which are far superior to what I have found at the grocery store. I promise you, if you love the feeling you get pulling a beautiful loaf of bread out of the oven, just wait until you lay your eyes upon your first loaf of creamy, handmade oatmeal soap. Your kitchen is about to become a whole new world. And so is your bath time!

URBAN COWGIRL

Artisan Beauty at Home

MOTHERHOOD IS LIKE A STORM

NOTHING CAN PREPARE YOU FOR THE HIGHS AND LOWS, the turmoil, the gut-wrenching range of emotions brewing in the heart of every mother. What is so incomprehensible to your own soul, so hard to explain to another human, is the way your thoughts, desires, fears, beliefs—the very paradigm you use to view the world—shifts the moment you become MOM. But that is what the storm is about. You are not the same person coming out as you were going in.

I entered the storm quite brutally one June night at three in the morning with my face pressed against my cold linoleum bathroom floor. I couldn't eat. I couldn't keep anything down, even small sips of water. Too weak to move, I listened to my worried husband whispering to an ER nurse on the phone. After three negative pregnancy tests, I was convinced I must be dying. I wondered if I was having a panic attack or worse. I was only twenty-six; could it be worse? A trip to the ER was my only solution.

"The good news is you're not dying!" the doctor said with a small smile. "You *are* pregnant. The bad news is you are about four days pregnant. Too soon for anything short of a blood test to pick up on, and if it is this bad now, it is only going to get worse."

Boy, did it.

That day I was diagnosed with a rare form of morning sickness called hyperemesis. I felt hopeless, and powerless, and sentenced to nine months of hell. The nausea got worse. I had to temporarily close my business, turn down a position on the local morning show, and spend most days reclined on the sofa with our dog, a small wastebasket, and the sonogram photo of my son nearby.

One day my mom and my grandmother "Mimi" drove the five hours from Dallas hell-bent on cheering me up. They walked in and announced, "Let's just go out! We have to get you out of this house!"

"You don't understand how bad I feel." I burst into tears. "I am depressed, and my best friend is a trashcan. The only thing I have to look forward to is my bath every night."

"Well then, let's go buy nice bath stuff."

That got my attention.

And the rest is history. I lived in the bath. I lived for the bath. My knowledge of bath luxuries went from grocery store bubble bath to imported luxury bubble cupcakes (yes, they are a thing) in a matter of nine months. By the time the baby was born, my zeal for natural bath luxuries had transformed into the type of persnickety snobbery reserved for wine connoisseurs sniffing a choice Bordeaux. I was only interested in the good stuff. And I was beginning to understand that as in cooking, the good stuff was fresh and handmade.

A FEW NOTES ABOUT EQUIPMENT AND SAFETY

THE BEST PART OF DIPPING YOUR TOES INTO this part of the book is you probably already have most of what you need in your kitchen. Bowls, spatulas, and small kitchen appliances are all you need for these recipes. However, you may find you prefer to use separate bowls specifically for your spa recipes if you enjoy scenting with essential oils or fragrance oils, so they don't leach into the plastic or so the scent doesn't carry over into tomorrow's meatloaf!

Weight versus Volume Measuring

Outside of this book, which serves as an introduction to handmade spa products, cosmetic recipes are usually given in weight measurements. This is because the degree of accuracy is so exact when weighing ingredients versus measuring with a cup measure. Because I know very few friends with a digital kitchen scale at home, I have chosen to give volume measures for all my recipes except the cream soap recipe, which absolutely requires a small scale to weigh out the precise amount of lye and oils needed. A small digital kitchen scale can be purchased at any home or kitchen store. Make sure to get a scale that has readings of both pounds and ounces with a good deal of precision.

Some Additional Tools You Might Need

PLASTIC SYRINGE BULB DROPPER: This is a little plastic dropper that will hold about a tablespoon or more of fragrance or essential oils. They are cheap and reusable. Pick up a few if you buy your essential or fragrance oils online.

SAFETY GLASSES: Available at the hardware store to protect your eyes

HEAVY RUBBER DISHWASHING GLOVES: To handle the lye used in soap making and wipe up any spills

APRON: To protect your clothes

CLOSE-TOED SHOES: To protect your feet

Some of the additional tools listed here are used only in soap making. These items are mentioned for safety purposes since one step of soap making involves handling lye, which is a caustic heavy alkali. This is very important to understand. Lye and water create a chemical reaction that produces heat. The lye water will rise to almost 200°F and must be handled as carefully as boiling water. Even once it cools, the lye water can burn your skin and eyes. Always handle it with proper gloves and safety glasses. Make sure there is plenty of ventilation and the area is free of children or pets. In the end the soap will not contain lye, because the oil and lye water have transformed through a chemical reaction into soap. It sounds intimidating, but with the right safety precautions it's a piece of cake.

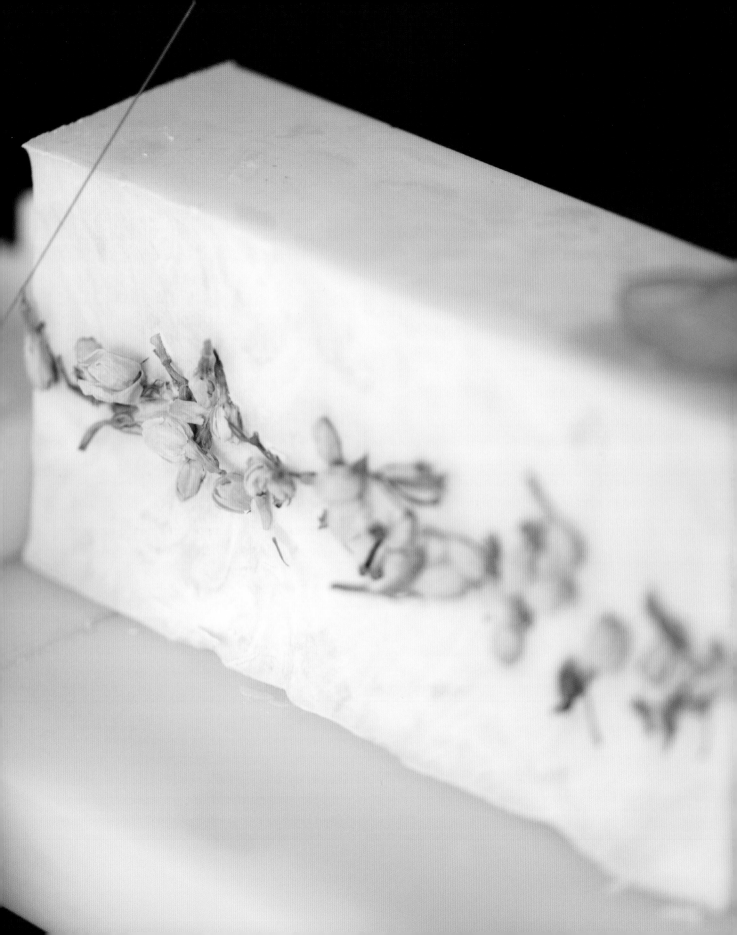

INGREDIENT DICTIONARY

I have tried to use ingredients in these recipes that are easy to obtain locally or at a larger grocery store, but if you think you have a suitable substitution on hand, give it a try!

COLLODIAL OATMEAL: An extremely fine powdered oatmeal available online. This finely ground powder is useful because you get all the skin soothing properties in oatmeal but it suspends in water instead of sinking to the bottom of the tub. If you like, you can also make your own by grinding fresh oatmeal in a high-quality blender or food processor, or you can purchase oat flour in the health food section of the grocery store for a close substitute.

DRIED CLAYS: Dried clays, which dry up excess oil and impurities, are available in natural food stores and online. Purchase in powdered form and blend with equal parts water. They come in many colors, from pink to green, and are often labeled by where the clay has been harvested. My favorite is green bentonite clay, for no other reason than it's fun to smear on your face and scare the children.

ACTIVATED CHARCOAL: With charcoal's ability to soak up toxins like a sponge, it's no shocker that it's being added to cosmetic formulas to achieve the same filtration for the skin. Activated charcoal has been chemically altered for cosmetic use and is not the same thing used in your charcoal grill! Purchase it online (only a little is needed) and add to your recipes to remove and draw out impurities. It will obviously turn any scrub or mask black, but it washes right off the skin.

DRIED HERBS AND FLOWERS: There are many dried herbs and flowers in this chapter, and I will discuss the benefits of each one in more detail in each recipe. Dried herbs and flowers are available in large cities at spice shops, apothecaries, and health food stores. Rather than getting your Google degree in every botanical you come across, I recommend experimenting with several that work for your skin type, are easy for you to obtain, and, most importantly, have a pleasing scent to your family. There is a rainbow of botanicals out there, but most of them are categorized in families that do the same thing: "reduce inflammation, calm the skin, purify and tone the pores, etc." There is really no need to have an exotic herb overnighted from the Amazon rainforest when there is probably a local botanical that will replicate the exact same results.

ROSEWATER: The by-product of acquiring rose essential oil through distillation is called rosewater. Real rose essential oil is one of the most expensive oils in the world, and rosewater is a more modestly priced luxury. I use it in a small atomizer in my purse for a refreshing facial mist, and I also use it in formulas for the romantic and relaxing aroma.

DEAD SEA SALT: Dead Sea salt is the crème de la crème when it comes to luxury bath enhancements because, in our experience, it really does increase relaxation and help you sleep. No, I do not believe any other salt gives the same effect. Real Dead Sea salts are from the Dead Sea in southern Israel. Look for pure, uncut salt with a slightly grayish tint to it. The gray tint is caused by the unusually large amount of natural minerals in the salt, including the relaxation minerals magnesium and bromide, the latter of which was sold as a sedative in the early twentieth century. The salts have been touted as curing all types of skin conditions and promoting a youthful appearance, but we love them for the gentle, calming effect of a Dead Sea soak and the sleep-like-a-log rest afterward. It works just as well on little babies and grumpy husbands.

WALNUT OIL: This wonderfully fragrant nut oil absorbs into the skin almost immediately rather than leaving a greasy feel. As opposed to coconut or olive oil, which leave you, well, sort of oily, walnut oil is rich in vitamins and minerals that soak into the skin, leaving a shimmery glow. Look for roasted walnut oil for an especially robust fragrance that blends well with essential oils.

DRY MILK POWDERS: Milk powders are dehydrated milk (goat, coconut, cow) that resembles fluffy, white flakes. It is found in the grocery store and online and is used primarily in bath soaks and soap-making.

CITRIC ACID: Citric acid is a white granular substance that looks like table salt and is made from citrus fruits. It is the fizzing component (reacting with baking soda) in a bath fizzy or bath bomb. It is available for the best prices online. It is also found in small amounts in the section of the grocery store where the canning supplies are sold.

BAKING SODA: This is citric acid's other half when it comes to making bath fizzies. The baking soda and citric acid react with hot water to release the fizzing, effervescent action. You can find baking soda in large boxes at the grocery store or even bigger bags at warehouse stores.

BEESWAX: Beeswax is a natural wax produced by honeybees that is used to give structure to balms and other cosmetic products, as well as enhance absorption into the skin. Found locally at farmers' markets and sold by beekeepers, it is also available at craft stores and online.

ESSENTIAL OILS: Essential oils are naturals oils derived from the plant or other source they are extracted from. The best prices are found online from sources that sell to candle- and soap-makers.

FRAGRANCE OILS: Fragrance oils are synthetic perfume blends. They can include natural sources as well, and in that case are usually labeled as EO/FO blends. Fragrance oils available online range from your favorite discontinued perfume (fragrance houses will often keep favorite fragrances long after the big brands have stopped using them in products) to fun fragrances like cookie dough or sleepytime. The best products are ordered online, and when searching you will need to confirm that the oil you are purchasing is body safe (i.e., not strictly for candle-makers).

TIP FROM MOM

ALL THE RECIPES IN THIS SECTION are great to make with the kids except Grandma's Cream Soap, which should only be made with older, mature children in full safety gear. Open the windows and restrict all pets and small children from the area.

HEAVENLY ROSE AND CLAY MASK

THE SMELL OF ROSES HAS GOTTEN A BAD REP in our generation for being old-timey and outdated, reminding us of grandma's house—but not in the nostalgic, wonderful way that burning leaves or freshly baked bread does. And I get it! But here's a secret: The rose smell granny used isn't derived from real roses, but from imitation, artificial rose scent combined with heavy talcum powder.

The rosewater I use here is as pure as plucking a blossom from your garden. The clay is just as wholesome, and when you buy it in the powder form, it lasts ages and can be mixed just right to actually do its job. This mask is naturally an excellent deep pore cleansing mask, but works even better on stubborn blackheads after a gentle steam. **YIELD: 1 MASK**

---

1 tablespoon natural bentonite clay

1/8 teaspoon activated charcoal

1 1/2 teaspoons rosewater

In a small bowl combine the clay, activated charcoal, and rosewater and whisk with a mini whisk or a fork. Whisk until smooth, adding an extra squeeze of rosewater if needed.

To prepare your face, run a clean washcloth under hot water; when it is comfortable enough to place on your face, lie back in a reclining position and place the hot cloth over your face, allowing it to steam open the pores. Repeat if desired. This mask also works well right after a hot shower.

When your face has been steamed, apply the rose and clay mask to your face and neck area. Apply up to a 1/4 inch thick and allow to dry and tighten, about 10–20 minutes. To remove the clay, wash with warm water, using a scrubbing motion with your fingertips. Towel dry and apply your favorite moisturizer.

HONEY CHAI MOISTURIZING FACE MASK

THIS IS A CHAI TEA LATTE FOR YOUR FACE. One of my favorite activities on a blustery, gray day is curling up in a cozy chair, a chunky cable-knit sweater wrapped around me, book in hand, and a chai tea latte steaming on the table beside me, filling the room with spice and sweetness. This mask will tighten pores, soothe skin, and fight inflammation while reminding you of quiet moments spent with a book you love. **YIELD: 2 MASKS**

2 tablespoons fresh local honey

$1/8$ teaspoon each cardamom, cinnamon, and nutmeg

In a small bowl combine the honey and spices. Microwave 15 seconds, whisk, and microwave an additional 5–10 seconds. Allow it to cool 10 minutes. You will know that it is ready when it comes back to the consistency of honey.

Bind back your hair. Coat your face with a thin coat of the honey mask, using sparingly around the eyes. Wash your hands and relax 10–15 minutes. Wash the mask off directly into the sink with warm water. The spices will gently exfoliate and help to remove the honey mask. Pat your face dry with a hand towel.

MAMA BEE'S HOMEMADE ORGANIC LIP BALM

REBEKAH, MY AUTHOR FRIEND AND URBAN COWGIRL TRIBE SCRIBE, has a mother with a thumb greener than fresh-cut grass. A few years ago, Rebekah's mom, Pam, decided she'd marry her love of nature with her love of bees and started a backyard bee colony. We've been the benefactors of a steady supply of beeswax ever since.

If you don't know Pam, you can get beeswax at your local craft store. It binds the oils together and is organic and natural. If you want a pop of color, you can always drop in a little dab of regular lipstick.

YIELD: 1½ OUNCES

---

2 teaspoons local beeswax from your farmers' market or local beekeeper (also at the craft store)

2 teaspoons extra-virgin olive oil

1 teaspoon coconut oil

2 teaspoons walnut oil

1 teaspoon castor oil

Several small cosmetic tins or jars with lids

NOTE: Any of these oils can be alternated or replaced with similar oils. The coconut oil, which is actually a butter, adds firmness to the balm, as does the beeswax, so these should stay in the formula. The castor oil adds shine to the final balm so that it is glossy, but it can be replaced if desired.

In a glass pitcher or measuring cup with a pour spout, combine beeswax and all the oils. Microwave in 10-second bursts until the coconut oil and beeswax are fully melted into the other oils. Pour into small jars and set aside to cool. Place lids on the containers and use to moisturize dry lips.

ROSE PETAL COCONUT SUGAR SCRUB

IT IS A TRUTH UNIVERSALLY ACKNOWLEDGED THAT WOMEN LOVE GETTING ROSES from their husbands. When my husband brings me roses, he knows that once they've wilted, into the food processor they go. I call it reusing; he calls it romantic carnage. Now you can benefit from my years of romantic repurposing! **YIELD: 1 SMALL JAR**

4 red roses

1 cup sugar

1/2 cup coconut oil

A small jar

Optional: vitamin E, favorite essential oils, half a vanilla bean

In a food processor place the rose petals of four roses topped with 1 cup sugar. Heat the glass jar of coconut oil gently in the microwave just until liquid. Portion out 1/2 cup coconut oil and pour in the food processor bowl. Pulse the mixture to just incorporate the ingredients, then turn on high for 10 seconds.

Remove the sugar scrub to a small jar and use immediately or refrigerate. This recipe keeps in the refrigerator for a long time. It will become solid as the coconut oil re-solidifies, but that just makes it easier to scoop. The coconut oil will re-melt into the skin during your scrub.

TO USE: Take a bit of the scrub and rub vigorously into the skin to exfoliate and soften. Rinse off with water. Scrubs are a great addition to bathing, but remember to keep this scrub refrigerated after use because it is truly all natural and does not include preservatives.

NOTE: Sugar scrubs are particularly good at polishing and removing dead skin off your lips during Chapstick season.

Vitamin E: Vitamin E is known for healing dry, chapped skin and can be purchased by the small vial or in gel capsules at the grocery store. Squeeze a couple capsules into the sugar scrub, especially when using this recipe as a lip scrub.

Essential Oils: A couple drops of essential oils will scent this recipe for use as a body scrub, and the scent will remain on your skin after you shower.

PRO TIP

FOLKLORE TELLS US THAT soothing scents like lavender and rose help to relax the mind after a hard day, while lemon and peppermint are best used to stimulate the mind and spark creativity.

QUEEN OF SHEBA OIL

IF YOU'VE NEVER EXPERIENCED A GULLY WASHER BEFORE, I don't think words alone can accurately convey the event. But I'll give it a go. Imagine the sky opens up like a zipper's just been yanked, and through the gap in the world Niagara Falls gushes down on you—into your purse, in your shoes, in places water shouldn't even be. These storms, unusual and peculiar even in the wide-open spaces of Texas, roll up out of nowhere, so you are seldom, if ever, prepared.

It was a bitter cold winter night. Two Urban Cowgirls, one gully washer, and an entire parking lot between us and the car.

We could run to the car . . . we could . . . Only we had eaten every single thing on the menu, and we were in that glorious post-étouffée daze. Running would ruin it. Besides, you can't run from a gully washer. You might as well let it baptize you, wash away every scrap of mascara and hairspray, then go home and take a long, hot shower.

Which is exactly the way it happened.

I whipped up a batch of oil that night for my chapped pink skin from some ingredients I happened to have lying around my bathroom, among the superhero bath toys and the make-up samples from Sephora. I plopped down on the bed, ready to watch a movie, and Tracey, my Urban-Cowgirl-Gully-Wash Compatriot, exclaimed, "Sweet Lord! What is that amazing smell?" (Only with adult language.)

She grabbed the little glass vial of oil and breathed deeply. Her eyelids fluttered closed and she sighed, "You smell like the Queen of Sheba!"

I scrambled for a pen and paper to scribble down the elixir I had just concocted in the bathroom, because who doesn't want to become a queen whenever she feels like it? Pretty much everyone reacts the same to this glorious post-shower oil, so I decided to share the goodness with my Urban Cowgirl readers. **YIELD: ¼ CUP**

¼ cup extra-virgin roasted walnut oil

25 drops lavender essential oil

10 drops jasmine essential oil

Mix thoroughly and use immediately or keep in a small glass vial for future gully washers.

LUXURY BABY MILK BATHS

SHOPPING FOR YOUR CHILDREN is a roller coaster ride of fun that also does a number on your wallet. In my perusal of store counters everywhere, I've noticed a phenomenon popping up all over: baby milk baths. Adults love luxurious bath products, so why wouldn't babies? They're tiny versions of us.

Baby milk baths are similar in almost every way to adult milk bath products, except they are usually unscented or lightly scented with a mild fragrance. And if you know how to make them at home, they are much more affordable and packed with extra love from you.

When I make these for my little ones, I add a couple tablespoons of Dead Sea salt directly to the water for extra relaxation before bedtime. Dead Sea salts contain magnesium and bromide, two minerals known to release feelings of tranquility and relaxation. Unfortunately, you can't add the Dead Sea salt directly to the mixture because these minerals are hydroscopic and attract water from the air, which would certainly contaminate the dry powder. Sometimes I add a couple drops of essential oils to the bath. The bonus of using powdered coconut milk is that it smells faintly of fresh coconut, which is always wonderfully scrumptious.

I sit beside them while they soak in the goodness I've made, counting all their little fingers and toes, and feeling perfectly, peacefully joyful to get those moments of bliss at bath time. **YIELD: 1 CUP**

1/2 cup finely ground oatmeal

1/2 cup coconut milk powder

In a jar with a secure lid, combine oatmeal and milk powder and shake well. Keep the milk powder dry between baths by using a dry spoon to scoop. Use 2 tablespoons to 1/4 cup per bath depending on the amount of water used.

DECONGESTANT BATH DROPS

WHEN I WAS LITTLE, I would hide under the blanket, feverish and coughing, just to avoid getting vapor-rub rubbed on my chest and under my nose. The gooey salve was good for soothing coughs, but the texture was the living worst. Who wants to be coated in gloopy glop? My toddlers weren't big fans of the amazing vapor-rub either, so I developed these bath drops to open up their airways and soothe their souls when they were feeling sick.

The essential oils in this recipe are sharp and pungent, and the heat from the bath activates the fragrance, filling the room with relaxing vapors. When you're sick, eucalyptus is the very best thing to open your airways and help you along the road to recovery. Soak in this bath and let all the discomfort drift away as your lungs open and your body heals. **YIELD: ABOUT 8 BATHS**

2-ounce glass apothecary bottle made for essential oil blends (it will have a special foam or rubber seal on the inside of the lid that prevents the oils from evaporating; repurposing a former essential oil bottle is fine too)

Plastic pipette with suction bulb or dropper, for portioning essential oils into the bottle

4 parts eucalyptus essential oil

3 parts fir needle essential oil

2 parts lavender essential oil

Using a plastic pipette with suction bulb or dropper, fill the apothecary bottle with the given amounts of essential oils. Replace the lid, tighten, and shake. The drops are ready to use immediately. Store in a safe, dry place away from children.

EUCALYPTUS BATH SOAK

1 dropper full of bath drops

1 cup Dead Sea salt, for intense relaxation and to ease tension in the muscles brought on by illness

For the soak draw a hot bath, dissolving 1 cup Dead Sea salts into the bath. Right before entering the tub, drop 1 dropper full of bath drops onto the surface of the water. Soak in the water, breathing deeply, and place a warm washcloth over your eyes if desired. Soak as long as you feel comfortable.

ALWAYS MONITOR SMALL CHILDREN and sick loved ones in the tub and on slippery surfaces.

BOO-BOO BALM

KISSING AWAY BOO-BOOS IS A COMMON JOB FOR A MOTHER, and while our children may believe our kisses have actual healing powers, we know they need a good antiseptic salve to make sure they heal properly. The ingredients in this salve leap above what can be found in store-bought containers. From extra-virgin coconut oil, which has antibacterial, antiviral, and antifungal properties and also moisturizes and strengthens skin tissue; to calendula, well known in skin care for its anti-inflammatory healing properties that date all the way back to ancient Egypt; to chamomile, which soothes skin and may assist in healing time—this balm is a champion. **YIELD: 2½ CUPS**

1 cup extra-virgin coconut oil

¹/₂ cup walnut oil

¹/₄ cup shea butter (alternatives include olive oil, cocoa butter, avocado oil)

¹/₃ cup dried calendula flowers

¹/₄ cup dried chamomile flowers

5 sprigs of fresh thyme

¹/₄ cup beeswax

1 tablespoon vitamin E oil

TIP
FROM
MOM

DRIED FLOWERS CAN OFTEN be found sold as dried herbal tea in the bulk section of health food stores.

INFUSING THE OILS: In a double boiler or in a small saucepan over low heat, melt the extra-virgin coconut oil, walnut oil, and shea butter until liquid.

Add the dried calendula and chamomile flowers and the fresh thyme sprigs. Bring the mixture to a low simmer, stirring to coat and incorporate all the herbs. Turn the heat down as low as possible and cover the pot with a lid. Allow this mixture to steep for 30 minutes, checking on it once to make sure it has maintained a low heat and does not boil.

After 30 minutes of steeping, prepare a small glass pitcher with a pour spout to receive the oils. (A glass measuring cup is perfect for this task.) Place a coffee filter in the fine-mesh strainer for an extra layer of filtering.

With one hand hold the fine-mesh strainer (containing the coffee filter) over the small glass pitcher and with your other hand pour the oil and herb mixture into the filter a little bit at a time. Occasionally, it is helpful to set down the pot and stir the mixture inside the coffee filter as it filters down into the glass vessel.

When almost all the oil has been filtered into the glass pitcher, collect the coffee filter (full of bits of dried flower) and squeeze and pinch it with your fingers to release the last and most potent bit of the oil. Discard the filters and dried flowers.

Fine-mesh strainer

2 coffee filters or cheesecloth

Optional essential oils: thyme, lavender, rose, or anything that blends well with the naturally sweet, honey-like scent of chamomile. I prefer to leave mine unscented because the dried flowers are quite strong on their own.

This infused oil will now become the base of the Boo-Boo Balm.

TO MAKE THE BALM: Add the beeswax to the glass pitcher. Microwave in 30-second bursts, stirring in between, until the beeswax is melted into the oil. Remove and allow to cool 10–15 minutes.

To finish, stir in the vitamin E oil and any essential oils that you desire. Pour into sterilized glass jars or tins, label, and use on any minor boo-boo.

FIZZING BATH BOMBS

BATH BOMBS, OR BATH FIZZIES, as they are also known, may be the coolest and cutest little things to hit water since the invention of bubble bath. Drop one of these little balls in water and they swirl and whirl around the bath in a flurry of activity, releasing beautiful colors, dried flowers, rich and buttery oils, and an explosion of pleasing scents. It's like an insta-spa, transforming your bath into a beautiful oasis that feels like you're soaking in cream.

Bath bombs are good for almost everyone and every occasion in which a bath is required. I even make baby bath bombs with little plastic toys in the center to convince my two dirty little boys that bath time is about more than just washing behind their ears! **YIELD: 6 MEDIUM OR 4 LARGE BOMBS**

---

1 cup citric acid

2 cups baking powder

1/4 cup cornstarch

Optional: 1 tablespoon ground oatmeal or oat flour,
1 teaspoon clay

1/4 cup coconut oil (specifically the jars of thick white butter that turns liquid when warmed)

1/4 cup any liquid oil such as walnut oil, sunflower oil, olive oil, avocado oil

1–2 tablespoons fragrance oil of your choice

In a bowl combine the citric acid, baking powder, and cornstarch and sift through the kitchen sifter or the fine-mesh strainer into another bowl so that it is well combined and powder fine.

In another microwave-safe bowl, add the coconut oil and the liquid oil. Microwave in 30-second bursts until the coconut oil is fully melted. Stir well and allow to cool for a few minutes. Meanwhile, fold the bath towel to make a cushy little bed for the delicate bath bombs to dry on. Place this near your work space and gather the molds and your spoon. Put on your latex gloves. When the oil mixture has cooled slightly, pour in the fragrance oil and stir.

Pour half to three-quarters of the oil mixture into the dry ingredients and stir well with your fingers. The oil must be fully incorporated into the dry mixture. One helpful technique is to collect the mixture into your palms and rub your palms together, letting the mixture slowly rain down into the bowl. Do this repeatedly until the mixture is moist throughout.

The mixture is ready to mold when it looks like wet sand (think of building sandcastles as a kid at the beach; the wet sand holds its shape best) and when you squeeze it into a ball with your fist, it stays in a ball after you open your palm again. This often means that you will not have to use all the oil. It varies greatly

TOOLS:

Kitchen sifter or fine-mesh strainer

Soft bath towel

1 or 2 plastic DIY Christmas tree ornaments from a craft store (They have the ability to be opened and items placed inside the ornament for crafting; instead we will use them as our mold. It is helpful to grab a couple of sizes to see what you prefer.)

1 large spoon from the silverware drawer

A pair of disposable latex gloves from the cleaning section of the grocery store (not necessary but very helpful)

Optional: herbs or flowers on top, such as rose petals, lavender, corn flowers, green tea, or herbs from the garden

I OFTEN HAVE A TABLESPOON or so of fragrant oil left and that's fine, save it for a bath tonight while the fizzies are drying!

from season to season and even where you live due to humidity in the air. Just remember your goal is to get it wet enough to hold a shape.

If needed, use more oil until it is the correct consistency, repeating the blending technique described above.

When the mixture will hold its shape, take a mold and open it so you have two halves. Scoop one half full of batter and pack it in with the palm of your hand. Pack more than enough so that the mold is overflowing slightly with batter. Set that half down and fill the other half with batter in the same way. Then take both halves and push them together, wiggling the halves until the mold closes and the excess batter falls back into the bowl.

Holding the (filled) mold in one hand and the metal spoon in another hand, give one side of the mold several light smacks with the back of the spoon. This should allow the batter to release from the mold and let you peel the first half of the mold off. If it won't release, try again until you get the hang of it.

Next, place the exposed bath fizzy batter-side down, gently resting in the palm of your hand, with the plastic mold facing up. Gently tap the remaining plastic mold with the back of the spoon until it releases the fizzy into your hand. Carefully rest the fizzy on the towel to dry and harden for 12–24 hours.

Repeat until you have run out of batter.

When the fizzies have hardened, they are ready to use. You can store them in a big plastic ziplock bag, which helps them to maintain their scent, or they can be packaged in cellophane candy bags for giving to friends and family.

HOW TO USE THE FIZZY: Fill the bathtub full of warm water. Place the fizzy into the water; it will begin to fizz and bubble, releasing the fragrance and skin-nurturing oils. Be very careful as the bathtub and your feet will be slippery after your soak.

IF YOU LIKE THE LOOK OF FRESH FLOWERS ON TOP of the fizzies, they are made in nearly the same way. I add a pinch of flowers or herbs into the first mold before I fill it with fizzy batter. They will adhere to the fizzy as it dries. This is an advanced technique, and you may want to experiment with basic fizzies first until you have mastered the task of removing the fizzy from its mold.

MAKING FIZZY BOMB BATTER IS A LOT LIKE MAKING PIE DOUGH! When you make fresh pie dough, you combine butter and flour, then drizzle in ice water until the dough can hold a firm ball shape that can be rolled out and molded into a pan. You never really know exactly how much ice water to add; a good baker watches until the dough can hold a ball shape. That is exactly what you do with a fizzy! Add the oil and blend well, drizzling in oil a little at a time, until the fizzy batter will hold its shape! That's the real secret to making bath fizzies. Like making pie dough, you watch for the visual clues.

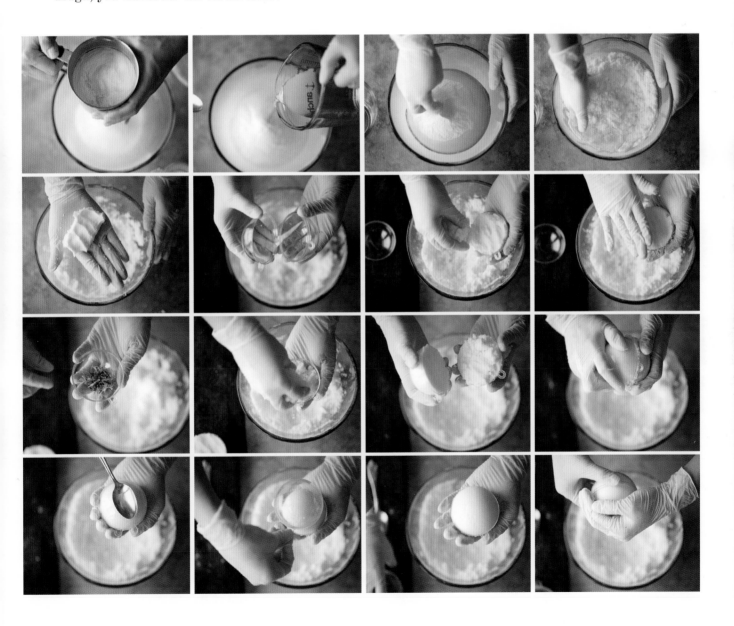

GRANDMA'S CREAM SOAP

THIS SOAP IS A THROWBACK to the old-fashioned and decadently creamy bar soaps that were beloved by our grandmother's generation. You've probably seen them at farmers' markets and in health food shops; now it's time to try it out for yourself.

I learned this method of soap making from my own grandmother, who would take me out behind her house, tie a gingham apron around her waist, and set up shop beneath the cover of evergreens and the sounds of birds chirping in the trees to make fresh soap in a kettle. It doesn't get more classic than this!

The only equipment necessary for making soap that you may not already own is a common kitchen scale, stick blender, and a thermometer, preferably a laser thermometer. These tools are inexpensive, and the laser thermometer is ideal because it doesn't require submerging into the soap batter. Because making soap is chemistry, it is crucial to measure by weight so you get exactly how much oil and lye you need to create a perfectly balanced, moisturizing soap. Measure all the ingredients listed by weight except the water, cream, and oatmeal powder. Follow these directions exactly, then let me be the first to say, "Welcome to your new addiction!" **YIELD: 20 OUNCES**

2.3 ounces sodium hydroxide (lye)

4 ounces water

5 ounces coconut oil

6 ounces olive oil

.5 ounce castor oil

5 ounces lard

1.5 ounces heavy cream

1.5 ounce essential oil or fragrance oil

1 tablespoon colloidal oatmeal

TOOLS:

Safety gear (safety glasses, heavy rubber gloves, apron, closed-toe shoes)

NOTE: Finding sodium hydroxide, or lye, has become more difficult in recent years, but your best bets are in the plumbing section of a hardware store or online. Lye usually looks like sugar or table salt, but some soap suppliers sell it in flakes. Either way, you must measure lye on a kitchen scale for accuracy. Lye and water create a chemical reaction that produces heat. The lye water will rise to almost 200°F and must be handled as carefully as boiling water. Even once it cools, the lye water can burn your skin and eyes. Read the safety information on page 204 again before starting this process.

NOTE: Read through the directions as many times as needed to feel comfortable with all the steps before you are ready to begin. Rehearse the steps to make sure you have all the supplies!

STEP 1: PREPARING THE LYE WATER: Put on your dishwashing gloves, apron, closed-toe shoes, and safety glasses. Remove all pets and children from the area.

Place a heat-safe container (that you will not eat out of again!) on the scale and measure out the amount of lye exactly. Be very care-

A plastic heat-safe container for the lye water, preferably with a pour spout

A large plastic bowl for making the soap

A long metal spoon for stirring the lye

Thermometer, preferably a laser thermometer

Rubber spatula

A stick blender

A soap mold—this could be a child's shoe box lined with freezer paper, a silicone mold, old Tupperware, margarine tubs, or a small soap box

Freezer paper

ful not to get any lye on the table, floor, or yourself. Lye is a caustic substance and can burn eyes and skin! When you have the correct amount of lye in the heat-safe container, set it aside and measure out the exact amount of water needed in another bowl.

I like to place the heat-safe container holding the lye in the sink (just in case) and then pour the water into it. Stir with a metal spoon until the lye dissolves in the water. At this time the lye water will get extremely hot. You will prepare the other ingredients while you wait for it to cool. Please instruct anyone in the house not to touch the lye water and certainly not to accidently drink it!

STEP 2: PREPARING THE OILS: In individual bowls measure out, by weight, the correct amount of each oil and the lard. Then scrape the lard and coconut oil, and pour all the liquid oils into one large bowl and place it in the microwave. Heat the oils until everything is melted clear, 30–60 seconds. Stop the microwave to stir occasionally, and be very careful not to splash yourself. Set the oils aside to cool.

STEP 3: PREPARING THE ADD-INS: Measure by weight the heavy cream and fragrance or essential oil. Portion out the tablespoon of colloidal oatmeal.

STEP 4: MAKING THE SOAP: When the oils and the lye water have cooled to around 120°F, you can start the soap making process.

First, to the bowl of melted oils, add the cream and oatmeal and, using the stick blender, blend them together well.

Next, you will very carefully pour the lye water into the bowl

PRO TIP

IN MOST CASES you will want to line whatever mold you decide to use with freezer paper. This helps when it comes to unmolding the soap in one beautiful loaf and protects your mold from wet soap batter. Using scissors, cut the freezer paper to fit snugly into the mold, lining it on all sides. You can use two layers if needed. If you use Tupperware, silicone molds, or disposable plastic containers as molds, you don't need to line with freezer paper. Wooden soap boxes will need lining, as will cardboard boxes.

of melted oil. *Do not* pour the oils into the lye water.

Place the stick blender into the bowl and, starting on a very low setting, begin to mix the lye water and oils. It helps to stir a little bit with the wand of the stick blender and then pulse a few times, until you see the mixture coming together. Blend on low until the mixture looks like thin vanilla pudding. Pour in the fragrance oil or essential oil and continue mixing. At this point we are waiting to see *trace*.

NOTE: Trace is the point in which the raw soap batter begins to thicken slightly, and when you drag a knife over the surface of the batter it holds long enough for you to see that ribbon for a few seconds on the surface of the batter. In cooking, bakers refer to this as ribboning. Same thing!

When the soap has reached trace, it's time to pour into the mold. Pour the soap into the prepared mold, using a spatula to scrape out as much batter as possible.

STEP 5: STORING AND CLEANUP: Put the soap to bed in a warm spot covered with a light lid where it won't be disturbed and is out of reach of small children and pets. Remember, it still contains lye until it goes through saponification (turns to soap) over the next 24 hours. You can store your soap in the garage, on a high bookshelf, in an empty oven, or in a closet where it will not be disturbed.

Most soapers place all their dirty bowls and tools in a safe place and clean them under hot running water the next day (once the batter has transformed into soap). If this is going to be a safety issue for you, you can rinse them out in the sink, but be aware that the soap batter contains active lye and you must wear your gloves the entire time you are handling raw soap. Also, clean the entire space thoroughly with paper towels and hot soapy water.

STEP 6: REMOVING AND CURING THE SOAP: In 1–3 days you can check the soap to see if it is firm enough to remove from the mold. Open the mold and remove the soap by pulling up on the freezer paper you lined your mold with. If the soap seems firm, unwrap the log and use a sharp knife to cut it into slices. Technically the soap is safe and totally usable now, but most soapers will rack the soap for 4–6 weeks to allow it to mellow, become more gentle for the skin, and firm up. This is called *curing* soap, and you will enjoy the soap much more by letting it cure. Think of it as aging a wine.

You can cure the soap in any clean, dry place that has plenty of ventilation. (I cure soap in my pantry.) After curing for 4–6 weeks, the soap is

ALL YOUR SOAP CONTAINERS will taste like soap and smell strongly of the fragrance or essential oil you use, so it's best to choose containers you can dedicate only to soap making. After you choose a bowl for your lye water, do not use it for food again.

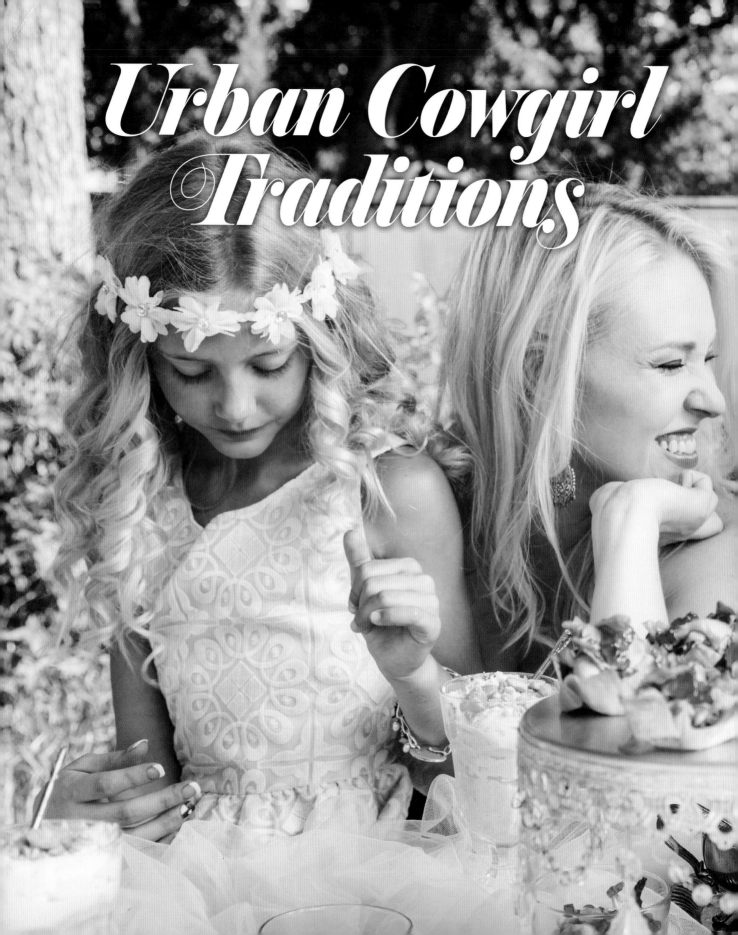

Urban Cowgirl Traditions

GROWING UP WE ARE TAUGHT FAMILY PASTIMES as a way to connect one generation to another. Our traditions are a way to pass along culture and create memories. In this chapter we explore the vast and varied traditions of the Urban Cowgirl tribe. We aren't just one family, with one set of experiences, located in one small town in Texas. The Urban Cowgirl tribe is as diverse in experience as we are numerous in size. I drew from my own life to build this chapter, delving deep into my childhood and carving out a sculpture of what the Urban Cowgirl life looks like when we come together as family and friends to share in a few sacred customs.

Pass it along to your little one, your friend, and your neighbor, because that's what traditions are for: to bring all together around the table.

Ladies Southern Tea

IF YOU'RE A WOMAN GROWING UP IN THE SOUTH, then you've probably been invited to tea in the garden. Maybe that garden was all manicured lawn and rosebush glory, maybe it was a container garden on your neighbor's screened-in porch, but if there is one thing that Ladies Tea requires, it's the scent of flowers and the sound of clinking glasses. The tradition of Ladies Southern Tea is long lived. I remember seeing sepia-toned photos of my grandmother in white gloves and a floral dress, hair curled and set, the hint of a smirk on her red-stained lips, sipping tea and eating dainty delicacies surrounded by flowers and females.

This is about as feminine as it comes. A moment to let modern sensibilities and the pressures that come with "having it all" fall away, allowing your inner Southern belle to take center stage. It's tiny, sweet, simple homemade goodies, savory morsels that can be eaten in one bite, grazing and picking and gabbing. It is gossip done right. It's for women, but if a man shows up, he better be dapper and daring, and he better have something clever to contribute to the conversation. The Ladies Southern Tea is centered around the idea that we should take time for each other, not just to celebrate special occasions, but also to celebrate the magic of being alive and connected. Now more than ever, we need to look each other in the eyes and listen with our hearts, not just our ears. And that gets easier when you have a piece of tipsy cake and a cup of ice-cold sweet tea.

The following recipes will provide ample inspiration to create your own Ladies Southern Tea, but feel free to experiment to find the right combination that works for you and yours. There is no one way to do tea, but whenever you can, you should.

URBAN COWGIRL ICED TEA

I AM NOT THE ONLY PERSON that dons a chef's hat in my family. My husband, Dereck, frequently finds his way into the kitchen to work alongside, or even instead of, me. He helped me create this twist on Texas Tea, and once again confirmed he was my perfect match. We use Earl Grey tea, which is regular black tea infused with bergamot oil, to make a richer, more affluent blend to rule over all others. This Texas iced tea is the tea you would serve the Lord if he showed up at your house looking thirsty. **YIELD: 2 QUARTS**

2 cups water

4 Earl Grey tea bags

Ice

Filtered water

Heat the water in a small saucepan and bring to a boil. Throw in the four tea bags and let simmer for 30 seconds. Remove from the heat and steep on the back of the stove 10 minutes or until cool. Fill a pitcher with ice and pour the cooled tea into the pitcher. Top it off with filtered water, and serve.

RED PEPPER JELLY CHICKEN SALAD
IN WONTON CUPS

THE POMP AND CIRCUMSTANCE OF SIGNIFICANT SOUTHERN EVENTS in an Urban Cowgirl family give the Dowager Countess and other *Downton Abbey* ladies a run for their money. After all, we consider ourselves our own royal families down here, laying claim to modern success stories rather than claims to some long-forgotten king. In the South royalty is made, not born.

And yet we all have the great matriarch of the family, our own Dowager Countess making sure the younger generation meets the demands and traditions of the family. Every proper Southern lady knows the challenges of having to find "the little bread" for the cucumber sandwiches . . . because you can't make little tea sandwiches without little breads, dammit!

The one time I dared to challenge tradition was at my own bridal shower, foolishly thinking I could actually get away with it that day. No one questions the bride, right? Except Grandma, of course. At first she pouted a bit at the absence of cucumber sandwiches cradled atop miniature rye bread, but in the end these beautiful wonton boats won her over. With a twinkle in her eyes she leaned in close, her long pearls swinging across her blouse, and whispered, "Well done, Sarah! Well done!"

And just like that, a new tradition was crowned. **YIELD: 40 WONTONS**

---

1 package wontons

3 split, bone-in chicken breasts

2 tablespoons olive oil

4 stalks celery, ribs and leaves

$1/2$ red onion

1 cup mayonnaise

1 (10-ounce) jar hot red pepper jelly

1 teaspoon kosher salt

$1/2$ teaspoon pepper

Juice of 1 lemon

2 giant handfuls of baby spinach

$1/2$ cup diced chives or green onions, for garnish

FOR THE WONTONS: Preheat the oven to 350°F.

Spray a cupcake pan liberally with spray oil. Place one wonton in each hole. It should make a little bowl with curled edges. Lightly spray the wontons with spray oil and sprinkle with salt. Bake the wontons for 10 minutes or until golden brown. Remove the pan carefully and transfer the wonton cups to a plate to cool. Repeat until you have the desired number of wonton cups.

This recipe makes a little over 1 quart of chicken salad, so we usually make all the wontons in the package and store leftover wonton cups in large ziplock baggies in the pantry if we have leftovers.

FOR THE CHICKEN SALAD: Preheat the oven to 350°F. Place the split chicken breasts on a foil-lined baking sheet and rub them with olive oil, then sprinkle with salt and pepper. Bake for 35–40 minutes or until juices run clear. Let the chicken cool completely.

Once the chicken is cool to the touch, pull the chicken off the bone, discarding the bones and skin. For the chicken either "pull it" into small strands or chop into bite-size pieces. Add the chicken to a large bowl and chill.

Rinse the celery well. Chop the red onion and celery into small dice. For this purpose the leaves and stalks of the celery may be used. Add to the chilled bowl of chicken.

To the bowl add the mayonnaise, 1/2 cup of the hot red pepper jelly, salt, pepper, and lemon juice. Fold this mixture until it is blended well.

Finely slice the two handfuls of spinach into long strands like ribbons. It's okay if they are not perfectly neat! This technique is called chiffonade, and it takes a bit of time to master. For this chicken salad, the spinach will blend into the mixture, so it's a good time to practice!

Fold the spinach into the chicken salad last and season to taste. Place into the refrigerator to chill at least 1 hour.

To serve, fill each wonton cup with a heapin' spoonful of chicken salad. Top each wonton with a small bead of hot red pepper jelly for color and interest. Garnish with fresh chives or green onions if desired.

FANTASY POPCORN

THE FIRST TIME I HAD THIS POPCORN I was sitting on a haystack with my childhood friend Nicole. Have you ever had a snack sitting on a haystack, just as twilight begins to envelop the sky with swirls of pink and magenta? Little lightning bugs flicker to life along the tree line. The smell of sweet hay, the wind in your hair, and the last rays of sunshine pouring down on your skin make everything seem magical. However, fantasy popcorn needs no help from fairy light and stardust.

It looks ordinary, like your basic white popcorn, but when you pop it in your mouth, the look of surprise on your face is always a treat for anyone watching. By design, it is a conversation piece.

As children it became our late-night haystack-sittin' favorite, and now it's our tea party favorite, because isn't that just the adult woman's version of a little time to unwind with the girls? **YIELD: 2 SERVINGS**

---

1 package lite microwavable popcorn, not heavily buttered, plain is best

1 cup white chocolate chips

Pop the popcorn according to the instructions, usually about 2–3 minutes. In a small bowl microwave the white chocolate chips in 30-second bursts until you can whisk them creamy and smooth.

In a large bowl, toss the popcorn with the white chocolate until well coated.

Turn the popcorn out onto a foil-lined baking sheet lightly greased with butter or spray oil.

Let the popcorn harden in a cool, dry place for 30 minutes. Break up with a spatula and place in a serving bowl or store in ziplock bags.

MANGO SHRIMP COCKTAILS

NEAR MY HOME IN DENTON, TEXAS, there is a little, unobtrusive taqueria set just off a major road. It's an authentic Mexican quick stop that has become an oasis of sorts to me. I don't tell many people about it because it's a place that I like to escape to all alone and recharge.

I can always rely on the little *abuelas* pressing tortillas to help me refill my mind with inspiration and my heart with gratitude. They smile brightly when I walk in. They wave, "Hola Chef!" I speak limited Spanish and they speak limited English, but that's okay because we all speak fluent taco.

Besides their sweet disposition and the strangely relaxing scent of tortillas cooking on the flat top, I come because they make the best Mexican shrimp cocktail I have ever had in my entire life.

Mexican shrimp cocktails are bright and fresh concoctions. They are usually served in tall, fluted sundae glasses or beer schooners so that the sweet and tangy tomato sauce drenches the shrimp and creamy avocado in juice. Herbaceous cilantro, red onion for crunch, and a bite of serrano or jalapeño adds interest and complements the juicy marinated shrimp, giving it just enough creeping heat to leave you longing for a cold cerveza. It is usually served with crackers and a long spoon for digging down and getting the last morsels of shrimp. Though, if you're like me, you'll want to lick the bowl.

The Urban Cowgirl version adds mango to enrich and sweeten the sauce. I originally designed it to be served in smaller shooters for parties—though you are more than welcome to pour it into the largest schooner glass you own and devour the entire thing in one sitting! **YIELD: 4-6 SERVINGS**

---

1 tablespoon liquid shrimp boil concentrate

1½ pounds Gulf Coast shrimp, shells on, deveined

Fill a large stockpot halfway with water and bring to a boil. Add the shrimp boil. Pour in the shrimp and simmer 4–6 minutes, or until the shrimp is cooked through. Remove the shrimp and drain well. Peel the shrimp and refrigerate.

In a blender or food processor, blend the frozen mango and the rest of the sauce ingredients. Blend well and taste for seasoning. Pour this mixture over the shrimp and chill.

Meanwhile, add all the chopped cocktail veggies besides the avocado, which will be added at serving time, to the shrimp cocktail. Marinate at least 1 hour.

At serving time cut the avocado into chunks and fold them in last, very gently. Serve in tall glasses with a shake of Tabasco if desired. Serve with long chilled spoons for a special touch!

This dish is traditionally served with tortilla chips or saltine-style crackers

FOR THE MANGO SAUCE:

1 cup frozen mango, defrosted in the refrigerator

$1/2$ cup Clamato

Zest and juice of 2 limes

1 garlic clove, minced

$1/2$ teaspoon minced fresh ginger

1 teaspoon fresh horseradish

$1/2$ teaspoon salt

1 teaspoon apple cider vinegar

Freshly cracked pepper

FOR THE COCKTAIL VEGGIES:

$1/2$ cup frozen mango, defrosted and small diced

$1/4$ cup small dice red onion

12 cherry tomatoes, quartered

$1/3$ cup freshly chopped cilantro

1 jalapeño, seeded and diced

1–2 Haas avocados

Optional: couple shakes of green Tabasco

Proper Fish Fry

WHERE I GREW UP, IF YOU SAY, "LET'S GO FISHIN' down there where the river starts," everyone knows exactly what spot you mean. When I was a little girl, my dad would wake my cousin Randi and I up late at night—or maybe so early in the morning it still felt like night—to take us fishing. We'd drive out that dark lonely road and park at that place everyone knew about but no one ever marked on a map, following the sound of frogs croaking until we stood at the edge of the river bottom.

My dad knew this place like the back of his hand, like maybe he as a little boy had been dragged out of bed in the dead of night to walk down to this very spot where the catch was always good and the lights from the nearby town were dimmer than distant stars. On my first walk I remember seeing the lightning bugs zip-zap past me. I remember chasing them with Randi, wondering what those magical little creatures were and what others I would find in this mystical, midnight woods.

We would fish, eating candy bars and listening to my Dad tell exciting stories from his rock-and-roll days until the sky changed over to purples and pinks. Then that night we'd have a proper fish fry, another tradition passed from my grandpa to my dad, from my dad to me, and now from me to my Tiny Texans.

CORNMEAL-BATTERED FISH
AND COUNTRY FRIES

NOW THIS ISN'T JUST A RECIPE, this is a walk-through of how to do an efficient Southern fish fry. We've spent many a summer day on the lake with friends and family, enjoying a cold drink and catching bass and catfish. What are you to do with a beautiful cooler full of freshly caught fish and a hungry family? Here's your action plan! It works just as well in your backyard as at a cabin on the lake! You may choose to serve this meal with a fresh garden salad with homemade dressing, fresh grapes, hushpuppies, coleslaw, potato salad, or the bourbon malt shakes also in this chapter. A fish fry is the perfect time to throw a potluck party. Assign the side dishes to your friends and send the kids out to bring home fresh fish with Dad! **YIELD: SERVES 4**

2 pounds (or more) tilapia, catfish, or any fresh-caught mild, flaky white fish, bones removed

Oil for frying, to fill roughly half of your cooking vessel

1 1/2 cups yellow cornmeal

1 teaspoon Creole or Cajun seasoning salt such as Tony Chachere's

1 teaspoon Old Bay Seasoning

1/2 teaspoon garlic powder

2 large russet potatoes

Additional seasoning salt

Lemons and fresh parsley, for garnish

In a large bowl filled with ice water, add slices of fish that have been cut to about the size of your palm or smaller.

In another bowl, add the cornmeal and seasonings. Begin heating the oil to 350–375°F. When the oil is at least 350°F, begin battering the fish. Pull each piece directly from the ice water, shake well, and place into the cornmeal batter. Make sure to only add as much fish to the pot that won't allow the oil to drop below 350°F, or the fried fish will be oily.

When the fish is golden brown, remove it to a baking sheet with a rack to drain off any excess oil. Season with Creole seasoning immediately and serve or continue frying fish.

When the fish is all cooked, there will be cornmeal in the oil, and this is a great time to fry up the country fries.

Cut the russets into 1/4-inch slabs and then cut very thin fries from the slabs. (Cut them thin if you like to get them crispy.) Increase the temperature of the oil to 400°F for this step. Fry them at high heat until golden brown. They will collect pieces of cornmeal, and they can also be dusted with leftover cornmeal batter. Salt immediately upon removing from the oil to drain.

Serve it all up with a dollop of Whizbanger Sauce, lemons, and fresh parsley.

WHIZBANGER SAUCE

WHIZBANGER SAUCE
YIELD: 1 ½ CUPS

1 cup mayonnaise

¼ cup diced onion

½ tablespoon sugar

1 tablespoon Tabasco

1 teaspoon vinegar

½ teaspoon paprika

This sauce is ridiculous. It's become a staple at our fish frys since we discovered it at a seafood shack outside College Station, Texas. I was commissioned with re-creating it, and the tribe has been in love with it ever since!

Combine all the ingredients in a mini food processor or blender and blend into a pink sauce. Taste for seasoning. Serve with the fish and fries.

PRO TIP

I PREFER TO DO THE MAJORITY OF THE FISH FRY OUTDOORS.

This is best accomplished with an outdoor deep fryer for large parties, or a simple table and electric cooktop set up for family parties.

For the table you will need a cookie sheet with rack for draining, a small cutting board and knife, tongs or a fry strainer scoop, fish and cornmeal batter, a large pot of hot oil over an electric or butane cooker, and preferably a laser thermometer.

BOURBON MALT SHAKES

THIS IS A SWEET TREAT SPIKED WITH BOURBON—so the five-star reviews write themselves. It's perfect to enjoy under the stars after a long day of fishing, frying, and frolicking in the water.
YIELD: 2 SHAKES

1/4 cup fine-quality bourbon

3 tablespoons chocolate malt powder

1/4 cup milk

12 heaping 1-ounce scoops vanilla ice cream (check your ice cream scoop to see how many ounces it holds)

In a blender combine all the ingredients. Blend well and pour into glasses.

South for the Summer

EVERY REGION HAS THAT PLACE. You know the one I mean. For New Yorkers and Jennifer Grey's "Baby," it's the Catskills. For New Englanders, it's the Cape. In Texas and Oklahoma, it's the Gulf. We pack up our trucks, strap in our little ones, and hit the 45 to Galveston, stopping at all the same truck stops, eating from the same kolache places and tamale trucks, buying that same brand of beef jerky and sampling that familiar fudge.

When we were young, going south for the summer meant spending our days building sandcastles, only to have them washed away overnight by the tide, or swimming in the ocean, chasing crabs, avoiding washed-up jellyfish. It was endless days of laughing with Mom and Dad, and being happy for once that you were still a kid.

As teenagers, we went for love. It was our chance to have that summer romance we'd grown up watching from afar. While our younger siblings built sandcastles, we stole kisses on the Wonder Wheel and ate cotton candy off each other's fingertips. Summer love was real when it happened beneath the lights of the Kemah Boardwalk. Hand-in-hand, we'd walk barefoot in the sand. We'd make promises that we couldn't keep. We'd make memories we'd never forget.

Then we got older, college bound, and summer became about getting a job, saving for fall, and life after graduation. Going south for the summer was our only escape, one where we could still ride the Wonder Wheel and search for seashells. We pretended that summer was sacred, even if now we knew that all too soon it would have to end.

We go back now that we're grown, with a mortgage and kids of our own, because going south for the summer is something the next generation shouldn't miss out on. That's the Urban Cowgirl way: never losing touch with our roots. We get to build sandcastles again and teach our kids to avoid jellyfish but never ignore a sparkling seashell gleaming in the sand. We get to watch teenagers fall hard, get heartbroken, and we pat them on the back and smile because we've been there.

Now, we're living our own happily ever after.

Summer on the Gulf is swimsuits and sandcastles. It's finding love, losing love, and then drowning your sorrow in the surf. It's growing up in Texas, but never growing old.

GALVESTON SHRIMP KISSES
WITH CARAMELIZED PINEAPPLE SAUCE

WHEN I WAS TWENTY-TWO, I moved to Galveston and spent my summer bartending on the beach where I met the man who would one day become my husband. We fell in love with Galveston's signature dish, Shrimp Kisses. (And we fell in love with each other, too.)

Shrimp Kisses are basically a shrimp en brochette—a bacon-wrapped shrimp stuffed with creamy cheese, jalapeño, or crab, fried crispy and personalized by each chef with an original sauce. From bourbon glazes to barbecue drizzles, every restaurant on the Island has a different twist on the recipe. Here's mine!

To complement the velvety cream cheese filling, I pair the shrimp with a sweet caramelized pineapple sauce. The caramelization adds complexity to the flavor, and the sweet pineapple makes you feel like you are on the Island enjoying a daiquiri. A dusting of chipotle powder adds a bit of heat and a whisper of smoke. It's the perfect coastal Texas dish. **YIELD: MAKES 18 LARGE SHRIMP**

---

18 XL raw Gulf shrimp, preferably local and brought in that day

1 package center-cut bacon

A box of toothpicks

1$^1/_2$ liters canola oil to fill a medium pot, for frying

FILLING

1 cup freshly grated cheddar cheese (about a 4-ounce block)

1 cup freshly grated Monterey Jack cheese (about a 4-ounce block)

2 green onions, sliced razor thin, green and white parts

1 (8-ounce) package cream cheese, softened to room temperature

Chipotle chile powder (optional) and cilantro, for garnish

Preheat the oven to 400°F. Place the pineapple cubes on a foil-lined baking sheet. Spray them with a little cooking spray or oil. Cook them in the oven for about 20 minutes or until brown. Try not to let many black areas develop. Brown is good, black is burnt!

You can also use your oven's broiler, but I would not recommend walking away from them. I would stand and watch as the color develops because it tends to happen very quickly.

Take the brown pineapple pieces and place them in a blender. Blend into a puree, adding a little water if necessary. Place the puree in a saucepan and add the butter, a pinch of salt, and a squeeze of lemon. Let the butter melt and stir in the cream. Heat the mixture gradually until it comes to a boil. Let simmer just until it thickens slightly. Taste and add additional salt or lemon juice if necessary. Keep warm while you cook the shrimp.

Peel all the raw shrimp. One at a time, use a sharp paring knife to slice halfway through the shrimp, butterflying it through the belly side and creating a place to stuff with the cheese filling. Do not cut all the way through the shrimp, only butterfly it. The shrimp should open up slightly, like a book. (The shrimp *can* be

CARAMELIZED PINEAPPLE
SAUCE

10 chunks of pineapple cut into
about 1 x 1-inch cubes (precut
fresh pineapple from the produce
section is fine; avoid canned
pineapple)

1/4 cup butter

Pinch of salt

Squeeze of lemon

1/4 cup cream

IT'S IMPORTANT TO
USE CENTER-CUT

bacon in this dish to ensure full,
even coverage of the shrimp.
Bargain bacon is mostly fat and
will melt off and into the grease,
allowing the cheese to melt out.

butterflied through the back, but the stuffing holds up better when it is cradled inside the shrimp by butterflying it through the belly.)

FOR THE FILLING: Make the filling by grating the cheese and adding it to a bowl with the sliced green onions and the cream cheese (microwave in 10-second bursts if you need to soften it). Mash the ingredients with a fork, mixing it all together until you get a mixture that you can make soft cheese balls from.

Open and lay out your bacon in front of you. Scoop up a small ball of cheese and roll it in your palm (about 1/2 inch in diameter). Take a shrimp and push the cheese ball into the butterflied belly. Mash it gently into the opening so that it fills up the space.

Take a piece of bacon and, holding the shrimp in one hand, wrap the bacon around the shrimp starting at the top and wrapping over and over toward the bottom until you have covered the cheese and shrimp. Secure with toothpicks. The shrimp and cheese should be fully encased in bacon.

Repeat with the remaining shrimp. When they're all done, place them in the freezer where they won't get smashed. We want to chill and firm them up, since they have been melting in your warm hands. Freeze 30 minutes.

Fill a medium-size saucepan halfway with canola oil and heat over medium-high heat to about 385°F. Place two to four freezer-chilled shrimp at a time into the hot oil and let them fry until the bacon is crisp and the cheese inside is hot and melty. Dry them off on a cooling rack or on paper towels. Remove the toothpicks before serving.

To plate, place a bit of sauce on a plate, top with the shrimp, and sprinkle with cilantro and chipotle chile powder if desired.

KEMAH SHARK EGGS WITH KICK IN THE PANTS RANCH

KEMAH IS A BAYSIDE TOWN NEAR HOUSTON with the largest marina in Texas and a boardwalk full of restaurants, carnival games, and rides like the Ferris wheel (which I always find particularly nostalgic and romantic because my husband took me on a Ferris wheel before we ended up on the beach with a little box and a shiny ring).

If you're anything like Dereck and me, you like a little snack with your romance, and we can never resist an order of shark eggs from our favorite Kemah hangout, T-Bone Tom's. We love them so much that I had to find a way to make them at home, so I fiddled with this recipe until it came out just right.

Shark eggs are a large, fresh jalapeño pepper stuffed with deviled crab, then breaded and fried crunchy to golden-brown perfection. I'm a sucker for fresh horseradish, which pairs well with seafood, so I thought I would invite it along for a sauce that's cooling and familiar with a zesty pop of spicy horseradish. The shark eggs are golden brown, crispy, and the perfect snack food to pair with a cold cerveza for a perfect day on the Gulf. **YIELD: 12–16 SHARK EGGS**

---

2 cups finely crushed club crackers (exactly one sleeve from the box)

3/4 cup cream

1 large egg

1/2 teaspoon garlic powder

1 teaspoon onion powder

1/2 teaspoon salt

1/2 teaspoon pepper

1 tablespoon chopped fresh parsley

1/2 teaspoon chopped fresh thyme leaves (about 4 sprigs)

FOR THE CRAB MIXTURE: In a large bowl combine the cracker crumbs, cream, one egg, all the seasonings and fresh herbs, pimentos, and the juice of one small lemon.

On a cutting board with a knife cut the jalapeño into small strips and then mince it finely. Slice the green onion (white and green parts) finely and add both vegetables into the bowl. Mix and toss well.

Before adding the crab meat, toss it into another bowl and pick over it finely, looking for any bits of shell. When you are sure it is clean, squeeze out any excess water into the sink and add it to the bowl of cracker mixture along with the chopped imitation crab. Using your hands mix in the crab meat. At this point I like to freeze the mixture for about a half hour or chill for several hours or overnight. This is not necessary but makes it much easier to handle and stuff the jalapeños.

1 (2-ounce) jar pimentos, well drained

3 lemons, 1 for juicing into the crab mixture, the others for cutting into wedges and serving alongside the shark eggs

1 jalapeño, deseeded and deribbed

1 green onion, white and green parts

1 pound crab meat (claw meat is fine)

$1/2$ cup well-chopped imitation crab

6–8 large jalapeños, split and cleaned

BREADING STATION:

2 cups flour

2 cups panko bread crumbs

2 eggs, beaten with a little cold water added to thin

1 quart oil (peanut, canola, safflower, etc.), for frying

Gather the jalapeños and the crab mixture. Using a spoon scoop a heaping $1/4$ cup of crab into the jalapeño and mold it well. It should look like a giant egg. Don't be afraid to really stuff a tall tower of crab mixture in there! Reserve and repeat with the rest of the jalapeños. Freeze for 15 minutes while you put together the breading station.

FOR THE BREADING STATION: You will need two large plates and a bowl for the egg wash. Pour the flour onto a plate, the panko bread crumbs onto another plate, and crack the two eggs into the bowl. Whisk in about $1/4$ cup water to thin out the eggs and create an egg wash. When the shark eggs are firm from being chilled in the freezer, take one at a time and dip the jalapeño side into the egg mixture and then into the flour on all sides (including the crab side). This is necessary to give the flour something to stick to besides the slick jalapeño skin. The flour will adhere to the crab mixture easily but the jalapeño side takes that extra step.

From the flour plate dip the entire egg back into the egg wash and then into the panko bread crumbs. Coat it well and apply gentle pressure to make sure the breading is tight. Place back on the plate and repeat with all the jalapeños.

Freeze the jalapeños for a full 30 minutes while you heat the oil.

FOR THE COOKING: Heat the full quart of oil in a medium saucepan at medium-high heat. Using a thermometer bring the oil to around 340–350°F. Place a cooling rack down on a cookie sheet to collect your cooked shark eggs, or a paper towel–lined plate works just as well.

PRO TIP

I LIKE TO CUT MY LEMONS into wedges and prepare a bowl of Kick in the Pants Ranch before I start to fry so the shark eggs are ready to enjoy as soon as they are golden brown!

KICK IN THE PANTS RANCH

1 cup milk

1 cup mayonnaise

1 packet ranch dressing mix

2 tablespoons horseradish (or more depending on your palate)

1 teaspoon coarsely ground black pepper

Pinch of cayenne pepper

One at a time take a shark egg out and gently place into the oil. Make sure to maintain heat above 325°F as you fry. One egg takes about 5 minutes and should come to a beautiful golden brown. Once you think you've got a handle on frying one at a time, you can add one more to the hot oil. I never fry more than two at a time because they cool down the temperature of the oil, making the shark eggs greasy.

Finish off the remaining shark eggs and serve hot with lots of freshly squeezed lemon and ranch dressing.

Once you think you've got a handle on frying one at a time, you can add one more to the hot oil. I never fry more than two at a time because they cool down the temperature of the oil, making the shark eggs greasy.

Finish off the remaining shark eggs and serve hot with lots of freshly squeezed lemon and ranch dressing.

PRO TIP

THE EASIEST WAY TO SPLIT AND CLEAN A JALAPEÑO: I was working the line during cooking school at a classy restaurant in Arizona when I saw a chef that I highly respected using a sharp paring knife to surgically remove the ribs and seeds from jalapeños before stuffing them. Delighted, I taught him this trick from back home that I had seen my grandparents do forever. Let's not overthink it. Stuffin' peppers is a country thing.

Wash the jalapeños, then on a cutting board with a sharp knife split the jalapeño from the top of the pepper to the bottom, where it points, by dragging your knife in a downward motion. You may choose to leave on the stem or slice it off (that's really up to you).

Using a small spoon or even a strong metal measuring spoon (look for one with a sharp edge), put the halved jalapeños in a bowl and over the sink, under cold running water, use the sharp edge of the spoon to scrape out the ribs and seeds. Repeat with all the peppers and wash the seeds and ribs down the drain. Wash your hands with soap thoroughly before touching your eyes, face, dog, or toddler.

Lonestar Christmas

FORGET HAM. FRUITCAKE CAN STAY IN ITS CAN. Prime rib is delicious but not essential. In Texas, we do tamales. Food should be shaped by culture, region, personal experience, and influence, and in Texas we have embraced this Mexican tradition as a staple of our own family gatherings. The corn *masa*-and-meat bundles—individually wrapped in corn husks and then steamed—are part of the traditional Mexican celebration of *las posadas*, which commemorates Mary and Joseph's search for shelter before the birth of Jesus.

This tradition is about more than eating—as most things connected to food are. The time-consuming and labor-intensive act of making tamales is also a chance for us to reconnect with each other, resolve conflict, gossip, and generally come together as a family before the food is even served. While the rest of the country prepares stuffing and gravy and an assortment of mince pies, we're assembly line–style creating tamales from scratch.

But it goes beyond tamales in Texas. In this section you will get a taste of a true Lonestar Christmas, and how that represents the diverse culture of this state and the incredible flavors we hold dearest. Because that is what Christmas is for, really, to celebrate what is dear and precious, the priceless gifts we are given as family, as friends, and as human beings.

TEXAS CHRISTMAS CHILI
WITH MEXICAN COKE

LIKE GUACAMOLE, CHILI IS A DISH WITH MANY VARIATIONS attuned to the purpose or celebration for which it was created. At Christmas, we make red and green chili. The red chili is usually cooked mild so that it can be eaten by the bowlful, topped with Fritos, cheese, and onions, and served to three-year-olds in boots and Santa hats. It is very different from the rich and often spicy chili gravy or chile con carne that you may associate with Tex-Mex. This chili is big on flavor but mild on spice and spiked with a little Mexican Coke (imported from Mexico and found in taquerias and Mexican markets) for sweetness. If it's not going to be served on tamales, I even recommend tossing in a can of ranch-style beans. If anyone gives you grief about that, you tell them to come talk to me. It's Jesus's birthday, if you want beans in your chili, you can have beans. **YIELD: SERVES 8-12**

2 pounds 85/15 ground beef, chili grind preferred

1 teaspoon salt

1 onion, small dice

3 large garlic cloves, pressed through a garlic press

1 poblano pepper, diced

2 Anaheim peppers, diced

3 tablespoons tomato paste

1 can stewed tomatoes

1 can diced tomatoes

3 tablespoons Mexene or Gebhardt Chili Powder

1 1/2 teaspoons salt

2 teaspoons cumin

Have the onion, peppers, and garlic ready to add to the pot. In a large, heavy-bottomed stockpot, place the ground beef and heat over high heat. Sprinkle with 1 teaspoon salt. Brown the meat well and add the onion and garlic. Cook for 2 minutes and add the peppers. Cook for 4 minutes.

Add the tomato paste and incorporate into the mixture. Add the stewed and diced tomatoes, breaking up any large chunks with your spatula.

Add all of the spices and the Mexican Coke. Cook down until the Coke is nearly gone.

Add the beef stock and simmer for 15–25 minutes. Add the beans now if you are using them.

To finish, add the tomato puree and the last measure of salt to taste.

Simmer as long as desired. Serve when ready, or chill overnight to develop the flavors. Top with the cheese, Fritos, Tabasco, and onion as desired.

1 tablespoon paprika

1 teaspoon granulated onion

1 teaspoon black pepper

2 teaspoons Mexican oregano

1 cup Mexican Coke

1 quart beef stock

Optional: can of ranch-style beans or kidney beans

TO FINISH:

1 cup tomato puree

2 teaspoons salt, to taste

TOPPINGS:

Medium sharp cheddar cheese grated from the block on the fine grate of the cheese grater

Fritos

Green Tabasco for the adults

Finely diced white onion

FOR MAXIMUM FLAVOR and ease, prepare this the night before your Christmas Eve bash.

CREAM CHEESE AND GREEN CHILE TAMALES

WHEN MY TRIBE GOT TOGETHER to make this recipe for the first time, there were a few skeptics in the bunch. They didn't like the idea of a veggie in a tamale. They weren't sure the cream cheese was a good idea. They didn't think the classic could ever be improved upon. And while I agreed that a classic pork tamale never goes out of style, I insisted they trust me. When the tamales came out of the steamer and my wary best friends grabbed a fork from the kitchen drawer, their doubts were quickly dispelled. This buttery, decadently roasted, cream-filled tamale quickly became a new tribe favorite. We love to gather together to make and enjoy, sharing stories but never sharing helpings!
YIELD: ABOUT 24 TAMALES

Package of corn husks for tamale preparation

FILLING

3 poblano peppers

1 pound cream cheese

1 teaspoon salt

MASA

1 cup lard

3 cups instant masa harina

1 1/2 teaspoons kosher salt

1 1/2 teaspoons baking powder

1/2 cup butter, melted

2 cups broth

You will also need: scissors, 2–3 ziplock baggies, kitchen twine (optional but helpful), tribe of friends or family, elevated steamer rack that fits into your stockpot with lid.

Begin by soaking the corn husks in a large bowl of hot water. You can add another bowl on top to help hold them submerged underwater.

FOR THE FILLING: Roast the poblano peppers (as seen in the "Urban Cowgirl Cooking School" chapter) and remove the skins and seeds. Place into a food processor with the cream cheese and salt. Blend well and set aside.

FOR THE MASA: Using a stand mixer or beaters, beat the lard until fluffy and whipped, about 2–3 minutes. Place the masa into a large bowl with the salt and baking powder. Mix well. Stir the melted butter into the broth and mash it into the masa with your hands, mixing well. Add the lard a little at a time to the masa, beating it well and keeping it fluffy and light. Taste the masa to make sure it is pleasantly seasoned. Add more salt if necessary.

TO MAKE THE TAMALES: Organize your tamale station with soaked corn husks, scissors for trimming the husks if necessary, spoons and spatulas, filling, masa, and two ziplock baggies per tamale maker.

Place a corn husk in front of you with the longest side running top to bottom. In the right-hand corner place about 2–3 tablespoons of the masa mixture with a spoon. Taking the ziplock baggie, press down on the masa and spread it out thin with your

fingertips. You want to get it ¹/₄–¹/₈ inch thick, about 4–5 inches long, and 5–6 inches wide. Put any excess back into the masa bowl. Remove the ziplock baggie from the masa base and place 1–2 tablespoons of filling in a line on the bottom third of the masa base. Start rolling the tamale up, and when you get halfway, tuck the tail of the corn husk in, then continue rolling up.

For videos of tamale making, check out my YouTube channel.

When you have six tamales done, you may choose to tie them all with kitchen twine in little bundles. This helps keep them standing up straight in the pot during cooking. Just make sure all the tail sides are down and all the open sides are up. Tie them into a bundle securely.

Repeat with the remaining tamales.

TO COOK THE TAMALES: In a tall-sided stockpot place an elevated steamer rack/tray. Pour water in so that it reaches just below the tray or rack.

Place the bundles of tamales into the stockpot with their open sides facing up and standing upright. You can use a small bowl to hold the tamales upright if you are not steaming enough tamales to fill the entire stockpot. Steam the tamales 40–60 minutes on a low, gentle steam.

Serve tamales in the husk. The person eating the tamale can unravel it as he or she wishes. Tamales are served with hot sauce and various condiments as well as chili (red and green), tomatillo sauce, or ranchero sauce. Take your pick!

PRO TIP

I MAKE OUR TAMALES WITH A HEALTHY HELPING OF BUTTER!

It's my secret ingredient!

GREEN CHILI WITH CHIMAYO BROWN SUGAR PORK

WHEN IT'S CHRISTMAS TIME, Urban Cowgirls really go the extra mile to make it special. That's why in our house Christmas Eve is probably the only night you will find red *and* green chili on the stove! And it *is* the green chili that makes the evening so special—green chili is made with tomatillos and green chiles to create a translucent, light green gravy. Traditionally I think most people would expect green chili to be made from chicken, but we love tender morsels of succulent brown sugar pork. It's the perfect complement to our Cream Cheese and Green Chile Tamales or for rolling up into a hot, buttery tortilla. I call the rub that I use on the pork in this green chili my Exotic Pork Rub. My husband doesn't understand what is so exotic about it—but cinnamon, Mexican oregano, and semi-rare red chile powder from our last vacation is anything but mundane. He shrugs, says, "meh," and walks away. Chef husbands are spoiled rotten! But I think you will love it. **YIELD: SERVES 8–12**

3–4-pound pork loin

Butter and oil, for frying

SARAH'S EXOTIC PORK RUB

$^1/_2$ cup brown sugar

2 tablespoons cumin

$^1/_4$ cup paprika

1 tablespoon Mexican oregano

1$^1/_2$ tablespoons granulated onion

2 teaspoons salt (more salt will be added by the batch as the pork is seared)

$^1/_2$–2 teaspoons cayenne pepper (use $^1/_2$ teaspoon for kids, more for adult company)

1 tablespoon black pepper

On a cutting board dice the pork loin into $^1/_4$-inch cubes and place into a large bowl. In a small bowl combine all of the ingredients for the exotic pork rub. Pour 3 tablespoons of oil into the rub, stir well and pour over the diced pork. Mix well. Marinate while you prepare the sauce or overnight.

In a heavy cast-iron dutch oven or skillet, fry the pork in small batches so that it sears well. Add more oil or butter as needed (about a 1 tablespoon butter to 1 tablespoon oil ratio). Liberally salt each batch with kosher salt right when you put it into the pan so that the salt cooks into the pork and enhances the flavors. Sear each batch of pork and transfer with a slotted spoon onto a baking rack over a cookie sheet. Let the oil drain off and reserve.

FOR THE SAUCE: In a saucepan heat the oil on medium to high heat and add the onion. Dice the Anaheim and jalapeño peppers (remove the stem but leave in the seeds). Add to the pot. Cut the poblano open and remove the seeds and stem, rough chop it, and add to the pot. Cook for several minutes. Dehusk the tomatillos, wash them, and rough chop. You can leave the stem on the tomatillo; it's fleshy like the rest of the body. Add the tomatillos

½ teaspoon good-quality, strong cinnamon

2 tablespoons New Mexico chile powder (see the "Urban Cowgirl Ingredients" chapter; I use chimayo powder, but any mild powdered chile will work)

3 tablespoons oil, for marinating the pork with the seasonings

FOR THE TOMATILLO CHILE SAUCE:

2 tablespoons oil

1½ cups diced white onion

2 Anaheim peppers

2 jalapeño peppers

1 poblano pepper

15 medium- to large-size tomatillos

1 teaspoon salt

3 large garlic cloves

1 quart chicken stock

1 teaspoon salt

Juice of 1 lemon

Freshly chopped cilantro, Mexican crema, Cotija cheese, for garnish

and salt to the pot and sweat the vegetables an additional 5–8 minutes, turning down the heat if necessary.

Rough chop the garlic cloves and add them in. Cook 30 seconds and add in the chicken stock. Bring to a boil and then turn the heat down to a rapid simmer. Reduce the mixture by half.

Prepare your blender or food processor. When the mixture has reduced, ladle it into the blender and blend about 20 seconds or until pureed. Pour the puree back into the pot and add the seared, drained pork chunks. Bring to a simmer. Add 1 teaspoon salt and the juice of one lemon to taste. Taste for seasoning. The pork can cook another 30 minutes–1½ hours. It will fall apart the more it simmers. Garnish with freshly chopped cilantro, Mexican crema, or Cotija cheese.

This chili is one of those divine dishes that can be served by the bowl, inside fresh corn tortillas, or topping tamales. I have a feeling that after you make it, you'll develop your own ideas.

PRO TIP

FREEZING MEATS SLIGHTLY before cutting into small cubes or thin slices makes the process easier.

Competition Cookin' Teams

LONE STAR ATTITUDE. IT'S A REAL THING. It makes us fighters, resilient, steadfast, occasionally cocky, but always down for a high noon showdown. It's in our blood. Show up for a Southern cook-off, church potluck, or innocent PTA chili night and you'll see this is not a strictly Texan phenomenon.

I have competed in oodles of competition cook-offs and the feeling is addictive. Urban Cowgirls love to compete, throw shade, build alliances, and ultimately arise as the best. We're still a posse of Wild West gunslingers—only now the battle is decidedly delicious.

CHICKEN AND JALAPEÑO CHEDDAR SAUSAGE GUMBO

LOUISIANA IS THE GUMBO CAPITAL OF THE WORLD. On the map, compared to Texas, it may look small, but it's really just concentrated. The state packs a rich culinary history and numerous contributions to true American cuisine, while maintaining its individuality and unique antebellum spirit. They also love a good throwdown.

East Texas and the Gulf Coast harbor a unique fusion of food and lifestyle. It is here that two great cultures collide in cowboys boots and bikini tops under Spanish moss–draped tree, where little bayous blur our borders and our friendships create new traditions. Toto, we're not in Kansas anymore.

You've entered Texianna.

Southern coastal living is intoxicating. When I lived there, I plunged myself into a world of feisty cook-offs, buckets of juicy buttered clams, plump grilled oysters topped with pico de gallo, and succulent Creole sauces. The girls and I fully surrendered to the experience one evening on the Galveston Pier, fueled on invigorating sea air, fishin' poles, and crispy shrimp po' boy.

We were ready to join the world of competitive cooking, and on that starry night our team was born. As huge fans of the HBO series *True Blood*, my band of food fighters, without much debate, named ourselves Merlotte's Vampire Gumbo. It was the beginning of a rowdy, new chapter of our sisterhood.

Our first go-round, we won a coveted trophy and bragging rights!

Our competition gumbo is a celebration of what we were feeling on the pier that day, an appreciation for the regions that soften us, blending us in spirit. This gumbo is rich and classic Louisiana gumbo, spiked with a healthy helping of Lone Star attitude in our jalapeño cheddar sausage. We serve it with a cold scoop of potato salad instead of rice, 'cause *that's how we was raised.* **YIELD: SERVES 10**

TEXAS TRINITY

The trinity" is the name Louisianans have given to their favorite blend of veggies that appear over and over again throughout Cajun and Creole cookin'. The Louisiana trinity is 50 percent onion, 25 percent celery, and 25 percent green bell peppers (with a healthy dose of garlic!). I call this blend the Texas Trinity because it also includes a poblano pepper for a spicy Southwestern twist.

3/4 cup oil

1 chicken, skin on, cut into pieces, or 8 bone-in, skin-on thighs

Creole seasoning salt

1/2 cup flour, for dusting

1 medium white onion, medium dice

4 stalks celery, medium dice

1 green bell pepper, medium dice

1 poblano pepper, deseeded and medium dice

4–5 garlic cloves, pressed through a garlic press

1 cup flour

2 tablespoons minced fresh thyme leaves

1 tablespoon freshly cracked black pepper

1–2 tablespoons Creole seasoning salt

2 quarts good-quality boxed chicken stock (room temperature or warmed)

1 (12-ounce) package green chile and cheddar sausage

2 tablespoons green Tabasco sauce

1 quart Houston Rodeo Blue-Ribbon Potato Salad, for topping (see page 260 for recipe)

1 bunch green onions, chopped

Begin heating your gumbo pot (a heavy-bottomed pot with a lid) on medium-high heat with 1/4 cup of the oil. Season the chicken pieces with Creole salt and dust every piece of chicken in flour. Fry the chicken on all sides until golden brown. The insides will be completely raw and that is fine. We will add them back to the pot later. Remove the chicken to a holding plate, and when all the chicken has been fried, transfer the plate to the refrigerator.

Meanwhile, gather all the chopped "trinity veggies" (onion, celery, green bell pepper, poblano pepper, and garlic). Keep the veggies close by when you're making the roux, so that when it hits the right color you can add them quickly.

To make the roux, once you have removed the chicken from the pan you should have about ¼ cup oil in the pan. Add another ½ cup to reach ¾ cup oil. Add in 1 cup flour and whisk well. Turn on the heat where you feel most comfortable, anywhere between low-medium to medium-high, and begin stirring with a silicone spatula. Soon you will smell the nutty aroma of simmering roux. It will gradually smell more robust and intense as it becomes darker.

This process can take 30–50 minutes depending on your pot and the experience of the roux maker. I take the roux for this gumbo to a "copper penny" color. I cook the roux hot and quickly to a tan color and then slow the process down by lowering the heat and stirring patiently as the roux goes from brown to red-brown.

When the roux hits a dark red-brown shade, it is time to stir in the trinity! Swiftly pour in half the vegetables and watch as the roux goes dark brown and tightens up. Stir briskly with the spatula, add the rest of the veggies, and stir for 5 minutes on low. Add the thyme, black pepper, and 1 tablespoon Creole seasoning salt.

After the veggies have softened, switch back to the whisk and add the chicken stock slowly and in small increments. Whisk well until it is all incorporated. Turn the heat back up to medium-high and add the reserved fried chicken back to the pot. Cover the pot and bring to a very low simmer for 1–2 hours, stirring as needed to prevent the bottom from burning.

At this point you can let the gumbo stew all day if you like. I like to stew it until the chicken is falling off the bone. At that point you can remove the chicken, cool slightly, and debone and pull the meat. Add the pulled chicken back to the pot and discard the bones.

Dice the sausage into ¼-inch coins and pan-fry it in another small skillet. It seldom needs oil because the sausage will release fat as it cooks. When the sausage is seared, add it to the gumbo pot or, to keep it crispy, add it to the top of individual bowls of gumbo.

Finish with 1–2 tablespoons green Tabasco to brighten the dish, and additional Creole salt if needed.

I serve my gumbo in a large bowl topped with chilled creamy mustard potato salad and sliced green onions with extra green Tabasco! For the rice lovers this may seem totally bananas, but in cooking the contrast in temperatures and flavors is often what makes the experience jump off the plate! The hot, rich, and spicy gumbo is completely opposite of the light, airy, cold, and creamy potato salad; therefore they *enhance* each other and the entire experience!

PRO TIP

YOU CAN MIX UP THE OILS IN THE ROUX with bacon grease, clarified butter, oil, or a combination. We always try to use some bacon grease at competition for the rich flavor!

HOW TO MAKE A ROUX (ROO):

HOW TO MAKE A ROUX (ROO): A roux, which is equal parts flour and oil or butter, is the basis for many classic French sauces. Flour is cooked in fat and when added to liquid (stock, milk, etc.) and simmered, the starch molecules absorb water and swell, thickening the sauce. This is all great until you hit the colorful, eclectic tapestry of cultures that have created the cuisine of Louisiana! The brown roux of the Cajun and Creole heritage are not included to thicken a sauce per se, but to flavor a dish with intense savory richness. A brown roux is trickier to make, and success is a combination of patience and practice. The oil and flour are combined as in any other roux, but the mixture can be stirred and cooked up to an hour and a half as the roux reaches the desired color—from peanut butter brown to red-brown to intensely dark brown. All the shades of the roux rainbow impart subtly different flavor profiles, from toasted and full-bodied to nutty, rich, and stout.

COZY FIREPLACE CHAT

SOME TIPS TO HELP YOU TO ROUX MASTERY:

• Buy a gumbo pot! While many Cajun cooks swear by ordinary cast-iron skillets, I began to see consistent success after purchasing a fancy enameled cast-iron dutch oven. It holds and distributes heat so well, and so evenly, that I have yet to burn another roux. It is also convenient to cook the roux directly in the pot I will make my gumbo in.

• Switch from whisk to silicone spatula after the flour has incorporated into the oil. Stir it frequently and don't walk away. There is a reason native Louisianans share recipes by stating phrases like "make yourself a one-beer roux" or a "two-beer roux." They are referring to how many drinks they consumed while stirring the roux to the correct shade of brown! They bring their drink right into the kitchen and babysit that roux!

• Turn down the heat when it reaches the color of peanut butter. When the roux begins to resemble the shade of peanut butter, turn the heat down to low-medium. The darker you take the roux, the lower you should go to avoid burning it.

• It's always good to have a roux buddy! Someone to stand and talk to while you stir and with whom you can entrust the stirrin' if you need a quick break.

HOUSTON RODEO BLUE-RIBBON POTATO SALAD

THIS IS BY FAR THE MOST POPULAR RECIPE on the Urban Cowgirl blog, and I think that's because people just trust a blue-ribbon winner! The secret to potato salad is getting the dressing perfectly right and then adding as much dressing as it takes to make the salad moist and exploding with flavor. With this in mind, I have given you my secret dressing recipe separately so that you can make as much as you need and personalize the potato salad for your own little tribe! **YIELD: SERVES 8-10**

SECRET DRESSING

1 cup mayonnaise

2 tablespoons red wine vinegar

1 teaspoon sugar

A pinch of salt, to taste

1/2 cup white onion, minced

POTATO SALAD

4 large russets for fluffy potato salad or 5 large red potatoes for cubed potato salad

Salt and pepper, to taste

2 tablespoons red wine vinegar

1 red bell pepper

1 cup from a bag of julienned carrot sticks or 2 carrots, julienned

For perfect potato salad dressing, whisk together the mayonnaise, red wine vinegar, sugar, and salt (to taste) in a small bowl. Add the white onion and chill while you prepare the rest of the ingredients.

If you have chosen russets, peel the potatoes and discard the peels in the garbage. If you prefer the waxy red potatoes, you may leave the skins on.

Cook the potatoes in a covered glass bowl in the microwave with a little bit of water for about 6 minutes. Allow the potatoes to steam an additional 2–3 minutes. Test the potatoes to make sure they are fork tender all the way through. When they are cooked through, allow them to cool and then dice into bite-size chunks (about 1/2-inch cubes). Salt and pepper the potatoes well and sprinkle them with 2 tablespoons red wine vinegar. Let the potatoes marinate while you work on the other veggies.

On a cutting board, julienne slices of the red bell pepper to about the size of matchsticks. Then cut the sticks into thirds and place into a bowl. Add the carrots to the bowl. Chop the celery

PRO TIP

IF YOU USE REDS, THE POTATOES will stay in firm cubes; if you use russets, you will have potato salad that resembles mashed potatoes. It's personal preference, and this recipe works perfect for either style!

1 stalk celery

¹⁄₄ cup minced fresh chives

2 tablespoons minced fresh parsley

Optional: 2 hard-boiled eggs

1 teaspoon Dijon or yellow mustard

Dash of celery seed

into small dice and add to the bowl along with the chives and parsley. Chop the eggs (if using) and add them to the bowl.

Combine the potatoes with the chopped veggies and pour the chilled dressing mixture over everything. Add in the mustard and a couple shakes of celery seed if desired. Season to taste.

Chill 2 hours or overnight. It should be flavorful when you first make it, but the magic of this dish is letting those flavors combine in the refrigerator. The next morning dishes like potato salad are peaking in flavor as opposed to when they are just made. Garnish with additional minced fresh parsley or chives for a beautiful presentation.

PRO TIP

I LIKE A REALLY WET POTATO SALAD. If you do too, you will want to make as much of the dressing as necessary to get the potatoes filled with moisture. This recipe is perfect for waxy red potatoes, but russets absorb so much liquid that you may want to make a double batch of the dressing in case you need a little extra sauce.

ODE TO THE COBBLER QUEEN

JUDGING COMPETITION COOKING IS NEARLY AS FUN AS COMPETING, but the real fun happens after the judging is over and you're free to pull out a pencil and scratch some notes about your favorite contenders. I've never met a nicer food fighter than a little lady I like to call the Cobbler Queen. The night of her competition, I ate so much of her cobbler that I practically needed to be wheeled away in a wheelbarrow. Although her filling was a simple canned pie filling (which we will get to in a hot second), her cobbler topping was a true religious experience.

Her secret was even more staggering: boxed cake mix and butter. As she explained her simple procedure to me, I began to consider the many cobbler toppings I have loved and hated throughout my life. Some are dry and flavorless, others are cornbread-like, and still others are buttery-crispy-good, but don't really enhance the fruit. This cobbler topping was delect-a-moondo. Because the cake batter topping lacks the moisture necessary to rise and become fluffy, it absorbs the butter and caramelizes into a golden-brown, crunchy topping. Dare I say a bit similar to the crunchy topping on crème brûlée? *Yum.*

The cake batter beneath the crust tends to absorb the fruit juices and turns to soft cake. Do you see where this is going? It's heaven!

Let's get cobblin', y'all. **YIELD: 4-6 SERVINGS**

---

1 pound fresh or frozen fruit, washed and chopped
(This will be different for every fruit—strawberries are halved or quartered, apples are cored and cut into spears, cherries are pitted, and frozen fruit is fully ready from the bag.)

1/8 teaspoon salt
(basically a pinch)

1/8 teaspoon vanilla extract

Squeeze of lemon

2 teaspoons powdered sugar

1 cup yellow or white cake mix

6 tablespoons salted butter

Preheat the oven to 375°F.

In an 8 x 8-inch glass casserole dish or similar-size glass pie pan, spread the fruit and add the pinch of salt over it. Add the vanilla extract and lemon juice. Sprinkle with powdered sugar. Done. Faster than finding a can opener and you don't really have to measure any of this exactly. Just eyeball it and give it a stir.

Over the fruit, sprinkle a cup of dry cake mix and dot all over with butter.

Bake for 45–50 minutes, or until the top of the cobbler becomes golden brown and crisp.

Serve with ice cream. This recipe can be doubled for a standard glass casserole dish of cobbler, and additional fruit can be added for a heartier fruit filling.

PRO TIP

AS FAR AS CANNED PIE FILLINGS GO, I am not their biggest fan. I have a low goo tolerance. If you have easy access to pre-chopped frozen fruit, I would argue that canned pie filling isn't even that legitimate of a convenience product. After reading my cobbler-filling technique, you will no longer need a recipe, just a pound of your favorite fresh or frozen fruit and the Cobbler Queen's cake topping.

Barbecue

THE MOST ROMANTIC GIFT MY HUSBAND EVER BOUGHT me for Valentine's Day was a barbecue. I would rather have that than diamonds and rubies and one hundred red roses. Give me a barbecue over a spa day any day!

The tradition of barbecuing in Urban Cowgirl Country is so important that it feels like it's part of our collective DNA. We celebrate major life milestones and holidays with smoked meat. In spring we trim our trees and set aside the wood knowing it will get used or bartered as a form of barbecue currency. I can name all the local trees, not because I'm an arbor enthusiast, but because I keep my eye out for my favorite barbecue woods to flavor my meat. And don't think I'm above pulling over on the side of the road and liberating a fallen hickory branch from the culvert.

Brisket or sausage, brown sugar or Dalmatian rub, wood or electric—we can discuss our particular favorites all day long. As long as we're discussing barbecue, the Urban Cowgirls are in.

COCONUT COWGIRL MARGARITAS

WHEN MY TRIBE AND I MAKE THESE MARGARITAS, we enter *Fried Green Tomatoes* and *Divine Secrets of the Ya-Ya Sisterhood* territory. These are for afternoons surrounded by the people you love best, eating the food of your ancestors (in my case, that means barbecue), and chewing on tall tales and local legends. This is fellowship juice. **YIELD: 1 MARGARITA**

1/2 cup sweetened shredded coconut

1/4 cup Coco Lopez (available in cans in the mixer section of the grocery store)

3 ounces tequila blanco

2 ounces freshly squeezed lime juice (about 4 small limes)

1 teaspoon Grand Marnier

Pinch of salt

Ice

A small plate of Coco Lopez, for dipping the rims of glasses

FOR THE TOASTED COCONUT RIMS: Preheat the oven to 325°F.

On a baking sheet lined with foil or parchment, spread out a thin layer of shredded coconut. Bake 5–10 minutes, just until the coconut begins to turn very light golden brown. Watch the coconut closely, as this happens rapidly. Pour the toasted coconut onto a small plate for rimming the glasses.

FOR THE MARGARITA: Open the can of Coco Lopez and you will see the coconut butter and coconut liquid. For this recipe use the liquid and reserve the coconut butter for another purpose.

In a cocktail shaker, pour in the tequila blanco, fresh lime juice, 1/4 cup Coco Lopez (liquid only), grand marnier, and a pinch of salt. Pour in a cup of ice and close the lid. Shake for a full 30 seconds, breaking up the ice well into the mixture.

Take a martini glass and roll the edges in the saucer of Coco Lopez and then in the toasted coconut.

Remove the lid from the shaker and place the strainer over the shaker. Strain the margarita into the glass and enjoy.

A SMOKIN' HOT VALENTINE'S DAY

SOMETIMES THE GREATEST GIFTS are more about the gesture than the cost. I learned this valuable lesson on a chilly February morning that will forever be imprinted in my mind.

I was sipping fresh coffee and listening to the fire crackle in the fireplace while nursing my chunky and cheerful four-month-old Micah under a periwinkle quilt when my husband suddenly burst through the front door grinning ear to ear.

"Happy Valentine's!" he exclaimed, startling our other son, who was playing blocks near the hearth.

"Happy Valentine's," I replied, clearly a little touchy and disappointed that with two little babies and no grandmas nearby we wouldn't exactly be having the romantic, champagne-and-chocolate-fueled date night that I had looked forward to every year. Dereck was working. A lot. I was missing him, but also missing our former life, my former self. I was far from the girl who wore expensive dresses and ran a successful business, who felt relevant. Who made a footprint on the world, however small that foot might be.

Now don't get me wrong: I wanted to be a mother more than anything I have ever wanted in my life. But you experience a culture shock when you realize that you are stepping into a completely different role. It can create a little identity crisis.

And it's forever. It's worth it, but it certainly takes some time to adjust to the gargantuan commitment of motherhood and the abrupt sting of sacrificing your independence.

"I have something for you." Dereck smiled, scooping up our oldest and nuzzling him with Eskimo kisses.

My hopes lifted. I stood up with the baby, giving Dereck my hand to let him lead me out the door and into the garage.

Inside was an oversize cardboard box topped with a pink bow. Not what I was expecting.

It took a moment for me to realize what it was, and then my heart melted into my shoes.

"Is that an electric smoker?"

He beamed. Not a traditionally romantic gift, but it showed me that even with all the changes in our life together, one thing was certain: I was still me. Though my days of working the line until 2 a.m. were over, my days of experimenting in my kitchen with two little chef taste testers had just begun. And that new chapter was going to be a great one.

It was the best gift my husband could have given me.

SMOKED STRAWBERRY BARBECUE CHICKEN

A HOT-AND-SWEET BARBECUE CHICKEN, perfect for your Valentine. **YIELD: UP TO 20 PIECES OF CHICKEN**

1 (12-ounce) bottle of Frank's Red Hot

1 cup favorite barbecue sauce (preferably original or bold style, not sweet)

10–20 pieces of bone-in chicken thighs, legs, or wings (as much as you would like to barbecue)

1 tablespoon black pepper

$1/3$ cup strawberry jam

Pinch of salt

Combine the Frank's Red Hot and barbecue sauce in a large bowl or glass dish, remove a $1/2$ cup for the glaze, and reserve. Place the chicken in the bowl, turn to coat, and marinate 6–24 hours in the refrigerator.

Prepare your smoker and bring the temperature up to about 275–300°F. For this recipe I prefer pecan or hickory wood, but you can use whatever you like.

Place the chicken on the rack spaced out enough that no piece of chicken touches another piece.

If you have a water chamber or water pan, you can fill that with water or diluted apple juice.

Smoke the meat $2^{1}/_{2}$–3 hours. Keep the smoke heavy for the first hour to infuse the chicken with smoky flavor. Toward the last half hour of cooking, stir reserved sauce together with black pepper, strawberry jam, and salt in a small bowl. Microwave the bowl in 30-second increments until the sauce is well blended. Brush the glaze onto the chicken and then close the smoker chamber to allow the sauce to caramelize onto the skin. Repeat if desired for a thicker coating of sauce. Remove the chicken, let rest 10 minutes, and serve as desired.

CANTALOUPE AVOCADO SALAD
IN HONEY LIME DRESSING

THIS IS HEALTHY INDULGENCE IN A BOWL. You may be asking yourself, *How could that even be possible?* Avocados always feel like cheating, regardless of how many studies are published touting their health benefits. They are simply too delicious. Add in the sweetness of cantaloupe, a tang of salt and lime, and you have yourself a side dish you'll quickly run out of. **YIELD: 4–6 SERVINGS**

1 cantaloupe

3 avocados

1/4 cup minced chives

Juice of 3 limes

3 tablespoons honey

1/2 teaspoon kosher salt

On a cutting board with a sharp knife, slice both ends of the cantaloupe so you can stand it up lengthways. Starting at the top of the cantaloupe, slice downward, slicing the peel off in thin, brisk movements from top to bottom. Turn the melon clockwise and continue slicing the peel off until the cantaloupe is peeled.

Discard the peels and cut the melon in half. Using a spoon, deseed the melon and discard the seeds. Slice both halves of the melon lengthways into spears and then cut the spears into bite-size chunks. Place all the cantaloupe chunks into a large salad bowl.

Open the avocados as described in the "Urban Cowgirl Cooking School" chapter and dice into small chunks. Add to the bowl along with the minced chives.

Into a small bowl juice the three limes and add the honey and salt; whisk well until combined. Pour over the cantaloupe and avocado pieces, toss well, and serve immediately or chill and marinate for 1 hour.

The Southern Harvest

MY GREAT-GRANDMA VELMA SMITH was one of those special family characters whose stories creep closer to the edge of a local tall tale with each retelling. Like the tales of Annie Oakley or Sacagawea, I pictured her as a gun-toting wilderness woman, gritty and hard as nails. She was blessed with wild black hair and donned real cowgirl attire, and I imagined her perched on horseback atop bluebonnet-covered hills, peering down upon the farming settlement of Lloyd, Texas. Everyone in my family swore she had Native American ancestry and pointed to her coal-black hair as the proof, something I have yet to find any evidence of and suspect was added to her story somewhere along the way.

Despite the folklore, to me she was simply the little granny who made me cheese toast. I was about two years old when she died. The only thing I can remember was her blue nightgown and the little snacks we shared. So you can picture my complete and total astonishment the day someone told me that she was a chef. I was stunned.

She was certainly not a chef in today's sense of the word, but rather a farmer, restaurateur, and the head cook of every kitchen she came across, which is essentially what any of us who call ourselves chefs these days hope to achieve. I suddenly felt closer to this larger-than-life matriarch who was slowly transforming into the image of a devoted mother, a dedicated cook, and an early Texan who didn't seem at all different from myself.

In 1938 my great-grandmother Velma—the town's great cook—set up the first school lunch at the New Hope Grade School. The school was a wooden structure about the size of a two-car garage, with one potbelly stove they filled with firewood to keep the children warm in winter. This was in the early beginnings of the school lunch concept, and my grandmother remembers her mother dotingly teaching the children to help cook the food. Some of them enjoyed it more than the academic lessons, a tendency I can relate to.

At home, Velma and my great-grandfather, Roy, kept a truck patch, a garden planted with the intention of canning a great deal of food for the winter. They canned 400–600 jars of every vegetable you can imagine for my family and their best friends, the Conways. Velma made jams and jellies, slaws, and pickles, black-eyed peas, chow-chow, and tomatoes. They kept fresh, homegrown potatoes under the house for the winter. This was during the Great Depression, though my grandmother can't remember ever going hungry on that little Texas homestead.

The Conways' had cattle and hogs, and shared a smokehouse where they would sugar-cure hams and smoke meat. They would shell peas under the live oaks and pecan trees, eat one of her hearty lunches followed by buttermilk pie, and fall asleep on the porch.

Later, as my grandparents' construction business grew prosperous in the thriving town of Denton, they opened the PK Grill, a cafe with carhops, which Velma ran and cooked from. When that took off, they opened the Builder's Supply Café.

"I don't know if we ever made any money," my grandmother explained to me. "We were always trying to feed all of the kids, and cousins, and feed anybody who didn't have the money for a hot meal. We were robbed one night after the cafe was closed and locked up. When we discovered it in the morning we realized the thief had stopped and helped himself to a piece of Velma's chocolate pie! We weren't even mad! We all just laughed!"

"So why did you keep on opening restaurants?" I asked.

"Because it was fun," she smiled.

Velma may have been a family legend, but she was suddenly now more real to me than ever before. She was a real food lover, a lover of the earth and the land, the big blue Texas skies, the smell of tomato plants and fresh beans, the zip of homemade buttermilk dressing, and a cool dip in the creek. Most importantly, she knew she had it within her to do whatever she dreamed. She had gumption. She had swagger. She was an Urban Cowgirl.

In my eyes, the reality of who she really was turned out to be greater than the legend. When I learned the real story—with all my wild imaginings and childish fantasies removed—I realized I was also learning about myself.

The inspiration for this section came from growing up in Texas surrounded by bountiful vegetable and fruit patches. Whether you have a mansion or a one-bedroom apartment with a tiny patio, you can grow your own tomatoes. You'll have a neighbor offering you zucchini plants, and your mom will probably show up on your doorstep looking to get rid of a few of her watermelons come summer. You can always find ways to put that harvest to good use in the Urban Cowgirl kitchen, whether in a homemade sauce, a jar of gourmet baby food, or a sweet blueberry jam.

BABY FOOD

When I had my first son, Gabriel, it never crossed my mind that I would buy premade baby food. As a personal chef, I had already been preparing homemade purees for my clients and their babies. The reaction from my clients was always the same: "Next time, will you make extra baby food? We can't stop eating it!"

While the products sold in jars are perfectly healthy for your babies—even I have used them occasionally when I was busy—it cannot compare to the food you make yourself. This food tastes full of life, and it will also give your baby a better relationship with food from the beginning. When I made Tiny Texans Baby Food on *Food Network Star*, my slogan was "Today's Toddlers are Simply Tomorrow's Foodies." During filming, Bobby Flay said, "My daughter is eighteen, I don't need baby food recipes. But *this* is really cool."

Right now, your baby is developing food habits that will follow him the rest of his life. Start your baby off with a love of real food, so that when he grows up, he won't depart from it.

COZY FIREPLACE CHAT

BABY FOOD GUIDELINES AT A GLANCE: If you receive your fruit and vegetables from a local farmer or family member, make sure they understand that you intend to use this produce for baby food and you need assurance that it is pesticide free and organically grown. Go the extra mile to ensure you're getting the best for your baby!

Before giving your baby any solid food, you should first introduce foods individually, watching for signs of an allergic reaction. The recipes in this section all contain ingredient combinations, and you want to make sure before feeding your Tiny Texan any baby food that he or she is not allergic to any ingredient included in the recipe.

BLACK BEAN AND LIME PUREE

As a private chef, I cook for all types of people. One of them was a new mom whose daughter, Roxanne, was born five days after my first son, Gabriel. Needless to say, we were always sharing our experiences of motherhood together because we were both newbies on a wild ride! When I told her I was making baby food from scratch, she asked if I would make a little for Roxie during the next personal chef service, which I agreed to do.

The day after the chef service, I got a hilarious voicemail: "Hey Sarah, we *love* the baby food; in fact we're going to need more . . . we can't stop eating it."

This is the famous recipe! As a warm and comforting black bean puree, it's perfect for your baby, but with a little extra salt it's totally delicious for Mom and Dad to pop in a tortilla or serve as a healthy alternative to refried beans. **YIELD: 4-5 BABY-SIZED SERVINGS**

$^1/_2$ cup onion, finely minced

$^1/_2$ garlic clove, finely minced

1–2 tablespoons cold-pressed coconut oil or extra-virgin olive oil

Large can of organic black beans, rinsed and drained very well

Organic veggie stock, coconut water, or filtered water, for thinning

1 lime

$^1/_2$ can full-fat organic coconut milk

1 organic red bell pepper

Sweat the onion and garlic in a saucepan with 1–2 tablespoons coconut oil or olive oil, just until translucent.

Add black beans and a bit of stock or water to thin. Cook 5 minutes.

Add mixture to a blender along with the zest of one lime. Cut the lime in half and add a good squirt of the juice (about 1–2 tablespoons). Add the organic coconut milk.

Roast the red bell pepper and add half the pepper to the blender.

Blend, taste, and freeze in tiny BPA-free containers or ice cube trays.

TIP FROM MOM

THE BEST WAY TO store large amounts of premade baby food is freezing in BPA-free ice cube molds, popping them out, and storing them in freezer bags. Press out as much air as possible and sort them according to recipe. Defrost in the microwave, adding breast milk or formula if they are too thick for baby.

SWEET POTATO AND CINNAMON BABY FOOD

SWEET POTATOES ARE ONE OF NATURE'S BEST sources of beta-carotene, are full of antioxidants, and have superior ability to raise vitamin A levels in the blood. This recipe calls for steaming the sweet potato, which preserves the most nutrients for your little boo bear!
YIELD: 4–5 BABY-SIZED SERVINGS

1 sweet potato, skinned and cubed

$1/4$ cup filtered water, organic coconut milk, or breast milk

Pinch of organic cinnamon

In a glass bowl with a lid, place the raw sweet potato cubes in a little filtered water. Place the lid on and microwave steam the potato for 5–8 minutes depending on size. Check to make sure it is cooked through.

Place the sweet potato chunks in a blender with $1/4$ cup organic coconut milk, filtered water, or breast milk. Puree for 30 seconds to a minute, stirring if necessary and adding additional liquid if needed to puree completely smooth. Add a tiny pinch of organic cinnamon and puree thoroughly.

Cool and serve, or freeze in ice cube trays or small BPA-free containers.

CANNING

URBAN COWGIRLS LIVE LOCAL. In downtown Denton, where I was born and raised, we all still crowd into a tiny pink salon tucked in a corner of the Square, complete with little old ladies getting their hair set under the driers and doling out marital advice. This is the place we go to get our dirt, to get our hair done, and, thanks to Tammy, who has been my stylist since I was five years old, it's also the place to learn the art of canning—jams, jellies, pickles—from a local canning queen. Knowing my Urban Cowgirl tribe would be into developing this skillset, Tammy was happy to pass on her knowledge to a future generation.

HOT WATER BATH FOR CANNING

The number one rule for successful canning is keeping your jars hot and clean! Place your prepared canning jars (clean and scalded) in a large canner on the stove filled with hot water. (Keep the water very hot, but not boiling.) Place inside the pot the lids and rings to keep them sterile. Take out one jar at a time and fill it with your jam, jelly, or salsa ingredients. Make sure to follow the recipe precisely for adequate headspace. Usually ½ in is sufficient for the majority of recipes. Wipe the mouth of the jars with a sterile cloth if any food is spilled on the rim of the jar. Place a new sterile lid on each jar to seal off the air. While jars may be reused, you must use new lids each time to preserve the integrity of the sealing compound found along the rim. Add the screw bands and tighten. To process the jars add hot water to the canner until all of the jars are covered by about an inch of water. Place the lid on the canner and bring up to a boil. Begin the processing time when the water comes to a full boil. At the end of processing, remove the jars from the canner and place them on a kitchen towel to cool. Once cool, press a finger upon the lid of each jar. The middle of the lid should not bounce up and down but have a firm vacuumed seal. Any jars that have not been sealed can be refrigerated and consumed but must not be stored in pantry conditions.

TAMMY'S BLUE-RIBBON NECTARINE BLUEBERRY JAM

NECTARINE BLUEBERRY JAM IS SWEET SUMMER DECADENCE, preserved and ready to be sampled all year long. This recipe wins big for the swirls of orange and plum-blue fruit that curl together as the jam sets, reminiscent of a late summer sunset. **YIELD: ABOUT 7 CUPS**

5 cups peeled and sliced nectarines

1 lime, zested and juiced

2 teaspoons butter

1 package Sure-Jell

5 cups sugar

1 pint blueberries, rinsed and coated in sugar

About 7 (8-ounce) jars and lids for canning

Place the nectarines in a medium saucepan and cook on low-medium until tender. Add the lime zest and juice and the butter.

Add the Sure-Jell, following package instructions, then add all the sugar.

When ready to can, place the sugar-coated blueberries into prepared jars (clean and scalded) just to cover the bottom. Ladle in the nectarine mixture. Cook in a hot bath for 5–10 minutes. The color of the blueberries will rise to the top and create a gorgeous jam. Tighten the rims, cool, and store.

PRO TIP

ADDING 1–2 TEASPOONS BUTTER TO ANY JAM recipe will prevent the majority of the frothy foam from getting out of control. If the mixture does not set, you can always add another package of pectin and try again.

PICKLED GREEN BEANS

THESE SASSY LITTLE GREEN BEANS ARE PERFECT with a hot grilled cheese sandwich. Add as many little red chiles as you like if you prefer a hot pickle with creeping heat. **YIELD: 3–4 PINTS**

1$^1/_2$ cups water

1 cup vinegar

1 tablespoon kosher salt

2 tablespoons dill seed

$^1/_2$ tablespoon celery seed

1 tablespoon mustard seed

2 pounds ripe green beans, fresh from a home garden or farmers' market

3 garlic cloves, peeled

3–6 little hot peppers (bird's eye chili, pequin, Fresno, etc.)

Bring the water and vinegar to a boil. Add the salt and dill, celery, and mustard seed.

To each jar add a stack of freshly rinsed green beans packed in tight, 1 garlic clove, and 1–2 peppers. Pour the boiled water mixture over and into each jar to fill.

Put in hot water bath for 20 minutes. Tighten the rims, cool, and store.

PRO TIP

EXPERT CANNERS always stir with a wooden spoon so that the spoon won't overheat and burn your fingers!

TEXAS T MANGO SALSA

THIS SUNSHINE-COLORED SALSA is studded with a small army of bright and cheerful garden chiles. It will turn just about any pan-roasted fish fillet or slab of fajitas into dinner in a hot second! It also takes some time to make properly—so plan ahead. You'll need a couple of days.

YIELD: ABOUT A QUART OF SALSA

12 mangos, peeled and diced

2 limes

1 teaspoon salt

1 bunch cilantro

2 tablespoons oil

2 red bell peppers

2 red onions

3 banana peppers

4 jalapeño peppers

1 habanero pepper

3 garlic cloves

Zest and juice of 2 limes

1 cup vinegar

1/4 cup salt

The night before making the salsa, peel and dice the mangos. (See the "Urban Cowgirl Cooking School" chapter for tips on how to slice mangos.) Soak the mangos in cold water with the juice of two limes and 1 teaspoon salt overnight in the refrigerator.

The next day put the cilantro (stems and leaves) in a food processor with 2 tablespoons oil and process until well blended. Pour into a large stockpot.

Cut the red bell peppers in half, remove the seeds, and rough chop. Chop the onions into wedges. Chop the banana, jalapeño, and habanero peppers into pieces just small enough to fit into the food processor. (Remove the seeds if desired for less heat.)

Place the onions, peppers, and garlic in a food processor and run until finely chopped. Add to the large stockpot.

Drain the mangos that you prepared the night before and add to the pot along with the zest and juice of two limes. Add the vinegar and salt.

Cook over medium heat; as it comes to a boil turn heat to low. Do not overcook.

Follow the instructions for canning on page 284.

PRO TIP

USING A BLEND of hot and sweet peppers gives salsas lots of flavor!

CHRISTMAS JELLY

YOU KNOW IT JUST WOULDN'T BE CHRISTMAS down South without a cracker tray and soft cream cheese topped with this vibrant Christmas jelly. This red and green pepper jelly is sweet and spicy with a little tang from the apple cider vinegar. Serve it with buttery crackers and a slather of cream cheese. I enjoy a chilled glass of chardonnay with this appetizer every year, and it just might be one of my favorite Urban Cowgirl noshes! **YIELD: 2 PINTS**

1 1/2 cups freshly chopped hot peppers, red and green colors (jalapeño, serrano, habanero, Fresno, red bell pepper, etc).

Note: Spicy jelly will include seeds; mild jelly will discard seeds.

5 cups sugar

1 1/2 cups apple cider vinegar

1 (6-ounce) bag liquid pectin

Add the peppers, sugar, and vinegar to a pot and bring to a boil for 3 minutes. Add pectin, stirring constantly. Bring to a rolling boil for 1 full minute.

Can in sterilized jars. Put in a hot water bath for 5 minutes. Let cool on countertop until sealed.

Serve over cream cheese with crackers during the holiday season.

OUR FAMILY MAKES A BATCH OF MILD JELLY for the little ones and a batch of hot jelly for the adults!

HEAVENLY HABANERO ZUCCHINI JELLY

THIS JELLY IS HOTTER THAN A FANCY FOX in a pepper patch! But it's also sweet and wonderfully peculiar given the healthy dose of zucchini. I *would* tell you that you could use this on quiche, hot buttered tortillas, a little dab with your fideo, roasted corn cobs, and even fried chicken tenders, but the Urban Cowgirl tribe vibe is that this stuff could practically make an old boot taste good. It's just fabulous on everything y'all. **YIELD: 3 PINTS**

10 habaneros

5 cups zucchini, with seeds and peels

1 1/2 cups vinegar

7 cups sugar

2 (6-ounce) bags liquid pectin

Place peppers, zucchini, and vinegar in a food processor and blend until smooth. In a large stockpot, combine with sugar and bring to a boil. Lower heat and simmer 20–25 minutes, stirring constantly. Add pectin and bring to a full rolling boil for 1 minute. Remove from heat. Place into sterilized jars with lids. Put in a hot water bath for 10 minutes. Tighten the rims, cool, and store.

COZY FIREPLACE CHAT

CONFIRMING THE GEL: For every canning pectin out there that one family has been using for three generations, there is another angry canner who can't seem to get it to gel. Expert canners say the secret is in the hard boil. In canning, a hard boil is when you have a continuous or rolling boil while stirring. After about a minute of stirring at a hard boil, bring the wooden spoon up to check the thickness of the jelly. You can see when the pectin begins to transform the syrup and gel, because the liquid will drip slower from the spoon instead of a continuous drip.

This method of checking the mixture and *confirming the gel* is what separates the novice from the expert.

VIBRANT CANNED COLESLAW

THIS FANCY LITTLE SAUERKRAUT-CHANNELING COLESLAW is ready to go whenever you are! It's perfectly delicious chilled right out of the refrigerator, or you can add a dab of mayonnaise for a tasty, quick side to sandwiches and burgers. **YIELD: 8–10 SERVINGS**

INGREDIENTS FOR THE BRINE:

1 cup apple cider vinegar

2 cups sugar

1 teaspoon celery seed

1 teaspoon mustard seed

1 head cabbage

1 large carrot

$1/2$ diced onion

1 cup diced celery

2 teaspoons canning salt

Optional: red bell pepper for color and interest, if desired

To make the brine, combine the vinegar, sugar, celery seed, and mustard seed into a pan and bring to a boil for about 1–2 minutes, until sugar is dissolved. Let cool.

Shred cabbage and carrot and mix in a bowl with the onion and celery. Add canning salt and let stand for 1 hour. Rinse and drain the slaw. Add brine to the slaw. (Make an additional batch of the brine syrup to top off the jars if needed.)

Pack in hot pint jars, adding extra brine to fill in. Put in a hot water bath for 15–20 minutes. Tighten the rims, cool, and store.

Apple Cidering and Apple Wine

Drop by my house and I can guarantee you a cool glass of apple wine fresh from my stash any day of the year. My great-grandfather made wine from everything! Strawberries, blackberries, even wild grapes he found growing on our land. That tradition has been passed down to me, and it's one of the most cherished parts of my heritage!

The first time you make wine, it's understandably a little intimidating, but after that first batch you completely understand how you could do this with just about any fruit, or fruit juice. If you've made it this far through this cookbook, let me congratulate you!

You're a card-carrying Urban Cowgirl now. To be fully immersed in this lifestyle, you've *got* to learn Cider Chic!

Apple cider and apple wine are made in exactly the same way, and I include directions for carbonating your wine if you choose to do so.

I'll let you decide what to call it since you're creating your own new brew!

THINGS YOU'LL NEED TO GET STARTED

- StarSan: A common brand of sanitizer. A tiny 4-ounce bottle will do just fine for your first couple of experiments. You can get it online, at the homebrew shop, and at restaurant and bar supply stores. Follow the directions in diluting the concentrate to wash all your tools and jugs. In a pinch you can use bleach, but StarSan is cheap and odorless.

- Five-gallon pail made of food-grade plastic: Clean, never used for any other projects but brewing. It must have a lid with a small hole to place a rubber stopper with bubbler as described below. They also have these at your local brewing shop.

- Rubber stopper and bubbler: While brewing your cider, the yeast has two commands for you.

1. Keep them safe from foreign yeasts floating through the air (which you will accomplish by putting a lid on your pail).

2. Allow them to expel carbon dioxide gas without pushing the lid off.

Yeast expels CO_2 while making alcohol—it's basically like breathing for your yeast friends. If you put a lid on the pail without some form of venting, the yeast will simply create so much gas the lid will pop off, and the open air will risk contaminating your brew. Nature is a force to be reckoned with!

To accomplish both goals, all you need is a bubbler, which is held in place by a rubber stopper.

- A bubbler (aka an airlock) is a little device that looks like a swirly piece of plastic pipe. They also come in a form that looks like a little cup with a hat. Both devices have a plastic shaft that is inserted into a rubber stopper that plugs up the hole in the lid. Now when the yeast expel CO_2 it will go up into the shaft, and as CO_2 builds up, gas is expelled through the bubbler. And, no surprise here, sometimes it looks bubbly . . . hence the name. Now no air and foreign yeast can get in, but the yeast can expel carbon dioxide to its heart's content.

- Spigot: The little piece of plastic that looks like a faucet and has a valve to release the contents of your bucket into any bottle of your choosing after the cider has fermented. It looks just like the water spout on the side of your house for the garden hose! There are other ways of getting the cider out and into bottles and jugs, but they are all messy and highly obnoxious. I recommend purchasing a bucket with a spigot or installing one yourself on your bucket. It can be done with a home drill and a spigot from the hardware store.

PRO TIP

WINE AND CIDER ARE TECHNICALLY THE SAME THING: fermented fruit juices. Although most people would refer to a carbonated beverage as a cider and a still beverage as a wine, this seems to be based more in current pop culture and regional vernacular preferences.

HARD APPLE CIDER

THIS IS THE SAME HARD CIDER I make year after year and the recipe couldn't be easier! After you have mastered this, you can create your own recipes to include other juice and flavor combinations that most authentically represent your tastes. **YIELD: JUST SHORT OF 5 GALLONS**

5-gallon bucket with lid, bubbler, and preferably a spigot

10 liters apple juice (any brand from the cheapest bottle to pure, freshly squeezed juice)

Note: The large 96-ounce jugs of apple juice are 3 quarts, which is roughly 3 liters; therefore, you will need to purchase four jugs, but we will only use about three and a half for this recipe.

1 ounce sanitizer

1 package sweet mead yeast (this particular strain of yeast leaves a little bit of residual sugar in the cider, which I prefer, but you can also use a package of champagne yeast or wine yeast for dry cider)

Roughly 8 liters of water, bottled or tap water, whatever works in your world, divided

4-pound bag granulated sugar

Always start in a clean space, usually the kitchen, and organize all your supplies so they are easy to access.

Check the instructions on the back of your yeast to make sure it doesn't require any additional steps. For example, the brand of sweet mead yeast I buy requires me to squeeze the refrigerated pouch in the palm of my hands to activate the yeast 3 hours before I want to use it. All the yeast brands are different, so follow the instructions on your package for best results.

In the sink fill your 5-gallon bucket with warm water and add 1 ounce sanitizer solution. Sanitize all the pieces including the inside of the 5-gallon bucket, the lid, bubbler, the rubber stopper, and inside of the spigot, and keep a bowl of the sanitizer solution reserved for your hands or tools before discarding the rest.

Fill a large stockpot with 3 liters of water and the whole bag of sugar. Bring the heat up to low, just until the sugar dissolves in the water.

Now it's time to make the cider, so you may want to place the bucket wherever it is going to live for the next month or so. For me, this is the top shelf of my soap cabinet in the pantry. The place needs to be clean and dry and maintain a constant temperature of 60–75°F.

When you have the bucket where you want it, pour the apple juice and the stockpot full of sugar water. Add in another 3 liters of plain water and "pitch" the yeast (that's brewer's code for pour in the yeast!).

PRO TIP

BREWING SHOPS ONLINE AND LOCALLY have these buckets for sale with lids and a small spigot at the bottom for filling bottles. They also sell bubblers and rubber stoppers as well as lids already fitted to the hole to secure the bubbler and rubber stopper in place. They're handy and reasonably priced.

At this point I check how much water I have left to add. The shaft of the bubbler should not touch the cider and I always leave a couple inches of room for bubbles or other yeast shenanigans. You should have about 1.5–2 liters of water left to add to reach 5 gallons of cider.

Put the lid with bubbler on, wipe up any spills, and forget about the whole thing for a couple of weeks. Within a day or two you will begin to see the bubbler bubble. The yeast is alive and working on your hooch!

TWO WEEKS LATER: Eventually the bubbler is going to quit bubbling, and that happens about two weeks later. This is a signal that fermentation is done. Cider makers usually wait another week to let the yeast settle and drop down into the bottom of the bucket.

When the yeast has settled, it is time to pull out those clean juice jugs or your favorite flip-top bottles and, using the spigot, fill them with cider.

We like to let the cider age another 2–3 weeks in the bottles because it mellows and enriches the flavor. At this point the cider is like wine and it benefits from aging. If you can wait several months, the cider will become fizzy and effervescent, but I usually just wait the recommended 2–3 weeks and then use champagne yeast and a pinch of sugar to make the cider fizzy using the same method I use for root beer (see "Homemade Sodas" in the "Urban Cowgirl Fuel" chapter).

You may prefer the taste of still cider, which my Papaw calls apple wine. When he places the cider into the individual bottles, he likes to stick cinnamon sticks or other holiday spices into the bottles for a festive Christmas treat.

PRO TIP

USE THE EMPTY APPLE JUICE CONTAINERS to measure your water. Also, keep the original juice containers stored away while the cider ferments. When the cider is done, you can use the original bottles to store the hard cider. Store them freshly washed with the lids on.

★ ★

MAKING APPLE JACK

JACKING IS AMERICA'S OLDEST METHOD OF DISTILLING ALCOHOL, and it is accomplished by freezing rather than steaming (which is how you make moonshine). While you usually hear about moonshining as the original bootlegged liquor, apple jacking was actually here first. My ancestors owned one of the first taverns in colonial Massachusetts, and they obtained their liquor through the old-fashioned method of apple jacking. And so can you.

Think of it like this: Many people keep their vodka or other hard liquor in the freezer because—as we all know—it will not freeze but keep the liquor ice cold. All you have to do is put apple cider in freezing temperatures and the water and alcohol will begin to separate. The water will rise to the top and freeze into an ice raft. Depending on the freezing temperature, what is left and poured off can be 30–60 proof.

To jack a cider, you'll place the cider outside on the porch during snowy weather, preferably in a plastic food-grade container with a lid. (The pilgrims used wooden barrels, but I was fresh out of those!) Every day ice will collect on the surface of the cider and you will want to scoop it off, concentrating the alcohol as well as the flavor of the apple jack. The colder it gets the higher the alcohol content.

If it doesn't get cold in your part of the country, you can jack a cider just as well in a deep freezer. You'll use the same procedure, skimming off the ice every day until the jack is ready. Then bottle it.

Disclaimer: The distillation of spirits—or in this case fractional freezing with the purpose of concentrating the alcohol content of spirits—is currently illegal in the United States. This information is purely educational, and is meant to encourage an appreciation of our collective culinary history.

IT'S NOT ALL ABOUT APPLES

Cidering is, and always has been, more about using whatever is around you in surplus to create something you can enjoy. Truth be told, I didn't grow up swinging from an apple tree as a child. My aunt and uncle had twin pear trees, and I grew up with a strawberry patch in my front yard that was larger than my first apartment. Today, our global pantry has made it easy to get everything from apples to goji berries delivered to your front door year-round. So I recommend trying the cider recipe with lots of different fruits like strawberries, peaches, pears, blackberries, and even honey. To carry the spirit of cidering into your life, use the ingredients that feel most authentically you.

Taco Therapy

Settle in. Prop up your feet. Take a deep breath and let it out.

All smart Southern women know that pearls and painted toenails go with every outfit. In the same way, the brokenhearted cowboy with a few bucks in his pocket, the girl who just got fired, or anyone who has ever drunk too much for their own good knows that a well-timed taco can transform even the darkest of days.

It's just a fact.

Tacos aren't fancy food. They aren't complex. But like the hug of a favorite sweater or the forehead kiss of a beloved grandmother, the taco holds the solution to life's most uncomfortable questions. We make taco runs when women go into labor. We bring them to wakes and memorials. Tacos are the fuel for late-night studying in college dorm rooms. They have been salvation to many hungover grooms on their wedding day and comfort to angry brides ditched at the altar.

Some of my biggest almost mistakes were prevented because I got a taco and mulled over my options. I've cried over tacos. I was really just crying over life.

Urban Cowgirls know one thing and one thing well: Taco therapy will cure any case of the blues, no matter the cause.

If you're ready to leave, thinking you've lost it, certain you've missed it . . .

Take two tacos and call me in the morning.

HOMEMADE PICADILLO
AND FRESH TACO SHELLS

TACO-TRUCK FLAVOR at home. **YIELD: ABOUT 15-20 TACOS**

---

1 1/2 pounds 85/15 ground beef

1/2 white onion, very finely chopped

1 jalapeño, destemmed, deseeded, and chopped

2 garlic cloves, pressed through a garlic press

1/2 teaspoon salt

1 1/2 teaspoons cumin

1 teaspoon pepper

1 teaspoon granulated onion

1 teaspoon paprika or any mild red chile powder

1/2 teaspoon Mexican oregano

Optional: 1 tomato or 1/4 cup finely chopped cilantro

Fresh oil, for frying

Fresh corn tortillas, for frying

1 block medium cheddar, grated on the finest grate (This creates the fine cheese commonly found in taco shops across the Southwest.)

Taco toppings: lettuce, sour cream, diced cherry tomatoes, taco sauce

In a large skillet brown the meat, using a fork or masher to break the meat up into little pieces. When it is seared, add the onion and jalapeño. Add the garlic, all the spices, and the tomato and cilantro (if using). Cook, stirring well, for about 8 minutes. The mixture can be diluted with a little bit of water if it begins to brown too much while cooking.

For the homemade taco shells, fill a skillet halfway with oil and heat the oil to about 350–375°F. Place a corn tortilla in the hot grease and let it get hot for 5–10 seconds. Flip. Using tongs, hold the top half up and out of the hot oil, allowing the bottom half of the tortilla to lie on the surface of the oil and fry. After 30–45 seconds, flip and fry the other side on the surface of the grease and hold the now-crispy side with the tongs up and out of the grease. This creates the "shell." When golden brown on both sides, remove from the hot oil and salt well. Place on a rack for draining while you begin the next taco shell. Repeat.

Serve these tacos with the freshly grated cheddar cheese, finely sliced lettuce, diced cherry tomatoes, sour cream, and taco sauce.

SQUEEZE BOTTLE TACO TRUCK SAUCE

THIS IS MY VERSION OF THE LOVELY RED CHILE SAUCE served in squeeze bottles at taco trucks throughout the land! **YIELD: ABOUT 1 CUP**

3 dried guajillo peppers or
3 fresh Fresno peppers

2 Roma tomatoes

1 tomatillo

1 garlic clove

1 teaspoon sugar

2 tablespoons salad vinegar

Salt, to taste

Squeeze of lemon

Place the dried peppers in a bowl and top with very hot water. Let them reconstitute while you prepare the rest of the sauce.

On a foil-lined and oiled cookie sheet, place the tomatoes, tomatillo, fresh Fresno peppers (if using), and garlic. Broil the tomatoes and tomatillo just until they are fully roasted and have black puffy skin. Remove the garlic as soon as it is done roasting (which will be sooner).

Transfer everything to a food processor and add the reconstituted guajillo peppers (if you went with the dried peppers). Add the sugar, vinegar, and a dash of salt and lemon juice. Blend well. Taste for seasoning.

TWO TEXANS CRAVING SALSA
FAR FROM HOME

THE LAST RECIPE I LEAVE YOU WITH is the first recipe I ever created. This is the one that started it all, before it ever really started.

I had just married Dereck and left my beloved Texas behind for the first time in my entire life. We were twenty-three, starting a new life in Arizona—the place where I would attend culinary school. The first thing I missed was chips and salsa, and so the first recipe we ever created together, with our boxes still packed, was chips and salsa!

We were in love with it from the first bite, and like any self-respecting foodie, the first thing I did was post it on the Internet. It's still there next to a picture of a very young and goofy newlywed couple. You can find it today plastered all over the web, but here it is from me to you. **YIELD: ABOUT 1 QUART**

$^1/_2$ cup fresh cilantro, packed into the measuring cup

1 (28-ounce) can whole tomatoes

2 seeded jalapeños, chopped (reserve seeds if desired for more heat)

Juice of $^1/_2$ a lime

$^1/_2$ teaspoon chili powder

$^1/_2$ teaspoon garlic powder

1 teaspoon salt

$^1/_2$ cup small-diced white onion

In a blender combine cilantro, tomatoes, jalapeños, and lime juice. Blend with just a few pulses. Add spices and salt.

The salsa will have a small bite from just the jalapeños, but I like to taste it now and, if desired, add in minced pepper seeds for heat. Remember to add only small amounts; jalapeños add the kind of heat that sneaks up on you. Pulse once more to combine everything. Then pour the salsa into a bowl and *put the blender away*. Otherwise you end up with spicy vegetable pulp.

Finally, add the small-diced onions (as much to your liking) to give it texture. Sometimes I leave out the cilantro until I add the onions, to give the salsa even more texture. Of course, you'll want to chop the leaves a little and then stir them in.

Serve salsa with tortilla chips and fresh tacos.

TO MY TRIBE:

Research has proven that people all over the world who consistently rank themselves as happy and fulfilled have one thing in common: They live in villages.

This tribe is a group of people who remain constant in your life. Your best friend, the kids you grew up with, your fairy godmother, or, in my case, a group of people I have known my whole life who support and influence me as much as my own family does. They really are family.

These little tribes share in life's most precious moments, from teaching you to tie your first pair of shoelaces to sharing the gnawing heartache of watching your last baby walk into kindergarten.

They're a troop of people who triumph in your accomplishments and weep with you in your losses. They don't have to RSVP because they're always there, usually bringing the ice you inevitably forgot at the grocery store along with extra napkins and a giant coffee. These are the people you can drop in on unannounced because they'll gladly set you a place at their table, or give you the spare bedroom after a wee bit too much holiday eggnog.

I believe magic happens when we connect with another person. When two hearts swell together, a little spark of pure genius is born. Like God is in the midst of them saying, "See, this is what I put you here for. This is how to live life abundantly."

I often wonder why this is. And the closest thing I can find to an answer is this: Abundant life is full of emotion. Emotion loves company. Sharing emotion amplifies the experience and satisfies the heart.

I thrive on connecting and collaborating, so it will come as no surprise that my most heartfelt thanks goes out to our tribe in and around Denton, Texas.

You are my crew, my pack, my family, and my village.

The truth is, this book is a collaboration of all of us and the life we've shared over three decades.

We worked on this book side by side, nitpicking food photos and contemplating true stories that helped breathe life into this snapshot of Urban Cowgirl Country. But we were always living that life, we just never knew it would be presented in this form. The rest of you raised us and star in the tales we divulge in this book, and for that I will apologize ahead of time. *Smirk*

I hope that you find that *Urban Cowgirl* is the product of the lifestyle it preaches throughout its pages.

Specifically I wish to thank a few very important people who climbed aboard the Urban Cowgirl mission and built her from the ground up.

The person I must thank first is my staggeringly creative cowriter, **REBEKAH FAUBION**.

Today, I sat across from her at Mr. Chopstick's with a platter of sushi between us. We drew *the line of death* (a line down the middle that separates the sushi even-steven) and continued brainstorming our work, just like we have since we were eleven years old—the age when we wrote our first screenplay.

Rebekah, what can I even say to convey how grateful I am that God put you in my life?

You were the first one down in the creative trenches with me, and like a potter, you and I crafted the *Urban Cowgirl* together. Not just the manuscript, but the very soul of the book. We learned together that first you create the essence of the book, and then the book tells you what it is and is not. If we lived in Harry Potter's universe I am quite certain this thing would be a Horcrux of both of us. The soul of our book communicates with you just as much as it does with me, which is the greatest compliment I can offer you.

Thank you for your patience, for tolerating the endless texts of "this isn't quite it" and "I think it's a little more like this" imposed upon your whimsical portrayals of the modern country girl. It is a common thing for someone to have a great concept in his or her head, but rarely can we articulate it, bringing it into the world with as much justice and gusto as we see it in our imagination. You did that. You are the doctor who delivered the baby. Without you, *Urban Cowgirl* would lack the depth and emotion that you challenged me to invest in it. Thank you for holding our book to that high of a standard.

CHEF GRADY SPEARS is as swashbuckling and handsome as a cowboy can get. I vividly remember being perched on the deck of a weathered log cabin overlooking the glass-like surface of Possum Kingdom Lake devouring his first book, *A Cowboy in the Kitchen*. It was the first time I had seen gourmet Texas fusion, and I was completely mesmerized.

Exactly ten years later, overlooking Lake Austin, we shared the most expensive bottle of wine that I have ever seen in real life, and Grady, the "King of Texas Cooking," insisted that *I* write a Texas cookbook. To say it was a significant moment in my life is an understatement. In that moment, Grady Spears turned the page on the next chapter in my life. Grady, the opportunity for me to write *Urban Cowgirl* came from the paths you forged writing the rustic yet refined cookbook I fell in love with on the lake that October day. You opened the door for me not once, but twice. First, when I was a young woman, you introduced me to high-end Texas cuisine, and then you inspired me to write my own chapter. I don't know what else you could ask for in a mentor. I love you almost as much as I love your chicken-fried steak.

I don't think it's possible for anyone who meets **DENNIS HAYES** to not completely adore him.

He is a cozy and gentle teddy bear man who loves his dogs and wears a bowler hat everywhere he goes. He has kind, honest eyes and a generous smile. Dennis is what you call a weaver. He weaves people together to produce stellar literary projects, a lot of them in food. He seems to always be handing me a glass of iced tea, which as a Texan is like someone always handing you a cupcake.

One rainy day as I was still coming down from the anxiety and turmoil of appearing on reality TV, we had a phone conversation on my back porch that forever changed my life. Dennis gave me an assignment. He said to me, "I want you to write some notes about the book you would do if you didn't have to answer to anyone, if no one imposed their opinions on you of what is marketable, or who they think you are." I thought that was a wonderfully freeing thing for someone to say.

A couple days later I e-mailed him a short selection of recipes with some rambling in between about my philosophy on cooking and life. I didn't censor my words or vision at all—after all, this was just between us.

He read the notes and I could hear the grin on his face as he chuckled and said, ever so gently, "Sarah, *you* are *the* Urban Cowgirl." His utter certainty turned on a light in me, illuminating what was already there. This person, the Urban Cowgirl, was ready to be introduced to the world.

I didn't think anyone would see those notes, but a few days later I learned that everyone in the world had, and Dennis had several soft offers on the book. If you're in publishing, you know this is utter insanity.

And that is the story of how Dennis Hayes became my favorite human.

Dennis, you are as compassionate and good-natured a person as any of us will ever meet,

yet you are also strategic and clever. You're like a duck gracefully floating on top of a beautiful lake but with your little feet madly churning under the water, taking us all to a carefully chosen destination. A better place.

God has a special reward for shepherds like you. Thank you, for absolutely everything.

Which brings me to the greatest editor a girl could ever hope for, **Erin Turner.** Erin is a person whose reputation precedes her. I can't count how many times I've heard, "Erin knooooooows Texas," referring to the number of long-term, best-selling Texas-y books she's produced, from folklore to gardening. And she's certainly an Urban Cowgirl if there ever was one. She'll say things like, "If you need me I'll be making pickles Saturday so just text but if I don't pick up I am probably hiking in Yellowstone and I'll get right back to you!" Rebekah and I will just stare at each other dumbfounded like, *OMG—she's one of us.*

Erin, you believed in this project from day one, and we all know that's because we're cut from the same dough. The thing I admire the most about you is the curious way you seem to know when to step back and let the little builder ants work—without bounds. *Urban Cowgirl* evolved and took form and you let it happen. You gave me the freedom to create without barriers. Thank you for having that much courage in your authors and the creative process. I think you've probably spoiled me for everyone else, and I'm hoping to work with you for many years to come.

Many people refer to **LEANN SQUIER** as my fairy godmother, but not just to me; she is a deeply influential person to the entire team here in Texas. Leann led the visual production of photography and stylistic choices we made for *Urban Cowgirl* and continues to determine every visual element we present with the brand, from wardrobe to food photography. She also happens to be my aunt. Leann's philosophy boils down to one simple concept: If God tells you to do something, commit to give Him your all. Don't do the thing *for the world*, do the thing *for God*, because He assigned it to you, and He deserves the very best. This woman is committed to producing excellence as an offering to God, a legacy she consistently imparts to the rest of us.

Leann, your perseverance in completing this project is nothing short of heroic! What is even more mind-boggling is that you never get cranky, you never snap, you're always cheerful, always leading the way. You became our great captain, mediating our disagreements and refusing to give up. You were a cheerleader and a referee and a therapist to all of us. Thank you for your bottomless talent and enthusiasm. You picked up where the writing left off and made *Urban Cowgirl* a tangible, breathtaking, country-chic universe that we all were proud to star in.

TRACEY LIGGETT, our food photographer extraordinaire. You worked tirelessly alongside Leann and me, climbing ladders or crawling on the ground to get that perfect shot. This project required heaps of bravery, was made of long hours and lots of coffee, and even when you probably wanted to quit, you stuck it out. I'll never forget our adventure into the heart of Texas, hanging out with cowboys and stuffing our faces with wagyu steak. Thank you for walking this through to the end, and producing some of the most stunning photos of food I've ever laid eyes on. My hope for you is this: a future full of purple and magenta Texas sunsets and mornings cuddled next to a cow dog in front of a toasty fire. You certainly deserve it.

ANDREW PENDERGRASS AND THE STAFF OF MARBLE RANCH: Thank you for inviting these city girls to your little slice of heaven in the middle of the Texas Plains. Many of the photos we took on the ranch populate this book and add to its beauty. Thank you for unforgettable evenings of wagyu steak and chocolate around the campfire! Thanks also for giving us the chance to experience a true Texas fairytale.

GABRIEL AND MICAH PENROD: My perfect little angel gentlemen, I am sorry for all the nights of peanut butter sandwiches punctuated with evenings of so much fancy food we had to buy another refrigerator. I know it was confusing to you. I hope one day you understand that being your mother is the most inspiring and influential part of my life. When you're older, I hope this book demonstrates to you that you really can do anything you put your mind to. Let God lead you and you will find your way. I owe you many days in the front yard throwing the ball and many trips to the park. Let's get started right now!

TO DERECK PENROD, who is the most patient husband alive, I owe you heaps of thanks for the past ten years, not just the time spent on this book. Marriage can be challenging between two people as motivated as we are with the added juggling act of raising two little boys. I am astonished at how far we have come since Surprise, Arizona.

In addition to the much-needed *thank you* for not divorcing me during the struggle of becoming an author, thank you for going one step further and holding me (and the food) to such a high standard. I adore you because you recognize my best work and you say something when you're not getting it. Every creator needs someone like that in his or her life. After this experience I have to doubt that masterpieces are created without a persnickety husband or wife nearby!

You are a magnificent father and husband, never once hesitating to sacrifice portions of your own career for this book to be created. To me that demonstrates the deepest level of love, but more importantly, respect for your partner. You are my best friend.

TO THE REST OF MY FAMILY: Thank you for the years of stories and dishes that make up this book. Thank you to my parents, Stephen and Kim, who, in living vibrantly and vivaciously, created a young girl with a thirst for abundant life, family, and tradition.

Thank you to my Nanan and Papaw for never letting go of where you came from and teaching me so many of the homesteading traditions in this book. I think the reason this book exists today is because you were so successful, even at times in your life wealthy, yet you still stubbornly and unapologetically made your own food. Somehow that statement has resonated in my heart and defined me. You never compromised your love of working the land given to you, harvesting what it reaps, and using the resources at your disposal to provide for your loved ones. You showed me that just because you *can* buy it, doesn't mean you should. It's never as good as homemade and from the heart! There is something important and fulfilling about doing it yourself.

Thank you to Mimi and Papa Wiggs for encouraging my Tex-Mex addiction. All the recipes you helped me cultivate from years of family gatherings and old Texas traditions became the backbone of this book. I hope you have many more to share.

Thank you to Texas, from Sweetwater to Denton to Galveston and beyond. You are the house that made me. I hope you find this book, its recipes and traditions, worthy of your collections.

With the deepest love and respect,

Sarah Penrod

September 8, 2017
Somewhere Deep in the Heart of Texas

★ INDEX ★

ABOUT THE AUTHOR

THE SOUTH IS HOME TO A NEW TYPE OF COWGIRL–the Urban Cowgirl. And no one knows that better than celebrity chef, television personality, and writer Sarah Penrod.

A seventh-generation Texan, Sarah is private chef to some of the most famous names in the Lone Star State. She's also charmed her way into the televisions of millions as the vivacious, hysterical Texpert on Food Network Star.

Hailed by food writers as a virtual evangelist for "the new modern Texan," Sarah is also a proud Daughter of the American Revolution. She fell in love with historical recipes after discovering she was the descendant of a rare female patriot who donated large quantities of steak to the American forces during the Revolutionary War.

When Sarah isn't poppin' bottles of homemade root beer on the back of a truck bed with her tribe of Urban Cowgirls, she enjoys making strawberry wine and her own homemade soap, playing catch with her sons, and dancing barefoot in the kitchen with her husband.

As a mother to two Tiny Texans, Sarah has devoted herself to promoting health in young people. She serves as an ambassador to the White House's Chefs Move to School's initiative, which is aimed at improving children's nutrition in public schools.

She resides in her childhood hometown of Denton, Texas, with her family, where she works every day to make the world a more delicious place!